Praise for *The Quest:*

"*The Quest* journey is one we all have the opportunity to take should we live long enough (and statistics show most of us will). The principles in this book helped give me the courage to see a future that no one else had dreamed for me and intentionally sail toward the reality of my true self. It combines the scientific study of anthropology, sociology, and philosophy with the tools and rich traditions of historically tested rituals. Randy explores the often neglected rites of passage in modern western societies and presents the cardinal directions you'll need to navigate your second half of life journey. *The Quest* gets my highest recommendation." -**JONATHAN FORD**, *Chief AV Engineer, National Institutes of Health*

"When I met Randy, I was crawling out of a 30-year history of being highly disembodied and trying to understand who I was in the world. *The Quest* not only allowed me to finally meet that person in solitude and wholeness but to see her as an integral part of humanity. It was an experience like no other—an altar giving thanks to who I had been and an edict welcoming who I was to become." -**ABBY LANE**, *Writer*

"*Quest* was a life-changing experience for me, and I reflect on it often. Last summer, I had the chance to take my family to Angel Fire. On Father's Day morning, my son and I hiked up to the same spot where I wrote my journal entry the day after *Quest* ended. (I recorded the GPS coordinates.) To sit there with my son seven years later, watching hot air balloons rise from the valley floor, was incredible. When I say *Quest* changed my life, I'm not kidding. But, be warned—it is not for the faint of heart, as *Quest* will push you to dive into your past and present areas that you might not do otherwise. I strongly recommend *Quest* for anyone desiring to live their very best life; it's a true game-changer." -**NEVILLE LETZERICH**, *VP, and Chief Marketing Officer, Fortune 100 Tech Company*

"*The Quest* is not only a book; it's an experience. Randy has been my mentor and a gracious guide both in person and on the page. He's been willing to travel fearlessly ahead and graciously alongside those willing. The question he and this book begs is, are you ready to go deeper and live your most expansive life? As I hope it is yours, my answer is a definitive yes!" -**MELISSA GREENE**, *Artist, Speaker, Writer, Co-Founder and Leader of IMAGINARIUM*

"I attended *Quest* five years after beginning to step away from day-to-day operations at our firm. At age 55, I found it hard to give up my "business marriage" and get past going back to the office most days! However, my time at *Quest* and the weeks, months, and years after were a chance to reflect emotionally on what I wanted to do with my future and how I wanted to give back. *Quest* showed me ways to pivot to the second half of life, and my goals and aspirations are once again unlimited, just as they were when I was younger. I'm thankful *Quest* gave me the tools and mindset to refocus on this valuable time of my life (and to give up going to the office!)"
-**JIMBO GULLEY**, *Partner, Texas Capital Partners*

"Almost a year out from my *Quest* conference and I still think on the personal and profound things I learned and discovered. The grounding in Jung's and Campbell's work was intellectually stimulating. The community was nourishing. And what I experienced during the rite will go with me for the rest of my life. I can't wait to read this book and can think of so many friends and colleagues who will benefit from it too." -**REV. DAN CLARK**, *Ohio Director of Faith in Public Life*

"*The Quest* experience opened my eyes to both the beauty and pain within the story of my life. Looking at the past (the first half of life) can be painful and enlightening. Randy skillfully walks participants through this process, with a specific focus on the potential treasures that lie ahead in the second half of life, particularly the freedom to be who we are. During *The Quest*, I received a special message from my heart and mind that was truly encouraging." -**JOHN PALM**, *CEO, Crossplan Financial Management*

"My experience attending *The Quest* event was truly transformational. I was in a time of enormous transition in career and identity. *The Quest* experience helped me face my insecurities and look forward with more incredible determination for accomplishing a mission. After attending, the image I saw in the mirror and who I needed to become wasn't blurry anymore."
-**RON ALLEY**, *CEO and Founder, Carpe Artista (Seize the Arts)*

"I experienced *The Quest* weekend during a time of fundamental change in my life—personally and professionally. The issues we grappled with throughout the weekend brought understanding and clarity. And it propelled me down the road of not just looking for answers but also learning how to spend time with the questions. As a result, I frequently return to all we explored as I continue my *Quest* to live a more intentional and authentic second half of life."
-**ERIC WYSE**, *Songwriter, Musician & Entrepreneur, Martingale Music*

The Quest

Discover a Way to Enjoy
the Second Half of Life

Randy Elrod

#TheQuestBook

Contact The Author

To inquire about a Quest Workshop or information about the live
Quest Experience
Email: randyelrod@gmail.com

For more information: www.randyelrod.com

cre:ate2.0
PUBLISHING

Bulk purchase and reprint permission may be requested from randyelrod@gmail.com

Printed in the United States of America

Library of Congress Cataloging-in-Publication Data has been applied for.

ISBN # 9780991471560

To JimBo Gulley

A friend, companion, confidant,

ally, and mentor

during my Hero's Journey

who believed in *The Quest*

from its inception over a decade ago.

Contents

Waypoints

Author's Note

We are growing older. When America became a nation, only one in five people lived to age seventy. Now more than *four out of five* do. The average life expectancy in America is currently around eighty years—and increasing.

This expansion begs the question, what are we to do with the second half of life that could last forty or more years? The additional time makes it inevitable that somewhere between age thirty-five and sixty, many of us will find ourselves at the cusp of a massive (and possibly catastrophic) transition.

Our culture provides no preparation for this upheaval, this unprecedented "mid-life crisis." Only the usual innuendos about sports cars, erratic behavior, and sexual escapades with a younger partner. But little practical help exists for the universal struggles with restlessness, dissatisfaction, and the nagging questions about what to do with all those remaining years.

Why has this ubiquitous transition not been adequately addressed? Let's begin with demography. Since the mid-19th century, Americans have been living longer. In 1900, the life expectancy of an average American at birth was approximately forty-seven years.[1] By 1930, it was still only fifty-nine. Therefore, our parents and grandparents did not expect life after retirement.

Life expectancy has increased as vaccines, antibiotics, and better medical care saved more children from premature death and effectively treated infections. Since 1960, however, longevity increases have been achieved mainly by extending people's lives over age sixty.

Instead of saving more young people, we are stretching out old age. At mid-life, for the first time in history, we face a long second life for which we have no plans. We have been busy building our sense of identity, importance, and security in first life, and we are caught unaware.

Psychologist Carl Jung studied the second half of life extensively. He said, "Thoroughly unprepared, we take the step into the afternoon of life. Worse still, we take this step with the false presupposition that our truths and our ideals will serve us as before. But we cannot live the afternoon of life according to the program of life's morning. For what was great in the morning will be little at evening and what in the morning was true, at evening will have become a lie."[2]

If this is true, and everything we believe and value becomes a lie, how do we navigate the second half of life? What happens when there are too many demands by the things we don't enjoy or believe anymore? And too few of the ones we do? Most of us believe there is more to this life, but we have no way of describing what "more" is.

In my twenties, I had chosen work that seemed to make the most of my interests, values, and strengths. However, as I stepped into the afternoon of life, I was increasingly trying to figure out if I could still do my career and remain healthy: physically, mentally, emotionally, and spiritually.

As I found myself face to face with this dilemma, I sought advice from older people I respected and was perplexed to find little help. Only now do I understand this was a question with which they had never grappled. They were surprised (some shocked) to have survived into their seventies, eighties, and nineties when expecting to live only fifty years.

Thus, my mid-life transition was made alone and without assistance. During my crisis (search for identity), I lost most of my family, friends, and community. For almost a year, I was homeless and alone. It was a devastating wake-up call after a lifetime of prosperity and undeserved good luck. Unfortunately, I was "thoroughly unprepared," and my painful transition lasted almost fifteen years.

A large American study found that I am not alone. Midlife is the time of least happiness, most tremendous anxiety, and lowest life satisfaction for both men and women.[3] It is a time when heroic ideals fade, and the journey forward is unclear.

But it does not have to be like this. The way we handle the shift to the second half of life is unique yet universal. Many people have walked this path before us. We can learn from them—from their suffering and victories. Mid-life finds us positioned between youth and old age in a way that provides a panoramic view of life. This perspective makes it possible to shorten our learning curve and enjoy the second half of life.

For the past two decades, I have been an avid student of the mid-life transition and finding ways to navigate the transition to second life better. My second life calling is straightforward: helping others make this journey far more efficient and pleasant. I was a shepherd in my first life, but I feel called to be a shaman in my second life. At first, I was reluctant to adopt this title. There is much misunderstanding about the term—shamans have been called witch doctors, new age gurus, medicine men and women, and magicians.

I learned much from the teachings of don Jose Ruiz whose Toltec ancestors have passed down more than a thousand years of oral instruction. The role in their community is a sophisticated combination of philosopher, spiritual leader, psychologist, and friend.

Ruiz and his father, don Miguel Ruiz teaches that shamanism is the wisdom of waking up, finding personal freedom, living in peace and harmony, and serving others and the planet. Those are traits I want to emulate in my second life.

Ten years ago, I created a live experience called *The Quest*. It is a secret rite of passage to the second half of life. The first adventure convened in Angel Fire, New Mexico, with six men. The participants were the CEO of a financial management company, the Vice President of an Austin tech company, a Senior Partner of a private equity investment and development group, a real estate broker and former mega-church minister, and a professional artist. Since then, I have guided nine *Quest* experiences in New Mexico and Tennessee with forty-seven alumni from all walks of life.

The experience has evolved and is now open to persons of any gender age thirty-five and up. My goal is to lead two per year with six participants each. The book you are currently reading (or listening to) expands those experiences. While there is nothing like attending *The Quest* in person, I hope this book will become a well-worn guide map for your journey into second life.

The Quest teaches that the path to finding your treasure, your holy grail, lies within you. Each of us has the truth we need deep inside ourselves. The way of *The Quest* gives you a language for your Hero's Journey inward: to heed your call to adventure, survive the trials, accept the rewards, and enjoy the elixir of wholeness. We must each find the words and symbols to describe our being.

The path of *The Quest* is a unique journey, and no two ways are alike. The many options can be disorienting. But fortunately, we have universal waypoints (intermediate points) that guide us to find the wisdom needed to make this journey of personal freedom. Therefore, I say each story is different, yet every story is the same.

Ten topics repeatedly appeared in the rituals, books, and resources I studied and in the conversations I've had with others going through the transition to second life. Jung calls such recurrences synchronicity or "meaningful coincidences." The ten waypoints (chapters) explore each recurring theme.

However, *The Quest* is not a sequential journey of ten easy steps to enjoyment. I realize that this book and experience would be more palatable to the modern consumer who lives for the next best-selling self-help guide to success in life. And if I were to cave in to this pressure (which I am not), the elevator speech would probably read something like this:

"WHAT IF I TOLD YOU THERE IS A SIMPLE WAY TO GET RID OF SHAME, FEAR, BOREDOM, GUILT, NIGHTMARES, DECREASE DEPRESSION, REVERSE THE AGING PROCESS, EXTEND LIFE AND MAKE IT MORE ENJOYABLE? WOULD YOU BE INTERESTED? AND GET THIS: THE COST IS ABSOLUTELY FREE! TOO GOOD TO BE TRUE? NOT IN THE SLIGHTEST! WELCOME TO THE MAGICAL WORLD OF THE QUEST. THIS HIGHLY-RESEARCHED AND WELL-DOCUMENTED THEORY IS BLOWING AWAY PEOPLE EVERYWHERE WITH ITS POWER AND ABILITY TO PERFORM SO MANY INCREDIBLE FUNCTIONS AND FIXES WHILE HELPING YOU STAY YOUNG AT HEART. LIFE REALLY DOES BEGIN AT FORTY!"

The messy reality reveals *The Quest* as an ever-changing experience charged with emotion. Although many aspects of the journey are similar, they are never identical. Because of these factors of sameness and difference, it isn't easy to simplify the infinite variations of the way of *The Quest* into a linear sequence.

I can do no more than present an honest picture of each waypoint from as many angles as possible and try to sketch their most typical features. My job is to guide *you* to a way to find *your* unique journey. I do not pretend to be *the* guide showing *the* way.

There are several ways to read or listen to this book to apply a semblance of order. Before turning the page or swiping to the next screen, please know this book doesn't always walk straight. As in real life, it meanders. You may traditionally enjoy it from beginning to end. But if you wish, you may read or listen to it in any order. Or you may choose to find a topic of interest and begin there—then progress naturally.

A word of advice—take it slow and don't get overwhelmed. This book contains over fifteen years of research and discoveries and a lifetime of themes, experiences, questions, and applications. Digesting a section and then putting it down for a while is okay. Others of you will devour it all at once and then return to explore relevant waypoints. Either way, I hope that *The Quest* becomes a handbook for the remainder of your life.

Furthermore, the book contains a section of fun and practical resources for your perusal, a selected bibliography, and a collection of mandalas (circles), quaternities, and sub-quaternities (sets of four) created for each waypoint. If you are listening to the audiobook, go to randyelrod.com/quest to find these resources.

The Quest is not for the faint of heart or those satisfied with the status quo. It is fraught with risks. In the words of Dr. Allan Chinen, "All are called, but few listen."[4] But the reward is a pathway of unique symbolism and universal emotion. It is a journey that bids us wake up and pay attention to our daily life's magic and gather the courage to explore the unknown regions of our inner being. For those who dare seek it, the holy grail offers the hope of enjoyment and enlightenment in life. What more could we hope for?

In the end, it is a travel planner. An adventurous journey into the vast depths of our unconscious, to discover the mystery and wonder of who we are. It is one person's attempt to make that journey less arduous for those who are not content to sleepwalk through second life.

A Few Words About Theory

Many people ask the following questions during the live *Quest* experience or after watching my YouTube™ video, *Be Who You Are Not What You Do*. "How am I to be who I am?" "How do I know who I am?" "What is the way to find who I am?" These questions prompted me to develop what I call "a theory of being."

A theory gives value and significance to new ideas. It forces an examination, from many angles, of a set of facts presented in a new context that few have studied to this point. Furthermore, a theorist hopes to inspire extended conversation and productive research. To that end, this book contains my Theory of Being, or, in a more accessible phrase, *The Quest*. Ultimately, it is a dynamic exploration of integration, in a word, wholeness.

The old gods are dead or dying and people everywhere are searching…

—Joseph Campbell

What is Enjoyment?

Is it an emotion? What is a joyful heart? Why do I experience a joyful heart in my physical body? Why does enjoyment feel so good? Why is it so contagious? How does joy make my heart feel contented, interested, and excited all at the same time?

How does it calm my spirit, make my mouth and eyes smile, and raise eyebrows? Why does it provoke sudden bursts of laughter, quick intakes of breath, face flushing, and mindful attention? Why do we scream Whew! Yayyy! Yippee! and OH! when we feel a joyful emotion?

Can enjoyment transcend the messiness of life? Is joy possible every day? Is childlike joy only possible in the first half of life? Are we doomed to be less joyful as we get older? Or, as longevity increases for many of us, will it open more opportunities to expand our enjoyment?

I have endless questions about enjoyment, about being who we are, and about successfully navigating the second half of life. I had time to explore all those things and more. That's where I've been for the past fifteen years. You might call it my *Quest*. Here are a few things I brought back from my journey.

Symbols

What Are Your Four Symbols?

In the words of Shrek to Donkey as they embark upon their *Quest*, "Ogres are like onions. They have layers. Ogres have layers. Onions have layers. You get it? We both have layers."[5] This observation embodies one of the *Shrek* movie's central themes: People are much more than what they seem on the surface.

Humans are intricate and multi-layered, and we need tools to help understand our deepest parts. Symbols are *tools of communication*. Like onions, symbols have layers and can help us decipher who we are.

The Quest sees life as a great dance with symbols. They point to things unknown or hidden and life-giving discoveries beyond the grasp of our consciousness. That is why we see them utilized significantly throughout history in the world's cultures and religions.

Few symbols are more recognizable than the Mercedes-Benz emblem. Every corner of the world recognizes its familiar three-pointed star as a synonym for prestige, luxury, and success. It signifies a layered meaning for the automobile company. The emblem represents a goal to motorize the whole world on land, water, and air. Three directions, three points, three aims.

Humans are a symbol-making species. Consider a few: flag, dove, rainbow, peace sign, cross, arrows, heart, skull, and phoenix. The list is practically infinite. We can use these images to function as eye-opening tools of self-discovery. Imagine a GPS app for *The Quest* and entering the destination "enjoy life" —one waypoint on the journey would be symbols. Waypoints are intermediate points on a route or destination.

A foundational principle is that *while all of our journeys are different, somehow, they are all the same.* Unique yet universal. Each of us must discover our unique path to the holy grail. And we can better do this by utilizing the human universals as waypoints.

This principle is true for symbols. They are unique yet universal. Part of the crisis at mid-life comes when the unique symbols that were invaluable for the first half of our life no longer hold the power they once did. They become broken and fragmented—useless. But be encouraged; we can find new unique yet universal symbols to help us survive and, yes, enjoy the second half of life.

For the author, the transition to second life necessitated changes from the symbol of the cross (goodness and religion) to the mandala (wholeness and spirituality), from the exclamation point (censorship and pat answers) to the question mark (curiosity and open questions), from the Bible (dogmatic and exclusive) to the classics (open-minded and inclusive).

In the Christianized versions of the mythical quest, the holy grail could be found only by a select few via the straight and narrow way. Only Sir Galahad was deemed worthy of the prize because he was sinless and pure in heart.

But never fear, for those of us who are more like the "sinful" Lancelot and Guinevere, this *Quest* is not a morality tale about right and wrong. Our holy grail does not require goodness or perfection—it asks only for the pursuit of wholeness. And happily, wholeness is a treasure attainable by saints and sinners alike—and it is a sure-fire way to enjoy life.

For many of us, somewhere around mid-life, our gods (our symbols) fell apart and are fragmented at our feet. Therefore, a pivotal aspect of *The Quest* is finding new symbols that are meaningful and beneficial for the second half of life. They are the language of communication between the conscious and the unconscious; they help us have a better conversation with our self than the one we are having now.

And we can learn this language for ourselves. So let's focus on four universal symbols that recur throughout history.

1. Mandala

The first symbol is the mandala, which means *circle*. It is a revered and time-honored tool that people have been using with great success for thousands of years. The cosmos (our universe) and nature work as a circle. The beauty of a circle is that we can create or draw one anywhere, set a center, and have a personal and orderly universe.

The astrological zodiac is a mandala, a circle. Indian spiritual practices developed fascinating mandalas, including the intricate colored sand versions created by Tibetan Buddhist monks. Furthermore, we find pictorial mandalas in Christian art; stained glass and murals portray Christ surrounded by the four disciples of the gospels.

Native Americans call this symbol a medicine wheel, and it has been used for generations to enhance health and healing. It has many forms. Over the centuries, they used stones (another powerful symbol) to construct hundreds of mandalas on Native lands throughout North America. We can still find them today. These medicine wheels typically employ the four directions, which symbolize the seasons and cycles of life.[6]

The four directions (north, east, south, and west) represent an example of a *quaternity* or a set of four. Four is a number of completion.

Quaternities are universal symbols that permeate the culture. There are four seasons (spring, summer, fall, winter), four natural elements (fire, water, earth, wind), four parts in music (soprano, alto, tenor, bass), four gates to an ancient city, four rivers of paradise, the four horses of Apollo's sun carriage, and many more. Discovering these sets of four has been fascinating. As a result, I have put together a companion book with over one hundred mandalas and quaternities found across the vast spectrum of my research.

The mandala we will use is in the form of an outer circle. Each waypoint quaternity comprises four inner intersecting circles, and an inner concentric circle represents the self. This combination will serve as the foundational symbol for our journey. As you will see, these circular drawings provide a simple yet profound way (a GPS) to discover the depths of meaning beneath our surface.

For *The Quest,* the mandala symbol is the infrastructure, the self is the foundation, and the essentials are the four pillars of our journey. They become mnemonic devices (memorable reminders) to chart the path and the waypoints of this extraordinary adventure.

Each day, psychologist Carl Jung sketched a new mandala (small circular drawing) to correspond with his inner situation. It was a crucial exercise for him, and he believed the illustrations provided an ongoing chart of life progress. Moreover, he thought they have the power to reveal the path to becoming who you are.

An internet search will return thousands of artistically rendered and intricate mandalas. Still, for *The Quest,* we utilize them more practically. One cannot minimize this symbol's importance as a memory device for the waypoints of our journey. See an example on page 297.

You will find a foundational collection of *Quest*-related mandalas in the Resources section. In addition, there will be a mandala, quaternity, and sub-quaternities to illustrate each of the ten waypoints. As you progress, they will inevitably spawn additional ones unique to your journey. Hopefully, your circles will soon begin to look like a pond spangled with intersecting ripples during a spring shower.

This powerful device helped me dive deeper into my inner being and explore myriad layers of myself. As a result, I created simple mandalas to chart my course. As of this writing, I have brought to life over two hundred mandalas that beautifully illuminate life's journey. They function as building blocks of true identity. They help us seek and create new meaning by interpreting the past, expanding horizons, and understanding and integrating the essence of being. And all this began with a simple exercise that you will find in the Essentials waypoint.

Seeing this growing interest, my wife used the first mandala I created to make a stunning mosaic for my atelier's wall. The symbolism of integrating hundreds of fragmented glass shards into a beautiful whole evoked powerful emotion as it took shape. It is truly a one-of-a-kind piece of art (a symbol in itself) that dynamically represents my identity in second life and the growing integration of my inner being.

2. Self

The second in this quaternity of symbols is the self. In the words of poet David Whyte, [*The Quest*] is about becoming a faithful and intimate companion to that initially formidable stranger you call your self.[7] If, as Carl Jung suggests, the mandala portrays the self in its ideal form, it would be to our advantage to discover and understand its layers. As the "central command center" of being, we represent the self by the innermost concentric circle on many *Quest* mandalas. See an example on page 298.

This section will explore the self as a mandala. The two upper quadrants represent the conscious self which contains the ego and the persona. The two lower quadrants illustrate the unconscious self, which holds the shadow and the gender (the inner masculine and feminine). In *The Quest*, these four aspects symbolize the quaternity of the self.

Ego

It may be helpful to consider the ego as a tiny sailboat tossed to and fro on life's ocean. The surface of this vast sea of life delineates the conscious and the unconscious. Above the surface is our conscious, which contains our ego and persona. Below the surface is the unconscious, which includes the shadow and the gender. We explore the conscious and unconscious further in other waypoints.

The self begins with an empty circle, and as life happens, it begins to fill up. Therefore, social compromise is necessary, for we cannot make our way in the world without it. But too much external domination spanks, combs, educates, and preaches the wonder right out of our being.

By their nature, institutions work to influence and control much of our lives—they want to write the rules for our self's physical, mental, emotional, and spiritual aspects. In addition, they tend to shame or discourage efforts that do not align with their preferences.

The Quest's calling is to be a unique being. Therefore, as we grow up, our values may begin to differ from the institutions (family, religion, education, and culture) of our life. There is a distinct possibility that our family will view this growth as a betrayal. And that religion will consider it as heresy, education as non-conformity, and culture may perceive it as rebellion.

But if we are to become whole and enjoy life, we must ask these questions:

- What do **I** want?
- What do **I** feel?
- What must **I** do to feel right with myself?
- What moves **me**?

A mid-life crisis (a better term may be a *search for identity*) happens when the symbols that formed our circle in the first half of life fragment. They no longer provide answers to the questions above. We will talk more about this in the Transitions waypoint.

Our calling is to live *our* wholeness and be who *we* are, not function like someone or something else. And for most of us, this requires new symbols; a tumultuous reckoning with all the people, places, events, values, and memories that have filled our circle of life.

The crisis freaks the ego out. For decades it had been smooth sailing on life's sea, and suddenly out of nowhere comes a catastrophic storm that tosses it around like a cork. When something goes wrong, the ego looks for the easy way out and looks for someone to blame; it goes into defense mode.

The ego always wants to be correct, and it begins blaming, projecting, denying, and suppressing. It activates all the classic defense mechanisms that Professor Freud taught us. We will look deeper into these protection devices when encountering the Emotions waypoint. At this point, it is essential to know there is no need to hold anyone accountable. Furthermore, we must recognize that self-blame is equally toxic as blaming others.

Personally, my ego invested the first half of life building up self-confidence and large-group charisma to stand on a stage and perform for thousands. Only to find me at mid-life with a restless and confusing desire to leave the performance stage and retreat to a place of solitude.

Jung's prescient words cannot be repeated enough, "Thoroughly unprepared; we take the step into the afternoon of life. Worse still, we take this step with the false presupposition that our truths and our ideals will serve us as before. But we cannot live the afternoon of life according to the program of life's morning. For what was great in the morning will be little at evening and what in the morning was true, at evening will have become a lie."

The stage, a primary symbol of my life's morning, became of little importance in life's afternoon. Unbeknownst to me at the time, the symbol of the table was to become of great significance. A drastic transition occurred from commanding the stage as a performer for large crowds to sitting around a table as an encourager for small groups. Thus, a radical change of one of my life symbols—from the stage to the table.

I built my ego identity around what I *did*—not who I *was*. Then, thoroughly unprepared for this crisis, all hell broke loose. My ego began to blame me and everyone for the bomb cyclone that had upended its peaceful voyage on the sea of life.

The time to ask which symbols of your first life may be fragmenting is before the identity crisis erupts. We might ask, what is this problematic transition, this brokenness, trying to show me? What can I learn? What new symbols do I need to find? We must force the ego to face these questions honestly. Only then will it submit to the conscious (persona) and unconscious (shadow and gender) aspects of ourselves.

Persona

The personas are the public roles required to function appropriately in Western culture. But when these roles (these masks we wear) don't allow the unconscious aspects to interact with the conscious, our personality becomes one-dimensional. This disconnect is where the ego allows defense mechanisms such as repression to kick in.

This split forces our natural personalities to adapt to the needs and demands of our institutions. Our family, church, school, and culture say we must act like a good little child. We must be a perfect spouse, a blameless Christian, an ideal student, a rousing success, and an excellent (socially and politically correct) person. *Don't* make waves, think too hard, or get big ideas. *Do* keep a low profile, stay in your own lane, and say yes even though you may not like it. In other words, we are to be and do what the influencers tell us we should. Others fill in our circle.

Institutions that authentically care about us should *promote* our personal development and never seek to suppress it. Unfortunately, as a rule, they refuse to allow us to be who we truly are, and we slowly begin to break apart inside. We must reclaim those parts of ourselves; salvage the treasures shipwrecked by institutional expectations, dogma, specialization, or prohibition.

At around age forty, while serving as an executive staff member, our chief operating officer organized a retreat where a professional consulting company administered a *DISC* personality assessment. It was extensive and returned over fifty pages of results. There were many interesting observations, but for me, the most impactful section contained two graphs. One illustrated the *natural* management style that reflected the real me, my "sweet spot." The other graph charted the *adapted* style, which showed how the work environment forced me to adjust to doing my job effectively.

The consultant told us that if the graphs show a substantial similarity between the primary and adapted styles, one probably feels comfortable being oneself in the work environment. But suppose there is a significant variance between the two types. In that case, that means something or someone in the environment motivates you to elevate or minimize aspects of your natural style. My two graphs were opposite. I was being forced to adapt my natural persona to succeed at my "dream" job.

This personality assessment was the first of several shattering revelations that prompted a mid-life search for identity. It hastened my resignation and subsequent transition to the second half of life.

Significant questions for the persona are:

- Who am I apart from my history and roles I have played?[8]
- What is the role I need *now* to be who I am?
- Do I need a mask at all?

An adapted persona fragments the self. Conversely, a natural persona integrates the self.

Shadow

The shadow contains the dark part of ourselves that we and others tend not to like—the faults and failings in ourselves that we usually hide, deny, or avoid. It is composed of negative characteristics (or those we believe to be negative) that we attempt to keep hidden to live the life required by family, church, school, and culture. In addition, elements of the shadow typically embody controversial aspects of human nature, such as anger, cynicism, all types of hatred, anxiety, and addiction.

However, we should not always equate the shadow with evil. It can also manifest helpful elements, treasures such as repressed memories, denied desires, and negative emotions that can be appropriately salvaged and used.[9]

One way to understand the shadow is through the negative characteristics we *project* on others. Projection is a defense mechanism that blames one's own unacceptable urges and actions on another.

The shadow answers these difficult questions: Why do good people do bad things? Why do people get stuck in a moment and can't get out of it?

The shadow can be individual and collective. We see the collective's dark power in a lynch mob and the January 6, 2021 insurrection attack on the US Capitol. What we hide in our unconscious can and will hurt us and others. The more we hide, the smaller and more fragmented we become.

However difficult it may be, we must bring shadow life to the surface of the unconscious as we confront the opportunity to grow and enjoy life. Or else we will be lost in a fragmented situation, get stuck, and inevitably digress.

People who refuse to confront the shadow in the second half of life are those we say are frozen in time. They are doomed to an existence that chains them to the dark forces of the past. The individual who denies self will grow increasingly ignorant of living their uniqueness.

Instead, they tend to be educated, influenced, and controlled as a subnormal social unit. We see this in the Nazi movement in Germany, the white supremacy movement of the American South, the Maga movement in the United States, and the cult of evangelical Christianity across the globe.

The arts abound with symbolic portrayals of this murky aspect of the self. A well-known example in literature is *The Strange Case of Dr. Jekyll and Mr. Hyde* by Robert Louis Stevenson. In *Star Wars,* Luke Skywalker's shadow figure is Darth Vader. Likewise, the theater characterizes the shadow with the symbolism of the phantom in the Broadway musical *Phantom of the Opera.*

Progressively discovering these fragmented, buried, and projected parts of ourselves and salvaging them deepens our journey and gives us practical work for a lifetime. As tricky as this shadow work may seem, it is necessary to experience psychological healing, inner growth, and healing relationships. We will further explore shadow work in the Enlightenment waypoint.

On a more encouraging note, the positive side of shadow work for *The Quest* comes as we gradually transcend the aspects of our dark side. Examples include converting anger to passion, cynicism to sensitivity, hatred to openness and acceptance, anxiety to contentment, and addiction to freedom.

Think of the shadow as the backside of your light side. The challenge is to bring treasures to the surface that life institutions have sunk deep in the unconscious. These are the aspects of ourselves that have been devalued, shamed, or given little support during the first half of life.

Too many of us made a terrible decision years before we knew better, and these compromises filled us with despair. Therefore, we repressed longings, denied creativity, stifled prophecies, squelched questions, and vowed never to consider them again. The poet Robert Bly asks this powerful question. "How many years must pass before a person finds the dark parts of themselves that they threw away?"[10]

To raise the positive values, the treasures, from that "ship graveyard" we call the unconscious, we have to know who we truly want to be. That knowledge requires much sorting through damaged goods to find the sunken treasure. And the realization that being your *whole* self—not your "good" self— leads to a life of enjoyment.

A healthy shadow helps integrate the dark and light aspects of self.

Gender

Understandings of gender continually evolve. This progression has perhaps never been more true than it is now. The data show that today's young people have significantly different interpretations of gender than previous generations, with consequences for all children, families, organizations, and institutions.[11]

Gender is the behavioral, cultural, or psychological traits typically associated with one sex.[12] Humans are born with biological characteristics of sex, either male, female, or intersex. Gender, however, is a social construct and generally based on the norms, behaviors, and societal roles expected of individuals based primarily on their sex.[13]

Gender identity describes a person's self-perceived sex: male, female, or otherwise. In recent years, expanding the public understanding of gender has freed many to feel more comfortable in their skin and live like the people they believe themselves to be. A 2015 poll of adults ages 18-34 in America found that most see gender as a *spectrum* rather than a man or woman binary.[14]

All of us are inundated with gender messages from the time we are born, yet with few opportunities to consider or understand this foundational aspect of self deeply. Societal ideas about gender will affect every critical part of one's life, from education to career, finances, relationships, and more.

While the gender spectrum and the desire for wholeness are universal—ultimately, gender is unique. Our individual intersection of identities, experiences, and personal characteristics informs each dimension of gender. Our gender is personal. While we share some aspects of self with others, the way these identities, influences, and characteristics come together is unique.[15]

Another distinction to make is the difference between gender and sexual orientation. Unfortunately, these contrasts are often incorrectly merged. In actuality, gender and sexual orientation are two distinct but related aspects of self. Gender is personal (how we see ourselves). At the same time, sexual orientation is interpersonal (who we are physically, emotionally, or romantically attracted to).

It is critical to distinguish between these two concepts. When we confuse gender with sexual orientation, we are likely to make assumptions about someone that has nothing to do with who they are. For example, what someone wears and how they act is about gender expression. However, you cannot tell what a person's sexual orientation is by what they wear. For that matter, you can't know what their gender identity is unless they tell you.[16]

We refer to people whose gender identity corresponds to their biological sex as cisgender. Transgender people have a gender identity that does not conform to their sex assignment at birth. People whose gender identity feels neither masculine nor feminine may identify as non-binary, and those who feel no gender identity may refer to themselves as "agender."[17]

Cisgender men may struggle to live up to notions of masculinity taught to them from a young age. Cisgender women may worry that sexism limits their opportunities. They fear that pursuing their goals will lead others to see them as less feminine and somehow less worthy. Especially if they do not dress or maintain their appearance as others expect them to.

Transgender people may feel profoundly disconnected from their true selves. Some who have experienced congruence (openly nonbinary or genderqueer) may feel more like themselves. However, discrimination often comes from those clinging to socially constructed notions about who men and women are supposed to be.[18]

The **feminine** (the Jungian term is anima) is the cumulative group of qualities traditionally associated with women in the unconscious. These traits may symbolize a masculine's emerging feminine side. They are the carrier and mediator of relational capacity—the relationship to the body, instinct, feelings, and emotions, to other feminines, and last but not least, to the unconscious.

Until we open up to this inner aspect of self, our journey will be troubled, and our intimacy with other genders will remain challenging. This awareness involves knowledge of the inner feminine and accepting it.

In mid-life, some people project the inner feminine onto another person. This attribution of ideas, feelings, or attitudes can cause a person to inexplicably and suddenly fall "head over heels" in love and declare that person to be "soulmate." One feels as if they have known this person intimately for all time, an infatuation that seems like utter madness to friends and family.

This attribution often results in a torrid love affair that can devastate a marriage and wreak havoc upon the families involved. The projection of one's inner feminine on another person is a desperate search for the traditionally understood "womanly" aspects hidden deep in the unconscious. It comes about primarily because of dissatisfaction with institutional masculine and patriarchal dictates during the first half of life. The healthy inner feminine has a burning desire for wholeness —to integrate and cultivate gender.

It is no coincidence that this often happens during the brokenness of the transition to the second half of life. Instead of doing the work to plumb our inner depths for the feminine treasure of who we are, we attempt a shortcut with someone who triggers the feminine characteristics of our anima. This other person's empathy serves as a drug for the brokenness inside.

This rapt attention from the forbidden other often comes as family and friends do not have the time to deal with the complex upheaval of the once "normal" person they knew. Therefore, they tend to ignore it—hoping it will go away with time.

But for those longing to be who they truly are, no matter the cost, these desires will not go away. On the contrary, a beautiful hunger for the feminine inner life will rise to the surface of the conscious. And they will deal with it in whatever way possible, ever fearful that external authorities will repress their longings once again.

For those who feel the cost is too great, the shame and regret that family, culture, and religion heap upon them becomes too much. As a result, they lack the courage to examine why this hunger gnaws deep within. Instead, they give up, ask forgiveness, and are content to return to "normal" and go back to living a fragmented and unexamined life.

On a positive note, in Jungian psychology:

1. If developed early, the inner feminine can help find the right marriage partner.

2. It helps dig out facts, feelings, and fantasies hidden in the unconscious.

3. The inner feminine puts one's mind in tune with congruent (cohesive) inner values. It opens the way into more profound depths.

4. The inner feminine acts as a mediator, or guide, to the inner world of the unconscious and the self.

The difficult task is cultivating and raising the inner feminine to the conscious's surface. We can do this by the painful (but simple) decision to accept our feminine feelings, desires, and fantasies seriously. But unfortunately, many cisgender masculines are taught to ignore feelings from the beginning of life. That feminine traits and longings are taboo.

At the urging of a life coach, I began painting watercolors in 2002. It was quickly evident that my enjoyment derived from painting nudes, particularly females. Not until years later did I realize these hundreds of paintings were self-portraits. My feminine acted as a guide to my unconscious, my inner world.

A further revelation was that my career as a musician and worship leader required utilizing the feminine aspects of my being. At a training conference, religious leaders stressed that a worship leader's role in leadership was that of "wife" to the pastor.

Dr. Allan Chinen cites other individuals who consciously reject traditional masculine roles and favor their feminine side, embracing feeling, intuition, nurturing, and sensitivity. He says artists, pacifists, healers, and gay men often fall into this group. These individuals honor the feminine and often lose touch with their masculine interests. These nontraditional men often lose contact with their male energy.[19]

My first life career required a primary identification with my feminine to do my job effectively. That is one reason why I now believe gender is a spectrum. A person with a male body can identify with feminine traits, and a person with a female body can identify with masculine characteristics. And we are only beginning to understand all sorts of variations on gender.

As I approached the mid-life search for identity, this became a primary example of a fragmented symbol. Was I to continue to embrace the feminine aspects of myself in my second life, or was I to elevate my masculine side? Or was I to become androgynous or non-binary? These questions helped me choose my mandala symbol for the *physical* aspect of my being. And I continue to process this "new" gender identity at the time of this writing.

If you could describe, draw, and paint your inner feminine, how would she look? Who is your ideal feminine? What actress or famous painting would best personify her? These answers may provide clues to the aspects of your feminine self.

A healthy gender identity helps integrate and cultivate your inner feminine and masculine.

The **masculine** (the Jungian term is animus) is the cumulative group qualities traditionally associated with men in the unconscious. It helps one express their deepest self, confidently and autonomously to the outer world. Many of the universal truths that apply to the feminine apply to the masculine. But because the world remains stubbornly patriarchal (institutions controlled primarily by men), there are some crucial differences.

The inner masculine is the carrier and mediator of one's most authoritative inner thoughts, impulses, and ideas. Dr. Clarissa Pinkola Estes' research and writings form the foundation of this section.[20] She says the masculine traits work as a helper, helpmate, lover, brother, father, and king in proper balance. However, the term king does *not* mean the masculine is the dictator of the feminine's inner being, as an injured patriarchal perspective might imply. Instead, it means a kingly aspect exists in one's inner being. When healthy and developed, the masculine roles act and mediate in loving service to one's true nature.

In the unconscious, a healthy masculine plays the role of a mentor and ideally helps realize possibilities and goals. It weighs the justice and integrity of things, strategizes when threatened, and helps unite one's inner being.

Confidence in decisions is lost if a dysfunctional father figure or patriarchal institution has relegated the masculine to a harmful or unhealthy role. Moreover, this fragmented role causes one to question the validity or reality of creative instincts, desires, and work.

Suppose one thinks about going back to college, attending an art class, learning a foreign language, starting a business, or fulfilling a lifelong dream of writing a novel. However, they stop the process, choking on a lack of inward nourishment and support. And we let others put the masculine in exile by asking questions such as: "But why would you want to be an: older student, artist, linguist, entrepreneur, or writer?" "Do you think you have the talent?" "Why would you think you have something to say that others have not already said?"

How does one develop the masculine to act as a champion or mentor in this messy world? Dr. Estes provides illuminating assistance. She urges those born feminine to practice graciously accepting compliments without disclaimers. To respond to all that goes on around them, let ideas loose, and begin something—*anything* to get started. She advises them to protect creative time and practice their goals every day. To stay with it, insist on quality time, and be sure to find nourishment for the creative life.

Finding and raising the inner masculine from the unconscious to the conscious's surface takes time and suffering. Jung says a feminine must realize who and what their masculine is and understand its emotional triggers. (We will explore this further in the Emotions waypoint.)

Instead of allowing others to subjugate one's freedom, we must confront these realities. In that case, the inner masculine can turn into a valuable inner companion who endows the feminine with the qualities of initiative, courage, confidence, independence, power, objectivity, and wisdom.

****

Gender diversity has existed throughout history. As one of the fundamental aspects of a person's self, gender profoundly influences every part of life. Where this crucial aspect is narrowly defined and rigidly enforced, individuals outside of its norms face innumerable challenges. Even those who vary only slightly from standards can become targets of disapproval, discrimination, and even violence.

This difficulty does not have to be the case. Through thoughtful consideration of the uniqueness and validity of every person's experience of self, we can develop greater acceptance for all. Not only will this create greater inclusion for one's who challenge the norms of gender, but it will also create space for all of us to fully explore and express who we are.[21]

Gender integration is the feeling of harmony in our gender:

- Experiencing comfort in our body as it relates to our gender.
- The naming of our gender that adequately corresponds with our internal sense of who we are.
- Expressing ourselves through clothing, mannerisms, interests, and activities.
- Being seen consistently by others as we see ourselves.

Finding wholeness is an ongoing process throughout our lives as we continue to grow and gain insight into ourselves. We find it most often through exploration. For some, finding congruence is fairly simple; however, for others, it is a complex process. Yet the fundamental need to find gender wholeness is true for us all, and any degree to which we don't experience it can be fragmenting.

A healthy gender identity helps integrate and cultivate the dimensions of one's gender.

3.   Myth

The third in this quaternity of symbols is myth. Unlike our modern understanding of the word, myths are not fantasies and superstitions. Instead, *Merriam-Webster* defines myth as a story told in an ancient culture to explain a practice, belief, or natural occurrence.[22]

Myths are stories that have permeated the wallpaper of our lives. Allan Chinen (a modern-day myth teller) writes they influence belief and behavior and infuse meaning into our lives.[23] They are universal stories so timeless that they echo throughout humanity. And we humans crave good stories like we crave good food.

These old stories haven't passed; they still have the power to connect our journeys to those of ancient gods, fairy tales, and folktales. When we find our self in a universal story, it lifts us out of our isolation and makes us feel that we are not alone. Furthermore, they contain a wealth of symbolism that can help replace the fragmented and broken symbols of our first half of life.

As you peruse these stories, notice if you feel drawn to one of the tales, heroes, heroines, gods, or goddesses. Because they are universal stories, I think that every one of us is linked to the essence of at least one. Sociologist Joseph Campbell believed this strongly. He said the essential thing in life is to find your personal myth.

Unfortunately, most of us know little of the stories that recount these enthralling journeys. Poet Robert Bly estimates that people in the West lost their ability to think mythologically around the year 1000. Perhaps because Christianity would not allow any new stories or new gods, or perhaps because the exciting pursuit of science after the Renaissance absorbed more and more imaginative energy.[24]

In recent times, America's education institution places little (if any) emphasis on these tales as old as time. For instance, how many of us know about Hephaestus?

In his delightful book *A Thing of Beauty*, Peter Fiennes retells the myth of this fatherless son of Hera, the queen of the gods. Hephaestus married Aphrodite (the laughing goddess of love), who often cheated on him with taller and stronger mortals. Although 'cheated' is not the right word to describe what a goddess may choose to do.

He took an ax and split open Zeus' skull when it was time for the goddess Athena to be born. Later (we don't know when, because time has no meaning here), Hephaestus pursued the beautiful but chaste goddess and tried to make love to her. She swatted him away, but in his excitement, he had spattered her thigh with his semen. She wiped herself down with a cloth and flung it to the ground.

And that is how one of the first kings of Athens was born, half-snake and half-human. Hera arose from the earth where Aphrodite tossed Hephaestus' sodden and embarrassing scrap of cloth. Ah, the classics.[25]

One has to admit there is a lot to unpack in this story, with more than a few relatable elements for many of us. And it is not hard to see why the prudish and censorious public education system acts as if these provocative stories do not exist. But alas, we are the worst for it.

No matter how the institutions of life attempt to suppress and purge these timeless myths—they prevail. They are a part of everyday life—yet we are often oblivious of their existence. Instead, we take them for granted.

Consider the concept of erotic love derived from the god Eros and the Gaia hypothesis, which posits the earth's living and non-living parts are a single organism. And the names of the planets Saturn, Mars, Venus, Mercury, and Neptune. The god Uranus inspired the name of the robust metal Uranium; the term superhuman and the fated ship *Titanic* are but a few of the namesakes of the Titan gods.

If one is truly serious about undertaking this noble *Quest*, it may prove advantageous to learn more. An accessible way to begin is *The Greek and Roman Myths: A Guide to the Classical Stories* by Philip Matyszak. For female archetypes, consider the books of Marie-Louise von Franz and Madeline Miller.

Furthermore, the masterful retellings by Allan B. Chinen, *In the Ever After*, *Beyond the Hero*, and *Once Upon A Mid-Life*.

We are not alone in our journey. It is possible to stand on the shoulders of those who have gone before us. Myths can serve as symbols, guides, and templates for our explorations—particularly in difficult life transitions.

Robert Bly says these ancient stories are vital because they are free from modern psychological prejudices. They have endured the scrutiny of generations of women and men, giving humanity both light and dark sides.[26]

Furthermore, they give us images to help our unconscious connect with our conscious—to discover our deepest parts. Finding and utilizing a personal myth is a crucial aspect of *The Quest*. Next are four (a quaternity) myth types to act as a starting point. There are many more.

First, we need to understand **archetypes**. The word archetype is used in Jungian psychology and refers to unconscious thoughts or symbols that seem to be universal. Luke Skywalker and Wonder Woman are two modern examples of the hero archetypes that first appeared in ancient mythology.

Jung posited that all humans unconsciously share specific thoughts or images expressed in fairy tales and mythology. For example, most cultures have similar ideas of the qualities of a hero. That similar *idea* is called an archetype, and the "hero" in a story would be a *specific* archetype.

We have inherited these wisdom structures, and they dwell deep within our unconscious. Archetypes possess great power for our *Quest* because they have the wisdom of collective humanity within them. Although it may not be possible to activate an entire archetype, we can embody parts of it. These characteristics are some of the treasures we discuss in the Unconscious waypoint.

At the risk of oversimplification, myth is the universal story. The archetypes are the universal ideas and models within the story that we can uniquely activate. The archetypes and myths give us powerful language and symbols to understand our *Quest*. Practically speaking, myths have provided guidelines for the conduct of life throughout human history.

The Hero and Heroine Myths

Joseph Campbell dedicated his life to studying universal myths in history and mythic figures in literature. He identified striking connections between Christian beliefs, such as the virgin birth of Jesus, and the religious beliefs of Native Americans. Because there were many similarities, he concluded that the views could not be coincidental.

The findings inspired Campbell to conclude that mythologies worldwide are related and that religions systematically misinterpret their own beliefs as exclusive. He called these common aspects the "Hero's Myth" or the "Hero's Journey." The journey symbolizes the rediscovery of the unconscious elements that the adult lost contact with while growing up.[27]

The hero myths are the most well-known in the world. For example, the *son of man* version includes some or all of these common aspects: a miraculous but humble birth, early proof of god-like strength or wisdom, a rapid rise to prominence or power, a small group of disciples, a victorious struggle with evil, the temptation to succumb to the "sin" of pride, a fall through betrayal or a "heroic" sacrifice that ends in death.

Sound familiar? It should. A few of the earliest myths that contained most facets of the son of man Hero's Journey were:

Horus, Quetzalcoatl, Buddha, Krishna, Zarathustra, and Jesus Christ.

After working with Campbell, Maureen Murdock wrote *The Heroine's Journey: Woman's Quest for Wholeness* to provide a less patriarchal outline. We will explore the steps of both journeys in the Transitions waypoint.

Most cultures have hero or heroine myths. These include well-known stories such as Achilles, Hercules, Odysseus, Atalanta, Gilgamesh, Thor, Beowulf, Samson, Saint Lucy, King Arthur, Joan of Arc, Davy Crockett, Luke Skywalker, and Mulan.

Disney, DC Entertainment, and Marvel Studios bring us hero myths for a modern generation. So, it should not surprise that it wasn't enough for America to have mere heroes; therefore, they created *Super*heroes. And we can't get enough. The seventies and eighties decades brought us the Superman and Batman movies and numerous sequels. In 2006 the *Marvel Studios* cinematic universe exploded with male and female characters from their immense treasure trove of over 7,000 comic book heroes.

The journey from struggle to strength is the heart of the hero or heroine's journey. There are countless tales in history and pop culture that tell of courageous people who overcome trauma—those who return to everyday life as better people for themselves and the world.

These journeys are invaluable for those in the first life as they struggle to establish a family, career, and identity. But when the mid-life transition looms, the hero or heroine's journey is often insufficient, and another universal journey may be necessary.

Who is your favorite hero? Heroine? Superhero? Why? To paint in broad strokes, the hero or heroine feels a calling to *save* the world.

The Healer Myths

These myths include chronicles of healers who were said to have the power of curing and wellness. Homer tells us that Asclepius is the Greek god honored by healers and physicians as the god of medicine in the Iliad. His serpent-draped staff, The Rod of Asclepius, is still found as the symbol of medical practice today.[28]

Other healing stories include Artemis, Brighid, Sirona, St. Luke, Jesus Christ, Florence Nightingale, and Theodore Roosevelt. An excellent modern retelling of the healer myth is *Circe* by Madeline Miller.

Today we associate healers of the body with physicians, nurses, psychologists, veterinarians, massage therapists, environmentalists, faith healers, chiropractors, and acupuncturists, to name a few. Characteristics they share in common include a calling to ease people and animals' suffering, serve the underrepresented, and protect mother earth. In addition, they tend to be highly empathic and sensitive. But if this myth calls to you, beware, for true healers have to be wounded themselves.

What healer archetype has proven most beneficial to you? Why? To paint in broad strokes, the healer feels a calling to *heal* the world.

The Shaman Myths

The term shaman probably originated in northeast Asia. Anthropologist Michael Brown notes that shamanism, not prostitution, is the oldest profession.[29] However, in modern times this revered myth and archetype has been misunderstood.

The Toltecs are an ancient group of Native Americans who reside primarily in Mexico. Shaman Don Jose Ruiz says that when his immigrant ancestors arrived in the Americas, shamans were called witch doctors, medicine men, and sorcerers. Despite the last syllable of the word shaman, they are all genders.[30]

He says that shaman means "the awakened ones" in his ancient tradition and is also the word for the life force energy, the divinity we all have inside us. Shamanism refers to the spiritual practice or religion of native cultures worldwide. These spiritual traditions are said to have certain things in common: a respect for nature, a respect for all life, and a respect for ancestors. But this is only the barest of beginnings of what it means to practice shamanism.

Ruiz continues that their roles in their communities were a sophisticated combination of philosopher, spiritual leader, medical doctor, psychologist, and friend. Shamanism is a complex and powerful practice available to all humankind. It personifies the wisdom of waking up, finding personal freedom, living in peace and harmony, and serving others and the planet.

This myth may have influenced subsequent vocations such as the minister, priest, guide, and mentor. Shamans believe their universal story can help one move forward to break the emotional cycle of suffering, to dream one's possibilities, and to manifest them to the world. With the notable exception of Christianity, most believe that the power to live out this myth comes from the wisdom within you—not external spiritual authority.

Be warned; it can be challenging to wade through the plethora of material (many are far-fetched and unsubstantiated) attempting to describe the shaman myth. In addition to Ruiz's books, another invaluable resource is *The World of Shamanism* by

Dr. Roger Walsh. He says that we have much to learn from shamans: the myths they live by, the training they undergo, the techniques they use, the crises they confront, the capacities they develop, the states of consciousness they enter, the understandings they gain, the visions they see, and the cosmic travels they take. For untold thousands of years, the world of shamanism has helped, healed, and taught humankind, and it has still more to offer us.[31]

The more one explores the shaman myth, the more it points to the unrecognized potential of our inner being. The shaman feels a calling to wake up inhabitants of the world and help them accept their personal and unique truth. To paint in broad strokes, the shaman feels a calling to *guide* the world.

The Sexual Myths

In the human course of *The Quest's* twists and turns, we inevitably encounter sex. As we mentioned, second only to shamanism, prostitution is the world's oldest profession. Archaeologists believe that the origins of the many aspects of sexual myths go back millions of years.

Scientists use skeletons of Amazon women, golden penis sheaths, charred remains of aphrodisiac herbs, and prehistoric erotic art to trace sexual practices back to their ancient origins. These include contraception, homosexuality, transsexuality, prostitution, sadomasochism, and bestiality.

Numerous myths surround sex—this most primal of our basic instincts. Throughout history, these stories vividly illustrate this biological instinct in sacred and profane ways. But despite its central place in history and biology, sex remains an often mysterious and poorly understood impulse encompassed by shame, anxiety, and guilt.

Sexual myths can point to a significant part of one's personal story. Our fantasies and proclivities tell us much about who we are deep within and how we developed in our first half of life. Unfortunately, however, the subject is shrouded in negative emotion, and we ignore or suppress these myths. But they are as old as time and have enormous relevance for our lives today.

We are all sexual beings, and because of the strong emotions that surround our desires and longings, we will spend a significant amount of time with the sexual myths.

Understanding the sexual aspects and symbolism of who we are is another path to wholeness. The myths, fantasies, and stories that resonate with us provide clues to salvage repressed events, people, places, and memories. Once we discover these "shipwrecks" in our unconscious, we can initiate *life repair*. We will explore this further in the Catharsis waypoint.

Discovering and redeeming our sexual treasures amid the repressed, suppressed, and denied shipwrecks of our lives is a vital task of *The Quest*. We may feel our deepest sexual longings are perverted or abnormal. But in reality, as we explore the symbolism of these myths, we realize that we are not alone; they have been around for thousands of years.

These myths come to life through the erotic stories of the Greek gods, Aphrodite, Pan, and Priapus. Other sex gods include Cupid and Venus (Roman); Rati (Hindu); Astarte (Canaan); and Ixcuiname (Aztec). Old Indian sex manuals such as the *Kama Sutra* still provide provocative and imaginative insight into our sex lives. While famous for its many sexual positions, it also espouses the art of enjoying life and the pleasures of love.

The Hindu *Upanishads* and *Bhagavad Gita* are replete with sexual symbolism. However, as R.C. Zaehner points out, this has often escaped notice due to persistent mistranslation.[32] And anyone who has read the *Holy Bible* knows that if it were subject to the Western rating systems, it would be rated NC-17 and labeled explicit subject matter.

Notwithstanding the graphic sexuality of these revered holy books, most novels and movies based on sexual myths have been habitually censored, banned, and burned by life institutions. A few examples of the many books include *Lady Chatterley's Lover* by D.H. Lawrence, *Tropic of Cancer* by Henry Miller, *Lolita* by Vladimir Nabokov, *Delta of Venus* by Anais Nin, and *The Story of O* by Pauline Reage. Movies include *Last Tango In Paris*, *The Last Temptation of Christ*, *A Clockwork Orange*, *Hail Mary*, and *Brokeback Mountain*.

Modern culture has dubbed personalities such as Rita Hayworth, James Dean, Marilyn Monroe, Farrah Fawcett, George Clooney, Jenna Jameson, Rihanna, and David Beckham as *sex symbols*. Considering the time we spend thinking about sex, craving sex, having sex, and viewing digital sex acts, it's no wonder we are overwhelmed. So, let's look at four of the most prevalent sexual myths.

Pleasure Myths. In ancient Greece, Homer and Plutarch told the story of Aphrodite, goddess of sexual intercourse. She emerged from the foaming semen of her father's castrated testicles. Likewise, mortal heroes such as Hercules have ravished fifty virgins in a single night. He also had an affair with his nephew and fell in love with another man with "curling locks."[33]

Greek men would claim adolescent boys and prostitutes as their lovers. Therefore, neglected wives found ways to satisfy their desires. The lesbian culture was associated with the stories of the Greek island of Lesbos "where burning Sappho loved and sung."

The literature contains many references regarding dildos made of padded leather and anointed with olive oil before use.

And, there were the Romans. One only has to watch the movie *Caligula* or visit the ancient city of Pompeii for graphic depictions of their sexual practices and excesses. Pleasure myths abounded, detailing the Bacchanalian festivals, which abandoned all restraint. The hedonism and lawlessness of these rites, with rampant orgies, was so pronounced that Rome outlawed public worship of Bacchus in 186 BCE.[34]

Unsurprisingly, Romans devoted much attention to developing contraception, a practice that is frowned upon by many religions to this day.

Worship Myths. Over 4,000 years ago in eastern Galilee, myths tell us that the people worshipped the goddess Astarte. Sacred prostitutes (human priestesses) who represented the goddess would dance in her honor at the temple and copulate with worthy men who were chosen and had paid for the sacred ritual.[35]

The Greek historian Herodotus writes about the worship of the goddess Aphrodite that required a woman, once in her lifetime, to offer herself to a stranger. The rite would proceed as follows: the woman would arrive at the temple, wait for the first man to put money into her lap, and speak the sacred words. Whether King or Shepherd, young or old, she would be obligated to have sex with him. Refusing was a sin, and her money was holy and remitted to the temple.[36]

During fertility rites in ancient Sumeria, the people expected the young king to show that his relationship with the goddess was strong. By bedding her chief priestess in full view of his subjects. The eager audience rejoiced if it appeared the coupling was a successful one—it would mean good crops and prosperity ahead.

Tantric Indian sacred sexuality is another elaborate worship myth representing a soul union with the gods. For example, in the *Mahanirvana Tantra,* the Tantric scriptures, a conversation between the god Shiva and goddess Shakti describes sexual behavior in graphic and lingering detail.

Modern-day Czechoslovakia still publicly celebrates bizarre fertility rites around the Easter season. Custom forces females to line the streets while the men whip them with cords. The women reward the men with a colorful Easter egg. The symbolism is evident; the whipping ensures the woman stays fertile, say Czechs. They whip women of all ages, from little girls to grandmothers. The rules say it is rude to leave any woman out, even if she's seventy years old.[37]

Procreation Myths. But then came the Christians. Around 1600 years ago, Christian moralists began to censor, rewrite, and destroy sexual myths. Many of the rules and taboos regarding sex originate in medieval dogma, such as the Old Testament. They persist to this day thousands of years later. For example, they teach that sexuality inhibits spiritual growth.

The church and clergy's threat of hellfire proved one of the most successful deterrents to pleasure ever invented. Lust and sex became associated with the original sin of Adam and Eve. The Christianized version of the hero myth, Jesus, was said to have been miraculously conceived without sexual intercourse.

The Christian Church forbade and severely punished adultery, incest, masturbation, oral sex, anal sex, and sex between men. Sex was allowed only within marriage and tolerated for procreation purposes only. In addition, they banned birth control because of its association with pleasure. To this day, these ancient procreation myths have transformed sex into a highly regulated activity loaded with fear, repression, and danger.

Religion censored the gods who represented the divine element in sexual energy, such as Aphrodite, Aurora, Shiva, Pan, Dionysus, and Hermes. Therefore, humanity lost many helpful archetypes and myths. As a result, our erotic energy lost much of its ability to mature and be expressed healthily.

Pornography and Fantasy Myths. As technology permeated the culture at the beginning of the 20th century, still photographs became moving pictures. However, it was only thirty years ago that the internet became ubiquitous and pornography increasingly available to enjoy in the privacy of the home. This virtually unrestricted access to all types of sexual pleasure and proclivities changed much of our lives. Far from the harmful effects first condemned from religious pulpits, many experts now feel we can use pornography constructively.

The highly respected psychologist Dr. Robert Stoller believes that pornography is a modern collection of adult sexual myths. In his provocative book, *Porn*, after years of scientific study, he writes that pornography (except for porn that uses little children) does little harm. He notes that banning pornography because it is harmful is like banning alcohol, automobiles, politics, vitamins, high-heeled shoes, computers, money, skiing, someone else's religion, and sunshine.[38]

In 2017 the internet site *Pornhub* released a fascinating list of the top ten all-time categories viewed by consumers of free pornography.

10. Hentai
9. Larger-than-normal penises
8. Well-endowed women
7. Anal
6. Ebony
5. Mature
4. Teen (18+)
3. Amateur
2. MILF
1. Lesbian

It doesn't take a psychologist to realize that the symbolic themes of pornography say much about our inner being, our desires and longings, sexual fantasies, and sexual myths. In the Stages waypoint, we see that the *primary themes* of the development stage are symbolized by numbers eight and nine on the list above. How we develop in the first stage of life significantly influences the formation of our sexual identity.

Most of us have never considered the symbolism of our sexual fantasies or preferences. Unfortunately, the absence of such awareness is often the result of shame. As a result, we frequently censor our sexual thoughts and feelings, even with ourselves.

Much repression of "dirty" or "naughty" thoughts and longings comes from the desire to be accepted by life's institutions, particularly during early development. The prudes, patriarchs, and power-mongers who tend to run countries and large institutions have long shamed the enjoyment of sex.

Therefore, a shameful view of the body and its forbidden desires permeate our culture. Yet as we see in the Emotions waypoint, these feelings are universal. Still, the way they trigger us determines the unique scripts (our personal myths) that play out on the stage of our lives.

Our scripts are made up of (in the words of Dr. Stoller) impulses, desires, defenses, falsifications, truths avoided, and memories of past events, erotic and non-erotic, going back to infancy. Nevertheless, they are a piece of theater whose story seems genuine because of the truth of the body's sensations.

Although the scripts of our fantasies seem to be spontaneous, they are far from it. Instead, they result from years of working to make them function efficiently. That is, to ensure that they produce excitement, with its end product, gratification, and not anxiety, depression, guilt, or boredom.

The type of pornography we prefer, and the sexual myths that please us, offer myriad clues to our life journey. If we can put aside the taboos, shame, and censorship of religious and cultural institutions, a candid and non-judgmental examination of these sexual symbols can bring us closer to understanding our true self.

In his book *Arousal*, Dr. Michael Bader says that our capacity for sexual fantasy is an enduring aspect of what it means to be human. But we often feel embarrassed about our sexual thoughts (our myths) because we assume that our thoughts define who we are.

For some of us who have grown up in highly restrictive or abusive environments, the only way to understand these sexual myths as symbols will require therapy. We will talk more about this in the Unconscious waypoint.

Salvaging the unconscious origins of one's sex life will help reduce the shame that restricts it. Furthermore, knowledge of symbols such as our preferred sexual myths provides vital communication tools. They help us identify the treasures and shipwrecks that have been forced to the bottom of the vast sea of our unconscious.

Finally, here is a word of disclaimer. This section on sexual myth does not take into account—nor does it intend to dismiss the reality of—sexual disorders or improper use of porn for revenge or the exploitation of children. It addresses people who do *not* have psychological disorders.

Understanding how sexual myths play out in our lives can help us accept who we are more easily. We should not view them judgmentally with a moralistic viewpoint. Instead, we should see them with compassion. Then we can look at our desires as healthy and not perverted.

****

Other well-known universal myths include stories about the trickster, warrior, the god-king, priest, good shepherd, the shapeshifter, mother nature, and mother goddess.

It is natural to feel drawn to several or perhaps all of these myths. After all, they are universal. But fellow travelers such as Joseph Campbell, Carl Jung, and Paulo Coelho stress the vital importance of finding your myth—your legend. We must seek to discover the story that fits our uniqueness, the myth that resonates deep within. But you may ask, how is one to know?

The story will speak to you. Words will leap from the page and become music, and voices will whisper in your ear. The characters will enter and exit the stage of your memory, trailing the scent of seductive pheromones. Find the myth that speaks the language you know, and it will be a tale or a song as old as time that sounds like you are hearing it for the first time.

You will know it. Achilles knew that he was born to be a hero, Circe a healer, Odin a shaman, and Aphrodite, a lover. If you are open to the ways of *The Quest,* you will not be able to escape your unique myth. And the aspects of the story will be like a personal treasure map guiding you through life.

Whether one calls it myth, legend, calling, purpose, or birthright, you will experience a resonance throughout your being when you discover the myth you were made for. As you begin to live your mythic story, a sense of enjoyment, peace, and wholeness will permeate your being.

Each of us already has a personal myth that drives us—although we may not be aware of it. So, questions for this symbol are:

- By what myth(s) am I living?
- Will my current myth survive mid-life?
- Should it survive?
- What's my story?

4. Art

The fourth in this quaternity of symbols is art. Creatives have transformed everyday objects and forms into symbols of beauty, depth, and meaning throughout history. These symbols endow the arts with vast psychological importance. The Spanish painter Joan Miró says, "Artists are often surprised at the shapes of their creation."[39]

Let's look at a quaternity (four types) of art. Then, as you read each genre, determine which speaks most effectively to your deepest being.

Cinematic

Motion pictures are the most consequential narrative art form in recent history. This technique adds depth and helps viewers see things in new and fascinating ways. Perhaps no one does it better than *Disney*. Their mythic masterpieces are some of the most symbolic films ever produced.

Consider *Beauty and the Beast*. Belle wears a yellow dress symbolizing a growing love between herself and the beast. A dark and stormy night represents the emotions of anxiety and terror. The castle is full of trash and dust, symbolizing desolation and neglect. The windows grow progressively larger until they fill the entire walls as Belle and the Beast get to know one another.

It is essential to pay attention to stories on the big and small screens that elicit emotion. One helpful way is to journal a film or scene that prompts a tear or a verklempt. Then, after a while, look for patterns and ask yourself why those moments impacted you.

Fortunately, creators of motion pictures love the great myths. Movies include *Indiana Jones* (hero), *Chocolat* (healer), *Dead Poets Society (*shaman*), The Brothers Bloom* (trickster*), Gladiator* (warrior*), The Outsider Series* (shapeshifter*), and *Sirens* (sexual*).*

Visual

Artists use pigments, canvas, and other materials to create art with painting, drawing, photography, and sculpture. From the 44,000-year-old cave drawings of mythological trickster figures on the island of Sulawesi to the American pop art of Andy Warhol, artists have utilized symbols to express their views of the world.

Consider Warhol's most well-known painting of Campbell's Soup cans. Thirty-two canvases represent all the varieties offered at that time. This symbolic work seems to manifest Warhol's interpretation of the booming prosperity America enjoys. He creates the experience of shopping in a huge supermarket. Yet, in doing so, this artwork celebrates and criticizes the expanding abundance of his day.

Art helps us get in touch with and express feelings that might remain buried or ignored. It concerns itself with the agony and the ecstasy of life. It has the power to say what we cannot. Artists commit their lives to expressions of emotion, to the ups and downs of real life. They reach deep into themselves to find raw feelings and experiences to express to the beholder.

It behooves us to pay close attention to the emotions of anxiety and terror evoked by Edvard Munch's painting *The Scream* and the towering statue by Giambologna, *The Rape of the Sabine Women*. And to contemplate the serenity and equanimity of Da Vinci's painting *Mona Lisa* and Michelangelo's sculpture *Pieta*. We should be aware of the feelings of repulsion or attraction exposed for Hokusai's woodblock print *The Dream Of The Fisherman's Wife* and Bernini's statue *The Ecstasy of St. Teresa*.

Who knew a few pigments, pieces of wood, and slabs of stone could be so frightening, painful, heartbreaking, peaceful, comforting, erotic, and orgasmic?

Performance

In the performing arts, creatives use their voices and bodies to convey ideas through mediums such as theater, dance, and music. And once again, we see a universal language that communicates uniquely to each person and culture.

Do you prefer rock (hard, soft, or metal), classical (orchestral, solo, or choral), rap/hip-hop (gangsta, trap, or cloud rap), jazz (smooth, Dixieland, or bebop), blues (urban, spirituals, or electric), country (hillbilly, outlaw, or bluegrass), or reggae, emo, easy listening, funk, folk, grunge, garage, Latin, k-pop, metal or Motown? The list of genres is endless.

Think of what you feel when you listen to your favorite song. Does it bring you to tears? Make you feel sad or happy? Does it transport you to another place—perhaps more reflective, peaceful and serene? Or does it make you want to celebrate?

The iconic symbolism and sensuality of dance are equally varied. Consider *Shen Yun*, Native American, *Alvin Ailey*, *Bolshoi Ballet*, *Riverdance*, hip-hop, and the recent television phenomenon *Dancing With The Stars*. Dance has been described as sublime to watch and poetry in motion. It can move us to tears, make us jump in celebration, or cheer on our favorite team. In fact, some experts believe that historically, dance precedes music which precedes language.[40]

Whether we realize it or not, the theater has embedded words and layers of meaning into the wallpaper of our lives. For example, Shakespeare's immortal lines "to be or not to be, that is the question" from *Hamlet* and "all the world's a stage, all the men and women merely players" from *As You Like It*. They have permeated our language. Memorable recent phrases include, "now life has killed the dream I dreamed" from *Les Misérables*, and "take me for what I am, who I was meant to be!" from *Rent*. And "death does not discriminate between the sinners or the saints" from *Hamilton*. These statements have become cultural mantras.

Consider the words of Victoria Hutter, a staff member with the National Endowment for the Arts. "The arts matter because I learn something about people and places I would have never known otherwise. The arts make my brain and heart stretch to make room for newness. Sometimes, parts of me are displaced and replaced by wiser stuff. And that's a fine thing."[41]

Literature

This medium includes poetry, drama, and story. English poet Robert Browning felt there were three kinds of writers—good, better, best. First, he wrote, the ordinary writer looks out the window and tells his readers that he sees something outside. The better writer gives his readers a detailed account of what he sees outside the window. Finally, the best writer, whom Browning called the "Maker-see," puts his readers at the window and lets them see for themselves. It is a great gift.[42]

Like Belle of *Beauty and the Beast,* literature transported your author, who was a child trapped in the poverty of the Appalachians, to magical and faraway places where the Greek and Roman gods reigned. King Arthur jousted, Blackbeard marauded, Marco Polo explored, Napoleon fought, Custer fell, Hemingway wrote (and drank), and John Muir roamed.

As an adult living the first half of life, my journey took me to every one of those exotic lands in a miraculous twist of fate. My childhood writers helped me see the places with vivid detail, and the subsequent visits felt like déjà vu, or synchronicity, as Jung calls it. The authors' layered symbolism made the Acropolis, the Forum, the Silk Road, the Round Table, Treasure Island, *Les Invalides,* Little Bighorn, Murchison Falls, and the Sierra Nevadas seem familiar places. They were symbols as old as time.

Literature details various *Quests* overflowing with symbolism in classic works such as *Steppenwolf* by Herman Hesse, *Magic Mountain* by Thomas Mann, "The Rime of the Ancient Mariner" by Samuel Coleridge, *Atlas Shrugged* by Ayn Rand, *The Magus* by John Fowles, "The Wasteland" by T.S. Eliot, and *Boy's Life* by Robert McCammon.

****

Art is miraculous symbolism. Any one of us can see the same movie, painting, musical, dance, or words on a page and experience completely diverse reactions. As with each waypoint on this journey, it is both universal and unique—the same but different.

Of all the symbols, perhaps art gives us the most straightforward windows into the body, mind, soul, and spirit—into our being. Therefore, you will find corresponding works of art mentioned throughout this book to help better learn the language of symbols.

If our *Quest* is free from censorship, art has the power to make life a sensual playground, fraught with curiosity, filled with mystery, fantasy, and imagination. In short, yet another way to enjoy life.

****

A fitting conclusion to this waypoint is to recall another bit of wisdom imparted to Donkey by Shrek. "You know, Donkey, sometimes things are more than they appear."[43] And so it is with the symbols of our lives.

Our journey will become more focused as we form our first mandala. And as we understand and integrate the aspects of self (conscious with the unconscious, natural self and adapted self, feminine and masculine, and our dark and light sides). And when we begin to identify our personal myth and express the layers of our being through the arts.

On page 297, you will find a blank mandala labeled *Quest* Mandala. Realizing these may change as you progress in your *Quest*, take some time to choose a symbol to represent each aspect of your being—body, mind, soul, and spirit. For example, I selected a stylized gender symbol for the body, a stylized question mark for the mind, a lyre for the soul, and a mandala for the spirit.

You may find it helpful to read the Essentials waypoint before choosing your symbols. Then, once you identify your essentials, there will be a reminder to return and complete this aspect of your *Quest*.

Essentials

What Four Words Describe Your Essentials?

Of all the words in the English language, *essence* is one of the most beautiful and most solid. It means the most significant element, quality, or aspect of a thing or person. And the word quintessence takes this to a greater level—the essence of an item in its purest and most concentrated form. So now, on to identify the essential layers of our self.

First, let's talk about fragmentation and wholeness. We are a divided world full of fragmented people. Our brokenness and complacency have unwittingly enabled our politicians and media to create divisive mosaics using pairs of opposite colors and phrases. Red or blue states, blue or white-collar, white or black skin, educated or uneducated, man or woman, Christian or Muslim, Republican or Democrat, weak or strong, rich or poor, liberal or conservative, socialist or progressive, pro-life or pro-choice, gay or straight, to name only a few.

*"Where there is no desire or pursuit, there is
no wholeness, but there are satisfactory lesser states, fragments."*
—Gore Vidal.[44]

We cannot be satisfied with lesser states, with a fragmented life. Our forefathers have worked in vain for wholeness in politics, careers, race, education, gender, religion, factions, strength, materialism, ideologies, and sexual identity. Moreover, today most of us feel more fragmented and cynical than ever. Essentials are the foundational aspects of our being; when these become fragmented, there are enormous consequences.

However, there is hope. In color theory, opposite colors are called complementary colors. In the world of color, contradictions make beautiful and inspirational statements. They balance each other through warm and cool characteristics that are often simultaneously stimulating and pleasing to the eye. The contrast can be bold and energetic or soft and soothing.[45]

I remain hopeful that our world teeters on the precipice of a new beginning, that is, a fundamental change of attitude toward the values and meaning of life. After years of thinking others have all the answers, we are desperately beginning to look within ourselves.

Physicist Stephen Hawking says, "When we see the world from space, we see ourselves as a whole. We see unity and not divisions. It is a simple image with a compelling message; one planet, one human race."[46]

These external divisions seep into our internal self-perception. This split could be the most urgent question we face in the twenty-first century: How, in all this fragmentation, all this division, can we lead lives of enjoyment and wholeness? It pertains to all aspects of our self, especially our physical, mental, emotional, and spiritual development.

We need to ask the *right* questions.

- What would a life of wholeness look like?
- How do we understand wholeness?
- How do we begin the path to put our lives back together?
- What could I do to make my life more enjoyable?

In these divided times, we can do our part to restore harmony. Once we better understand our inner being, we are farther on the road to the holy grail of wholeness.

Take particular notice of common metaphors utilized about you. For example, when people make comments such as: "You're an old soul," "You're a free spirit," "You are comfortable in your skin," or "You are a deep thinker." Ask yourself why they utilize those comparisons. They provide invaluable clues to identify your essentials.

1. Understanding the Essentials

As I entered mid-life and the "obligatory" search for identity that comes with it, I journaled that I felt like a piece of paper torn into little scraps and thrown into the wind. The fragments of my life were chaotic. Then, about the time I was finally able to think coherently, a friend gave me a book called *Essentialism*. Author Greg McKeown writes these three words: "Less but better."

He goes on to say, "Essentialism is not about how to get more things done; it's about how to get the right things done. It doesn't mean doing less for the sake of less, either. It is about making the wisest possible investment of your time and energy to operate at our highest point of contribution by doing only what is essential."[47]

Words of wisdom. Therefore, let's make the wisest possible investment of our time and energy and explore the essentials of our being.

Our **physical essential** is the body. It includes our ability to survive in the material world. Developing the physical level of our being involves learning to take good care of our bodies and enjoying them.[48] It means developing the skills to live comfortably and effectively in the world.

Our **mental essential** is the mind, our ability to think and reason. Developing the cognitive level of our being allows us to think clearly, ask questions, remain open-minded, and discern intelligently.

Our **emotional essential** is the soul. Some people may choose to refer to this essential as the heart. It encompasses the ability to experience life deeply and relate to ourselves, one another, and the world on a feeling level. Developing the emotional level of our being allows us to appreciate the full range of the human experience with the senses.

Our **spiritual essential** is the spirit. It is about ethical living according to personal moral guidelines, values, and beliefs that may be sacred or secular. This spiritual ethos may come through religious or spiritual teachings; for others, it comprises a secular ethic of responsibility.

Developing awareness of the spiritual level of our being allows us to experience a feeling of "fulfillment" in the universe, to acknowledge a deeper meaning and purpose in our lives.[49]

All four of these essentials are of vital importance. For example, suppose we desire to feel whole and find enjoyment in life. In that case, we need to focus time and attention on understanding, identifying, healing, integrating, and cultivating each aspect of our being.

Some layers may need extra attention because we are wounded or have suffered trauma in that area. For example, strict religious beliefs may have injured you. As a result, you reject or diminish the spiritual aspect of life. In addition, we all have suffered disappointment or hurt that has left us emotionally injured and fragmented.

Take a few moments to consider which of your four essentials are well-developed and which one(s) may need a little more attention or expression in your life. Furthermore, know that your essentials will be in flux and will change as you grow during *The Quest*.

2. Identifying the Essentials

Body

Are you physically healthy and active? Do you like your body? Do you feel comfortable in your skin? Do you enjoy your sexuality? Are you able to rest peacefully? Are you a lover of food? Do you have physical phobias? Allergies? Are you in good shape? Are you well-coiffed?

List eight words that best describe your body—your physical self. Immediately following the eight blank lines are some concepts to help jumpstart thinking.

1._____   5._____
2._____   6._____
3._____   7._____
4._____   8._____

Agile
Animated
Athletic
Aristocratic bearing
Attractive
Balance
Body Scent (Pheromones)
Casual
Competitive
Confident (Head High Up)
Demonstrative
Endurance (Stamina)
Energetic
Exercise
Expressive
Fitness
Flexibility
Frenetic
Graceful (Motion)
Health
Height

Hygiene
Hyperactive
Image-Conscious
Mobility
Neat
Posture
Powerful
Radiant
Resilient
Sensual
Sexy
Slow-Moving
Smile
Speed
Strength
Style
Symmetry
Verbal
Voice
Youthful

Next, narrow it down to a quaternity, the top four words that best describe your body—your physical self. Now write them on your essentials-body mandala on p. 305.

1._____
2._____
3._____
4._____

Now choose the ONE word that epitomizes your body—your physical self.

1._____

Mind

Are you satisfied with your intellect? Can you think and express yourself clearly? Do you have a knowledge system that supports you and works for you? Are you open to new ideas? Are you a questioner?

List eight words that best describe your mind—your mental self. Immediately following the eight blank lines are some concepts to help jumpstart thinking.

1._____   5._____
2._____   6._____
3._____   7._____
4._____   8._____

Accurate
Achiever
Action-Oriented
Adaptive
Alert
Aggressive
Ambitious
Analytical
Anxious
Assertive
Brave
Calm

Capable
Cautious
Cerebral
Challenger
Composed
Complacent
Competent
Confident
Confrontational
Control
Creative
Critical

Curious	Love of Learning
Decisive	Mentally Tough
Determined	Motivation
Dislikes Change	Open Book
Dominating	Open-Minded
Driven	Optimistic
Easy-Going (Relaxed)	Orderly
Enthusiastic	Perfectionistic
Energetic	Positive
Entrepreneurial	Pragmatic
Excelling	Precise
Firm	Pre-Occupied
Flair	Perseverance
Flamboyant	Perspective
Focused	Purposeful
Forthcoming	Rational
Goal-Oriented	Reading
Hard-Working	Referee
Imagination	Relentlessness
Impractical	Resourceful
Indecisive	Risk-Taker
Independent	Scattered
Individualist	Scheduled
Indomitable	Self-Assurance
Innovative	Self-Confident
Inquisitive	Self-Reliant
Inventive	Self-Talk
Knowledge	Slothful
Leadership	Spirited
Learner	Straight-Talking
Likes Challenge	Strong-Willed

Stubborn

Success

Suspicious

Takes Charge

Teachable

Teamwork

Tenacity

Thoughtful

Troubleshooter

Unrealistic

Vigorous

Vision

Visualization

Vitality

Willful

Work Ethic

Narrow it down to a quaternity, the top four words that best describe your mind—your mental self. Now write them on your essentials-mind mandala on p. 306.

1._____

2._____

3._____

4._____

Now choose the ONE word that epitomizes your mind—your mental self.

1._____

Soul

Are you in touch with your feelings and able to express them appropriately? For example, do you allow yourself to feel the full range of emotions: fear, anxiety, and anger, as well as excitement and enjoyment? Or do you find that certain emotions make you uncomfortable? Are you able to set appropriate boundaries with people? Can you relate to others in a close, intimate way?[50]

List eight words that best describe your soul—your emotional self. Immediately following the eight blank lines are some concepts to help jumpstart your thinking.

1._____   5._____
2._____   6._____
3._____   7._____
4._____   8._____

Affection
Agreeable
Angry
Anxious
Appreciative
Arrogant
Bold
Charming
Communion
Community
Complacent
Content
Defiant
Detached
Distractible
Dramatic
Dreamer
Dreamy
Easygoing
Eccentricity
Empathy

Enthusiast
Easygoing
Emotional Intelligence
Engaging
Entertainer
Equanimity
Excited
Expressive
Extrovert
Fearful
Fun-Loving
Group-Oriented
Happiness
High-Spirited
High-Strung
Humor
Impatience
Impulsiveness
Intense
Intimacy
Introvert

Intuition
Isolated
Joyous
Lusty
Melancholy
Mixes Easily
Moody
Non-Demanding
Nurturing
Optimistic
People-Pleasing
Perceptive
Pessimistic
Playful
Possessive
Promoter
Prudence
Reactive
Reassuring
Rebellious

Receptive
Relational
Reserved
Satisfied
Scattered
Secretive
Self-Absorbed
Self-Aware
Self-Conscious
Self-Pity
Social Intelligence
Spontaneous
Stable
Suspicious
Sympathetic
Temperamental
Utopian
Versatile
Withdrawn
Zest for Life

Now, narrow it down to a quaternity, the top four words that best describe your soul—your emotional self. Now write them on your essentials-soul mandala on p. 307.

1._____
2._____
3._____
4._____

Now choose the ONE word that epitomizes your soul—your emotional self.

1._____

Spirit

Do you feel a relationship to your spiritual origin? Are you able to spend time in spiritual practices such as meditation or journaling? Do you have a relationship with your inner wisdom, values, beliefs, or intuitive guidance? Do you have moments when you feel at one with everything or part of something more significant? Is nature vital to you?

List eight words that best describe your spirit—your spiritual self. Immediately following the eight blank lines are some concepts to help jumpstart thinking.

1._____	5._____
2._____	6._____
3._____	7._____
4._____	8._____

Accepting	Certitude
Achiever	Committed
Advocate	Compassion
Agnostic	Courage
Anarchist	Cunning
Atheist	Defender
Avaricious	Discipline
Awareness	Doubter
Beauty	Equality
Caring	Equanimity

Existentialism
Fairness
Fearful
Freedom
Forgiveness
Generous
Gratitude
Harmony
Helper
Holistic
Honesty
Hope
Humility
Iconoclast
Identity
Independence
Initiative
Insightful
Inspirational
Integrity
Interpersonal
Investigator
Judgment
Justice
Karma
Kindness
Love
Loving-Kindness
Loyal
Meaning

Mediator
Modesty
Motivator
Nature
Nihilism
Open-Hearted
Patience
Peacemaker
Principled
Productive
Progress
Protector
Purpose
Reformer
Reliable
Responsible
Ritual
Self-Controlled
Self-Honesty
Self-Indulgent
Self-Reliance
Self-Regulation
Sensitive
Serenity
Servant
Service
Significance
Skeptic
Spirituality
Success

Supporter   Truth
Sweetness   Useful
Tradition   Wisdom
Transcendence   Work
Trustworthy

Narrow it down to the top four words that best describe your spirit—your spiritual self. Now write them on your essentials-spirit mandala on p. 308.

1._____
2._____
3._____
4._____

Now choose the ONE word that epitomizes your spirit—your spiritual self.

1._____

Note additional thoughts and feelings and consider how well you currently experience each of the four essentials. Are there any actions you can take toward growth, wholeness, and enjoyment?

_____
_____
_____
_____

Here is an invaluable step to this process. Once you determine your best words, give three trustworthy people the opportunity to add or dialogue about the terms and then rank them in order of importance. This feedback is critical. It would be best to have objective and honest, loving, and trustworthy input to make your mandala the best possible investment of your time.

3. Piecing Together the Essentials

Now the fun part! Let's piece together your top four essentials for each aspect of your being into a personal mandala on pages 305-308. This visual is where your unique personality emerges. Next, narrow it down, and put the top word you have chosen to represent your body, mind, soul, and spirit on the essentials mandala on p. 298.

This profound but straightforward tool is powerful. It is much different from *Meyers-Briggs, DISC,* and the *Enneagram* assessments. It does not squeeze you into a predetermined box with a limited number of categories. Instead, the possibilities of the mandala, when you gather outside input from your closest acquaintances and add additional layers, are infinite.

You know yourself better than anyone. And once you have feedback from trusted friends or family, narrow the list down to the four words that best represent your essentials.

Symbols give us a powerful communication tool to discuss the nuances of our essentials. So, having chosen your quaternity, read the last two paragraphs of the Symbols waypoint and create your symbols mandala.

Stages

How Were You Formed By The First Two Stages of Life?

Consider this universal fact of history: we are born and we die. In between, the lucky live by developing, establishing, enjoying, and consciously aging. You are fortunate if you read these words. Not because you get to read these pages, but because you have the disposable income to purchase this book. You have the education and spare time to read it, and the freedom to seriously consider ways to enjoy the second half of life.

For most of my life, I felt I was a self-made person. My success, my part of the American dream, happened because of hard work and tenacity. I progressed from a life of poverty in the Appalachians to the pinnacle of success in my field.

Or so I thought. The truth is, I've come to realize the doors of opportunity were wide open for a person like me. In the early 1980s, the paths of success were ideal for an American, white, heterosexual man with a conservative religious background. Furthermore, I was fortunate to come from a lineage of hard workers and quick learners.

I vividly recall the day an alpha-male friend (with a long and successful career as a futures trader in the pit of *Chicago's Mercantile Exchange*) screamed at the top of his lungs. We were strolling through a crowded mall. "Elrod, you've got a golden horseshoe shoved up your ass!"

And you know, I've come to understand he was right. If you are reading this book determined to find your holy grail in *The Quest*, you probably have one shoved up yours as well. We live in a world where over 700 million people live on less than $1.90 a day. A moment of gratefulness would be appropriate as we savor the luxury of allocating the priceless commodity of time to consider the days of our lives.

Let's assume we have one hundred years or approximately 36,500 days. Due to lifestyle choices such as diet, exercise, low stressful environment, and extraordinary advancements in medical care, centenarians are now one of the fastest-growing demographics in the developed world.[51] *Annuity Digest* tells us that in the United States, the centenarian population is doubling every decade.

To illustrate, during the live experience of *The Quest*, participants gather before a sizable outdoor mandala constructed of stones from the land. While standing amid this multi-layered symbol, I teach that (much like the number twelve on a clock) the northern axis represents our birth. It proceeds chronologically in a clockwise direction to the eastern axis, which symbolizes age twenty-five, the end of the first stage of life.

This *circle of life* then advances to the southern axis, to age fifty, representing the end of the second stage of life. Then it progresses to the western axis, age seventy-five, the end of the third stage of life. Finally, it returns where it began, to the northern axis, somewhere around age one hundred, the end of the fourth stage of life. A visual of this mandala appears on page 309.

We will spend extended time exploring the first two stages of life in this waypoint. These periods are where we encounter the most unhealthy and challenging people, places, memories, and events. And inevitably, these wounds will scream for our attention as we approach the mid-life transition and the third stage of life. Therefore, we will explore the third and fourth stages of life at length in the last two waypoints.

Stage One: Development

The first 9,125 days begin at birth and range until approximately age twenty-five, which we call the development stage. There are early and late bloomers; therefore, the stage could end about five years earlier or later.

More than any other, this stage determines the formation of the waypoints of our self, essentials, emotions, conscious and unconscious. This stage impacts (in both healthy and unhealthy ways) the remainder of life. Robert Bly writes a powerful and poetic illustration of this truth. When we were tiny, our "horse" had all four legs, and it joyfully lived in whatever sensualities it could gallop to. By the time a child in our culture is twelve, one of the legs at least will be crippled by shame, whether it lives in a "dysfunctional" household or not.[52]

During the first stage of life, our focus tends to be primarily on self. Let's focus on four (quaternity) crucial influencers of development—attachment, play, basic themes, and institutions.

Attachment

The first development influence is attachment. We now know that infants' early parental or caregiver experiences (the first eighteen months) profoundly impact their adult relationship skills. A wealth of knowledge comes from a concept developed in the 1950s by Dr. John Bowlby, a psychoanalyst. He researched the effects of separation between infants and their parents.[53]

This concept is called *Attachment Theory*. The experiences with our caregivers as an infant make up a system that guides us in our patterns and habits of forming and maintaining relationships, particularly in our intimate and romantic relations as adults.

A child's attachment style is primarily a function of the quality of caregiving in their early years. For example, those who received support and love from their caregivers are likely to be secure. In contrast, those who experienced inconsistency or negligence from their caregivers are likely to feel more anxiety surrounding their relationship with their parents, and thus, other people.

Once children reach the toddler stage, they begin forming an internal working model of their attachment relationships. This model provides the framework for the child's beliefs about self-worth and how much they can depend on others to meet their needs.

In Bowlby's theory, children's attachment styles based on their early interactions with caregivers form a range of emotional control from anxious to disoriented.

Research shows that infants placed in an unfamiliar situation and separated from their parents will generally react in one of four ways upon rejoining them.

Secure Attachment

Upon separation, these infants showed distress but were easily comforted when the parents returned. They are generally more likely to see others as supportive and helpful—and themselves as competent and worthy of respect. They relate positively to others and display resilience, engage in complex play, and are more successful in the classroom and interactions with other children. They are better at accepting the perspectives of others and trusting them.

Anxious Attachment

A smaller number of infants experienced more significant levels of distress upon reuniting with the parents and seemed to seek comfort. But they also tried to "punish" the parents for leaving. As a result, they likely lack self-confidence and stick close to their primary caregivers. In addition, they may display exaggerated emotional reactions and keep their distance from their peers, leading to social isolation.

Avoidant Attachment

Upon separation from the parents, these infants showed little or no stress and either ignored or actively avoided the parents upon rejoining them. Children with an avoidant attachment style are generally less effective in managing stressful situations.

They are likely to withdraw and resist seeking help, which inhibits them from forming satisfying relationships with others. They show more aggression and antisocial behavior, like lying and bullying, and distance themselves from others to reduce emotional stress.

Disorganized-Disoriented Attachment

Subsequent research added a fourth attachment style which refers to infants who have no predictable pattern of attachment behaviors. Children with a disorganized-disoriented attachment style usually fail to develop an organized strategy for coping with separation distress and display aggression, disruptive behaviors, and social isolation. In addition, they are more likely to see others as threats rather than sources of support. They thus may switch between social withdrawal and defensively aggressive behavior.

****

As you can see, many behaviors and emotional styles result from a child's attachment style. The previous descriptions of behaviors and emotions illustrate how attachment style in childhood can lead to significant relationship benefits or challenges in adulthood. Click the reference for a link to assess your attachment style.[54]

Play

Play is a crucial influencer of the second period of the development stage. The way we frolic in childhood determines to a great extent how we approach playful (enjoyable) situations as an adult. And in adulthood, it contributes to physical, mental, emotional, and spiritual health.

Physical play encourages exercise. Mental play stimulates thought with surprises and exploration. Emotional play strengthens social bonds, and spiritual play enhances awe and well-being.

There are many theories and studies about *why* we play and the *outcomes* of play, and they are worthy of further research, but for *The Quest*, let's discuss *how* we played as a child. It is valuable to remember the simple and forgotten things of childhood. And for mnemonic purposes, we will again look at it in quaternity form.

Physical Play

Some children love to get dirty. They make mud pies, revel in the smell and feel of a sandbox, run along the curbs, splashing wildly after a spring rain. Some play hopscotch, jump rope, ride bicycles, and play with sticks, nets, and balls. These kids perpetually have bumps, bruises, scratches, and broken bones.

Physical kids throw frisbees, ride the surf on a boogie board, skip rocks, and climb trees. They usually have pockets full of frogs and jars filled with insects.

What were your physical play experiences as a child?

Mental Play

Other children enjoy pretending. Whether they build a sandcastle, play with dolls, or read a book, their imagination runs wild. They sprout wings, fly over their neighborhood, fight dragons, and win at Quidditch. These kids enjoy time alone with their imagination.

Mind-focused kids cast spells, ride the sky on a magic carpet, skip with fairies, and climb beanstalks. They usually have pockets full of books and jars filled with potions.

What were your mental play experiences as a child?

Emotional Play

Some children are highly emotional. They are the first to have a best friend, a boyfriend, or a girlfriend. Whether they are playing house, doctor, schoolteacher, or parent, they are emoting. These kids most enjoy time with others.

Emotional kids tell jokes, are the life of the party, and many have already developed empathy. First, they cry crocodile tears; the next moment, belly laugh until they cry again. They usually have pockets full of tissue papers and jars full of gags and gifts.

What were your emotional play experiences as a child?

Spiritual Play

A few children seem to have an unusual grasp of spiritual things and enjoy playing priest, psychic, or healer. They may be intensely attracted to church activities and consider it fun. They love to play with animals, crystals, and plants and love spending time in nature. They experience flashes of light, hear things, or have other unexplained occurrences.

Spiritually focused kids seem much older than their age. They chant scripture, share the sky with angels, skip with "imaginary friends," and climb stairways to heaven. Unusual experiences are interpreted as signs from the spirits.

What were your spiritual play experiences as a child?

****

When Carl Jung was at the height of his career as a world-renowned psychoanalyst, he would set aside time between appointments to go outside. He would escape to a private place on his estate and play with stones as he did as a child. During his intense confrontation with the unconscious, Jung felt he had no choice but to return to his childhood and "take up that child's life."[55]

He believed that when a memory of playing as a child touches a good deal of emotion, it means there is life remaining in those things. Evidence that one's inner child is still around and has creative energy forgotten over time. Playing as an adult can help bridge the gap from the present to the wonder of childhood. Jung believed with certainty that play was a path to discovering his personal myth. (See Symbols waypoint.)

I recall sketching and doodling endlessly with a pencil as a child. Upon reading as an adult that the foundation of watercolor is a good pencil sketch, I was immediately interested. That prompted me to buy a set of pencils, brushes, and watercolors; the subsequent paintings have resulted in many of the most joyous and life-giving moments of my life.

Over the past two decades, these creations, prompted by my unconscious, have led to myriad revelations. And they functioned as crucial tools of communication for many invaluable memories that were lost, repressed, and forbidden in the vast sea of my unconscious.

If you have known me long, then you probably have heard me quote these words. They are from the introduction to *Boy's Life* by Robert McCammon and sum up the details for this section on Play perfectly.

"See, this is my opinion: we all start out knowing magic. We are born with whirlwinds, forest fires, and comets inside us. We are born able to sing to birds and read the clouds and see our destiny in grains of sand. But then we get the magic educated right out of our souls. We get it churched out, spanked out, washed out, and combed out. We get put on the straight and narrow and told to be responsible. Told to act our age. Told to grow up, for God's sake. And you know why we were told that? Because the people doing the telling were afraid of our wildness and youth, and because the magic we knew made them ashamed and sad of what they'd allowed to wither in themselves."

Basic Themes

The third influencer of stage one focuses on primary themes of development. These themes involve radical change. Dr. Donald L. Nathanson tells us that nature delivers its bounty along a bell-shaped curve. The great majority of us are given normal ranges in each of these development themes. But a small number have much less or a lot more.[56]

Inevitably, pride is associated with "normal," and shame is attached to "abnormal." The healthy and unhealthy emotions heighten these differences during adolescence. It is a time of significant physical, mental, emotional, and social change. Hormones radically erupt as puberty begins. Let's look at four basic themes.

Size and Shape

Some people are obsessed with size, focused inordinately on attributes relating to the axis of big and small. Embarrassment and pride fill the adolescent world; therefore, tallness, shortness, and size of body parts are matters of tremendous importance. (See the most searched terms on *PornHub* in the Symbols waypoint.)

More young teens request plastic surgery in the modern age of selfies and social media. In 2017, the American Society of Plastic Surgeons reported that more than 200,000 teens had a cosmetic procedure. These operations have jumped 200% percent since the year 2000 for all ages, with patients spending more than $6.5 billion.[57]

We could fill a library of books with the many nicknames, slurs, and jokes designed to deal with the embarrassment associated with genital and breast size. Likewise, the porn industry exasperates this perceived disparity. The enormous penises and breasts featured are extremely rare or digitally manipulated—yet the industry markets them highly desirable.

Through most of our years of development, we experience shame and pride about size and shape matters. And remember, the experiences in the first stage of our lives carry with us throughout our years.

Dexterity and Physical Skill

Clumsiness brings shame in our hyper-competitive and sports-obsessed world, and grace and skill foster pride. Who has not felt the embarrassment of adolescent fumbling or failing to hit, hold, kick, or catch a ball? Or fall, stumble, or get out of sync with a dance move? Or not being able to complete a gymnastic exercise?

Unhealthy emotions and memories forever enmesh the middle school years for many of us who developed physically later in life. But, again, this perceived disparity is frustrated by expectations that we all should play basketball like Michael Jordan, football like Tom Brady, dance like Julianne Hough, or do a floor exercise like Simone Biles.

It is vital to remember that abilities and attributes that lie dormant in a growing child's body (and mind) "come online" at different periods of development. Few of us can be athletic stars, and many of us were late bloomers.

Dependence vs. Independence

Our feelings about dependence and independence result from years of emotional development. They also link with our "attachment style." Some families create a cult-like atmosphere of closeness, reluctantly releasing their child to marry. They use every psychological trick to regain control and proximity of the "lost" family member. Yet other parents send children off to camp and boarding school as soon as possible.

A parent who raises children to be confident and independent reinforces the association between skills and childhood pride. But the parent that experiences those skills as a threat will weaken the linkage of confidence and independence by instilling negative emotions such as distress, anger, disgust, or shame.

The adage of "cutting the apron strings" takes on layers of meaning. The string quickly becomes a chain not easily broken. Our successes and failures (and experiences of shame and pride) depend greatly on our independence from parents and caregivers throughout life.

Dr. Nathanson says that any definition of the typical adult must consider how they handle both solitude and community, dependence and independence.[58] As it turns out, all of humanity is more or less dependent on each other. Still, the degrees of dependence vary significantly due to influences during our development.

Cognitive Ability

Adolescence is a time of rapid cognitive development. Cognitive ability means the growth of a child's development to think and reason. This growth happens differently in each youth. To cope with differences, adolescents delineate the "smart" kids, the "jocks," the "in-crowd," and the "marching band" kids.

Again, we must remember the abilities and attributes that lie dormant in our minds during growth "come online" at different periods of childhood. For example, from ages twelve to eighteen, we grow in the way we think. We moved from concrete thinking to formal logical operations. But not all of us grew at the same pace.

Those of us brought up in a home that championed curiosity, critical thinking, and book knowledge most likely excelled cognitively in the early years of adolescence. In contrast, those with emotional issues have problems developing thought in more complex ways. Each of us as children progresses at our own pace in cognitive ability.

That pace determines the levels of shame or pride we experience to a large extent. The thoughts, ideas, and concepts developed at this period of life considerably influence one's future life and play a significant role in character and personality formation.

Institutions

The fourth influencer of the development stage focuses on institutions. They form the quaternity of family, religion, education, and culture. These collectives spawn most of the healthy and unhealthy emotions of adult life. They constantly attempt to chip away and fragment the essentials of who we are from birth. Our attempts to make a successful life as adults often depend on the images we carry from life institutions.

The rules and demands of these institutions are written very early into the textbook of a child's mind. Consider the words of the poet, e.e. cummings. "To be nobody-but-yourself—in a world which is doing its best, night and day, to make you everybody else—means to fight the hardest battle which any human being can fight." So let's examine these institutions more closely.

Family

The first institution is family. In an intriguing article in *The Atlantic*, David Brooks makes some thought-provoking observations. First, he asserts that the family structure we've held up as the cultural ideal for the past half-century has been a catastrophe for many. Then, thoughtfully, he says it's time to figure out better ways to live together.

How many of us have the following memory? Dozens of people celebrate Thanksgiving or some other holiday around a makeshift stretch of family tables—siblings, cousins, aunts, uncles, great-aunts. It's the family in all its tangled, angst-ridden, loving, exhausting glory.

However, we've moved from big, interconnected, and extended families, which helped protect the most vulnerable people in culture from the shocks of life. And we have relocated to smaller, detached nuclear families (a married couple and their children).

People who grow up in a nuclear family tend to have a more selfish mindset than those in a multigenerational extended clan. They tend to romanticize the nuclear family. Yet, we're likely living through the most rapid change in family structure in human history. The causes are economic, cultural, and institutional all at once.

Those in disrupted families have more trouble getting the education they need to have prosperous careers. People who don't have thriving careers have problems building stable families because of financial challenges and other stressors. The children in those families become more isolated and more traumatized.

All forms of inequality are cruel, but family inequality may be the most brutal. It damages the soul. The blunt fact is that the nuclear family has been crumbling in slow motion for decades. Many of our other problems—education, mental health, addiction, quality of the labor force—stem from that crumbling.

Brooks concludes with this plea. For decades we have been eating at smaller and smaller tables, with fewer and fewer kin. It's time to find ways to return to the big tables.

Religion

Religion is the second institution. It gives answers to the questions of life and creates dogma to explain the mystery. But unfortunately, the answer to most of life's questions is a resounding "no!" Particularly when it comes to pleasure, sexuality, and the body.

Fundamentalism magnifies this negative response to the many questions that arise during adolescence. This movement is a strict, literal adherence to religious doctrine accompanied by a rejection of intellectualism and the many things they condemn as "worldliness."

All religions can experience a rise in fundamentalism. Among Southern Baptists, for example, fundamentalism has been steadily on the increase since the seventies. Another example is how the Taliban regime in Afghanistan enforces fundamentalist Muslim doctrine.

Central to many religions are variations of the concept of total depravity formalized by St. Augustine and advocated in many Protestant confessions of faith and catechisms, especially in Calvinism. The doctrine teaches that, as a consequence of the "fall" of man, every person born into the world is morally corrupt and enslaved to sin. As a result, they are apart from the grace of God, utterly unable to choose to follow God or choose to turn to Christ in faith for salvation.[59]

During stage one (the most formative time) of our life, at least three negative emotions are triggered repeatedly in those with a hyper-religious background. Our "sinful" actions and our "depraved" nature trigger *shame*. The threat of eternal punishment for those sins and our sinful longings triggers *fear*; the constant reminder of our sins triggers *distress*.

Religion has successfully adopted a quote from Aristotle, "give me a child until he is seven, and I will show you the man." They have developed sophisticated children and youth programs and pastors to groom them, much like sex traffickers.

The Church distorts our sense of self. Furthermore, the Hebrew Bible demands that we deny ourselves. Religion discourages the integration of gender, the feminine (anima), and the masculine (animus). And the Church rewards an adapted persona—not a natural one.

Because of religious teaching, many of us have shipwrecked our longings and instincts and repressed, denied, or projected them; many of the most unhealthy people, events, memories, secrets, and places hidden in our unconscious result from false religious teaching. The deep trauma of this unnatural distortion haunts and hurts us for the remainder of our lives.

Education

The third institution is education. Thought leaders often talk about the fallacies of our educational institutions. And few have expressed it more eloquently than the late Sir Kenneth Robinson. Consider only a few of his extraordinary insights.

"Children are not, for the most part, suffering from a psychological condition. They're suffering from childhood."

"I believe this passionately: that we don't grow into creativity, we grow out of it. Rather, we get educated out of it."

"If you can light the spark of curiosity in a child, they will learn without any further assistance, very often. Children are natural learners."

"If you sit kids down, hour after hour, doing low-grade clerical work, don't be surprised if they start to fidget."

"Kids prosper best with a broad curriculum that celebrates their various talents, not just a small range of them."

"The answer is not to standardize education but to personalize and customize it to the needs of each child and community. There is no alternative. There never was."

"We have sold ourselves into a fast-food model of education, and it's impoverishing our spirit and our energies as much as fast food is depleting our physical bodies."

In light of these statements, how does your education compare? How has it impacted your life? Your career? Your self-esteem?[60]

In 1976 I had the unusual distinction of being the first family member ever to graduate high school. As a young boy of around nine, I helped teach my grandfather to read and write.

Here is an excerpt from my memoir *A Renaissance Redneck* that recounts the challenges encountered by our current educational system for a creative and sensitive child raised in an uneducated family.

"One of my first memories of elementary school was being placed in a 'gifted' class. This was about when the American education system was trying to figure out how to provide an education to students who are now called 'special needs' children. So they called them gifted.

Now if you can picture a fair slip of a boy walking into class on the first day of school, wearing a big silly smile sort of like Gomer Pyle, talking incomprehensible jargon with an accent as thick as the mountains, and nary a measure of social skills, you might rightly understand why he could possibly be singled out for reassignment.

First thing in the morning, on the second day of school, the teacher asked me to step outside, saying, 'Honey, I'm happy to tell you, you are being moved to what we call a class for the gifted. I'm sure you are going to love it.'

Straight off, I was escorted to another room downstairs. As I walked the sterile hallway, I ruminated on how much I liked being described as gifted. No one had ever called me that before.

The first thing I noticed as I entered the class was there were only half as many students, and three times the number of teachers. A nice lady greeted me and showed me to my desk. She had a dear face, talked slow and distinct, looked me directly in the eyes, and possessed a nice smell and manner about her. She told me I was free to wander about the class, find a book that looked good, and locate a comfortable place to read. She said to take all the time I needed. There were shiny new books everywhere and I commenced to read them. It seemed like heaven.

About a week later, that nice lady came up, gently took my chin, looked me in the eyes, and said, 'Randy, dear, how many of these books have you finished?' I did my best to keep my eyes and voice from quivering, and answered, 'All of them, ma'am.' She abruptly dropped my chin. Things happened quickly after that. It seemed that 'all of those' books were supposed to have been enough to last each member of the class the whole year. Something wasn't right. I reckoned I wasn't gifted after all.

Next day, I was returned to my original class, the one for 'normal' people, and to the same line of uncomfortable desks, sitting alphabetically and stuck somewhere between 'D' and 'F.' There was only one teacher way up front who sat behind her desk and talked in a disinterested manner most of the day, without eye contact, to the thirty of us rowdy and smelly six-year-olds crammed in the room. Longing for the freedom of the 'gifted' class, I was reminded not to move or talk, and the monotony dripped on for the next five years."[61]

Unfortunately, our educational institutions have put children to sleep for years, all the way through graduate school, and some never wake up again.

Culture

The fourth institution is culture (society). Perhaps this is the most significant cult of them all, "cult"-ure. Children and youth are forced early to function in culture; it shapes one's identity. Culture affects the way we learn to think and behave. It does this with expectations, rewards, punishments, and examples.

The self (ego, persona, shadow, and gender) develops through interaction with peers, relatives, and the media. Each of us responds in our unique way. Unfortunately, but unwittingly, we also began to internalize and adopt influencers' attitudes. As a result, there is intense pressure to conform to social norms.

Psychologists have spent decades studying the power of social influence and how it manipulates our opinions and behavior. Specifically, social impact refers to how individuals change ideas and actions to meet the demands of a social group or perceived authority. [62]

While social influence can positively affect behavior, its disadvantages have been a motivating factor behind research into conformity by psychologists such as Stanley Milgram. [63]

He found that conformity to a narrow set of behaviors and views can discourage the nurturing of new ideas which could improve the lives of a person or group. Conformity prevents its members from questioning and debating the beliefs and practices held by the majority of a group. We observe this behavior in cults, where members are often reluctant to publicly doubt the group's authority for fear of being rejected by their peers.

Another form of social influence—minority influence—has also been used historically for malign purposes. For example, the followers of tyrants such as Adolf Hitler and Donald Trump have accepted and internalized the leader's radical views without question.

When we are young, we feel the need to be informed by accurate information. When we lack confidence in our knowledge, we turn to others hoping they will provide us with the correct information. Regardless of whether it is accurate, accepting this information subjects us to social influence. We banish our unique qualities to the unconscious.

An excerpt from the Persona section of the Symbols waypoint bears repeating. This conformity forces our natural personalities to adapt to the needs and demands of our institutions. As a result, we become what others tell us we are. We fail to realize groups that authentically care about us—should *promote* our personal development and never seek to suppress.

In the way of *The Quest*, stage one is a time to focus on self.

Stage Two: Establishment

The second 9,125 days, which I call the establishment stage, begins at about age twenty-five and ends around age fifty. Again, there are early and late bloomers; the timeline varies with the individual. We establish our work, home, worship, and identity in this stage. Our decisions during this time dramatically impact the mid-life transition to stage three.

During the second stage of life, our focus tends to be primarily on *others*. There are many, but let's focus on four (quaternity) crucial aspects of the twenty-five years comprising stage two.

Career

The first aspect of the establishment stage is a career. Fresh out of school, we are ready to carve our niche in the world. For some, the world is full of opportunities to explore and find the "perfect" job. But for many, whether they know it or not, a career choice has already been made. The institutions of life have pre-determined it.

Afraid to buck the systems of family, education, culture, or religion, we consent and conform to the wishes of others and let them choose this crucial aspect of our circle of life. But unfortunately, this choice often forces us to work without utilizing our natural persona and strengths. As a result, it leads to a greater failure rate and a lack of joy.

This all-too-common scenario caused comedian Jim Carrey to say, "why fail at something you don't enjoy? At least fail at something you love!"

Instead of types of careers, let's look at types of workers. First, determine how you function best to get more joy and fulfillment from your work. Shelly Prevost posits an intriguing theory with an article for *Inc. Magazine*.[64] She lists four (quaternity) working styles: doers, leaders, lovers, and learners.

Doing

Provost says that doers make things happen. They come alive when completing tasks, checking lists, or tackling projects. They typically have intense focus and are detailed in their efforts.

Doers are usually highly focused. However, they may forget to look up and communicate *what* they're doing.

Doers also tend to dive into work with little forethought. They believe that everyone should "fire, ready, aim" and tend to devalue the important work of planning.

Leading

Leaders create the vision and inspire others to believe in it. You can't help but listen to, admire, and follow them. Without leaders, we would be spinning in a hamster wheel with no real vision.

However, leaders can be detached from others, not completely understanding *all* that goes into executing their vision. Moreover, they sometimes forget to check in with the people following them because they're out front.

Loving

Lovers are relationship-builders. Believing that we are stronger together, they thrive in harmony, working hard to manage relationships and build consensus.

People strong in the loving working style are sensitive and empathic. They have a finger on the pulse of every other person on the team. So if you want to know how others on your team are feeling, ask the lover.

But lovers can suck at follow-through and more detail-oriented work. Left to their own devices, they can out empathize with anyone and make people feel great but not provide a "tangible" result.

Learning

Learners are the researchers. These engineer types love learning and meticulously understanding the nuances of a problem. They are deliberate, disciplined, and think more strategically than most people.

Without others, however, learners wouldn't get much done. To execute their best-laid plans, they need a team ready to act. Their strategy is only as good as the problems they solve—not in theory, but in reality.

****

Which working style resonates with you? Are you able to operate in your natural strengths and skills? Or do you feel compelled to adapt to succeed?

Family

The second aspect of the establishment stage is family. A friend once told me there are only two decisions one needs to get right to have a joyful life. First, what kind of work you choose, and second, whom you marry. Ah, if it were only that simple. But he does have a point. Those decisions are two of the most crucial ones of our life. A Chinese proverb says:

Happiness is somebody to love,
Something to do,
And something to hope for.

Companion

For many of us, we base the choice of a companion on institutional influences. We bow to the power of family, culture, and religion. As a result, the options of a same-sex partner, someone of a different race, culture, or socioeconomic status, and singleness are often deemed unacceptable.

We enter blindly into a lifetime contract without taking time to honestly evaluate personal desires, attachment styles, personality, or family backgrounds. Vowing serious and frightening commitments that are not lightly shed, if ever, future divorce or not. Furthermore, as the years go by and our paths diverge—family, friends, and religion make negotiating an amicable separation virtually impossible.

A lucky few are independent and dare to freely and thoughtfully choose a companion. But even then, the odds of staying together are dismal, at around fifty percent. Maybe that is why in 2017, nearly half of American adults chose to remain single.

And then there are the "lifers." Culture tends to applaud the fifty-plus-year marriage without knowing what happened to the souls of those in the relationship. Despite what religion teaches, longevity and replication of values are not automatic virtues.

The real test for a successful relationship is that both partners care deeply about encouraging each other to become who they truly are. When mutual enlargement happens, few things bring greater joy to life no matter how long the relationship lasts. Companionship is a profound commitment to another person, officially or unofficially. It is a longing for daily physical communion with a particular person.

The philosopher Nietzsche once observed that companionship is a conversation, a great dialogue. Genuine relationship springs from a conscious desire to share the journey and grow nearer to the mystery of each other's wholeness through the bridges of conversation, sexuality, and compassion.

Children

Bringing children into a relationship is one of the most pivotal decisions of life. Whether through procreation or other means such as surrogacy or adoption, adding additional people to a home permanently changes everything. There is little middle ground, and children usually bring the best or worst of times. Many of the structures that once supported the family no longer exist in today's world.

Let's hear from David Brooks once again. He says families have gotten a lot smaller over the past two generations. The American birth rate is half of what it once was. In 2012, most American family households had no children. There are more American homes with pets than with kids. In 1970, about twenty percent of households had five or more people. As of 2012, only around nine percent did. Once a dense cluster of many siblings and extended kin, the family's story has fragmented into increasingly smaller and fragile forms.

But a new and more communal ethos is emerging, consistent with 21st-century reality and values. Recently a new paradigm has appeared called *chosen families*—and they transcend traditional kinship lines. The modern chosen-family movement came to prominence in San Francisco in the 1980s among gay men and lesbians. Many of them had become estranged from their biological families. They had only one another for support in coping with the trauma of the AIDS crisis.

These gay men and lesbians insisted that family members are people who are "there for you," people you can count on emotionally and materially. "They take care of me," said one man, "I take care of them."[65]

These groups are what Daniel Burns, a political scientist at the University of Dallas, calls "forged families." Tragedy and suffering have pushed people together in a way that goes deeper than merely a convenient living arrangement. They become, as the anthropologists say, "fictive kin."[66]

Whether your children are biological, adopted, or chosen, it is crucial to remember this fact. Children temporarily pass through our bodies and lives en route to the mystery of their own life. When we as parents at mid-life can accept this, the ambivalence of parenting will gain its proper perspective. If we truly take this to heart—we can avoid much disappointment.

Place

The third aspect of the establishment stage is place. A relatively new term, "sense of place," has become a buzzword used to justify everything from a nostalgic appreciation of a safe home in the country to selling large suburban enclaves. According to the United States Census Bureau, a typical American will move 11.7 times during their life.[67]

Let's examine how our body, mind, spirit, and soul view the places that look and feel like home to us. I label them geographical, demographical, psychographical, and ideological on the mandala. These are the cultural preconceptions that shape how we respond to an environment. They make up our sense of place.

Geographical-Physical

This aspect relates to our family history and genealogy—being born in, and growing up in a place. The geographical element of a sense of place develops over time and can prove extremely strong. When we speak of "going home," it usually means geographically. These solid and enduring relationships are attachments based on our personal history with a location. They are characterized by a strong sense of identification and a long-term residence.

In geographical relationships, a sense of place is a physical part of our history. They require significant time to develop and are most influential when they contain extensive experiences and memories. These become part of your individual (sense of self) and environmental (sense of place) identity.

Geographical relationships sound like this statement: "This place *looks* and *smells* like home."

Demographical-Mental

This aspect describes the statistical data relating to the people within it. Americans hail from areas as diverse as the rural south, the academic northeast, and the free-spirited western states. A defining characteristic of the demographic relationship is a rational choice, the ability to choose a place with the best possible combination of desirable features.

Demographic relationships have little or nothing to do with personal history. Because they are founded on your list of desirable traits, demographic relationships typically result from dissatisfaction with a former community and the quest to find a more desirable place. We base this relationship on the match between the attributes of a location. What one thinks is a "perfect" place. Not surprisingly, your perception of the ideal community changes across the life cycle.

Demographical relationships sound like this statement: "These people *reflect* my worldview."

Ideological-Spiritual

This relationship is about ethical living according to one's moral guidelines and responsibility to a place. The ground rules may be sacred or secular and come from religious or spiritual teachings. For others, it is a secular ethic of responsibility. The ideological relationship embodies a profound sense of belonging. In spiritual terms, it often feels mystical. We form ideological connections on values and beliefs that relate to physical places. The defining characteristic of ideological relationships is a well-articulated ideology about *living* in a place.

Ideological relationships sound like this statement: "These people *believe* as I do."

Psychographical-Emotional

Psychographics is a methodology used to describe psychological attributes such as personality, values, opinions, attitudes, interests, and lifestyles.[68] These emotional and intangible feelings form a sense of belonging. It encompasses one's traditions relating to a place through stories.

Psychographics include family histories—and social, political, and fictional narratives. These aspects are often the most robust and enduring relationships and create an emotional attachment to a place.

Psychographical relationships sound like this statement: "This place *feels* like home."

****

Every place has its unique influence on how we relate to it. However, it is essential to remember that our *relationships with* and *attachments to* places are interrelated to our personal history and the essentials of our being. Therefore, how one feels in one place is influenced by other areas' positive and negative feelings.

A sense of place is an experience created by a person's essentials combined with the environmental setting. In other words, to some degree, our understanding of self guides our sense of place in this world. But ideally, they do not exist independently of each other.

Integrated community and spatial relationships benefit our whole being—our body, mind, spirit, and soul. A cohesive sense of self and space will enhance our physical, mental, spiritual, and emotional health.

Community

The fourth aspect of the establishment stage is community. Yet another crucial decision in stage two of life as we deal with increasing diversity and mobility—is the friends, cultural, and religious groups we associate with. I say much about this in my book, *The Loss of Belonging*. It addresses the challenges we face when losing our community and finding a new (and better) one.

There are many valuable things in life, and our community is one of the most important. To live life without the experience of belonging is a life without living. Group relationships are essential to our success and well-being.

Communities have greatly evolved over the years. If you go back a couple of thousand years, humans generally belonged to one tribe. The individuals in a person's circle and the group overlapped.

Today, we have many individual connections along with a large number of group connections or communities. We are probably better at identifying and correcting individual connections than we are at groups. Author John Chancellor believes that the groups we belong to can have a stronger influence on our mental state than most of our individual connections. Far too many people are willing to disconnect on an individual basis rather than forsake their group.[69]

I experienced this first-hand at mid-life when I left the evangelical Christian community. Recently, many others have had similar, if less intense, disruptions in their individual vs. group connections. Consider the families and friends who no longer talk to each other because of Trump, vaccines, face masks, gender identity, sexual preferences, and race relations.

We are often aware of the impact of our individual connections on our state of happiness. We are less aware of the impact our group connections have on our state of enjoyment. Furthermore, when we talk about community, we are often far too general. We fail to distinguish a community of individuals from a large group. For example, friends from the religious community, co-workers from the political group, etc. Certain communities—such as religion, political party, and the NRA, can have a major impact on how one thinks, and that leads to how we act and feel.

Take a moment and consider your community's impact on your life. Consider the things you value most—your essentials and strengths—and if your community adds layered nuance to whom you are becoming. Healthy communities help piece together the fragments of our lives. They complement *who we are* until what emerges is whole, meaningful, new, and better.

*****

Some choose a primary community from the people with whom they worship. Unfortunately, most of the world's significant religions build on medieval ideologies. Choosing a path contrary to our church community can create devastating problems, mainly if we have outgrown the dogma that often seeks to restrict, censor, and control.

A loss of confidence in one's moral ideals can result in a significant identity crisis (see Crisis Mandala on page 322.) In many religions, questioning or abandoning one's faith often risks ex-communication or ghosting. In the case of Islam, it is death. Suppose we build the majority of our community around those with whom we worship. In that case, it can result in a total loss of community—friends, family, and our image of God.

To address this crisis, Psychologist Marlene Winell has coined the term *Religious Trauma Syndrome (RTS)*. She describes it as the condition experienced by people struggling with leaving an authoritarian, dogmatic religion and coping with the damage of indoctrination. One may be going through the shattering of a personally meaningful faith and breaking away from a controlling community and lifestyle.

RTS is a function of both the chronic abuses of harmful religion and the impact of severing one's connection with one's faith and can be compared to Post Traumatic Stress Disorder (PTSD).[70]

Dr. Winell details four aspects of Religious Trauma Syndrome.

1. Cognitive Symptoms: Confusion, poor critical thinking ability, negative beliefs about self-ability and self-worth, black and white thinking, perfectionism, and difficulty with decision-making.
2. Emotional Symptoms: Depression, anxiety, anger, grief, loneliness, difficulty with pleasure, and loss of meaning.

3. **Social Symptoms:** Loss of social network, family rupture, social awkwardness, sexual problems, and being behind schedule on developmental tasks.
4. **Cultural Symptoms:** Unfamiliarity with the secular world; "fish out of water" feelings, difficulty belonging, and information gaps (e.g., evolution, modern art, music).

If you are experiencing or anticipating the loss of your religious community, Dr. Winnell's books, videos, and website (journeyfree.org) may prove helpful and cathartic.

****

As we approach the mid-life transition and the culmination of stage two, we face an excruciating choice to deepen or weaken commitments to career, family, place, and community. Many of us feel trapped in lives that seem not to fit anymore.

The development stage shows that our parents, teachers, religion, and culture influenced our identity. Institutions force us to "fit in." Consequently, we develop emotions, behaviors, and beliefs that have us acting in the ways they taught us. Not in the ways that make us feel like our true selves.

Psychologists call this version of our identity the "Adaptive Self"—the part of us that prioritizes fitting in, getting along, and doing what we're told. When these actions begin to feel unhealthy, the Adaptive Self constricts our lives.

To remember and recover one's true identity, we need to discover our "Authentic Self;" the self that prioritizes living according to one's essentials—not the demands of others.

Unfortunately, for most of us, our Authentic Self is buried deep in the unconscious, where its treasures remain hard to remember, identify, and salvage. But, as we will see, the deep dive required is well worth it.

The four stages of life (development, establishment, enjoyment, and enlightenment) are social constructs that enable us to describe and support life's significant changes. We will explore life's third and fourth stages in the final two waypoints.

This saga now turns to the transitions in life, which inevitably lead to a crisis of identity, when our first half of life dreams collapse and fragment. We have grappled with symbols, essentials, and the first two stages of life. But, for many, now comes the time when a call to adventure becomes increasingly urgent, an intense longing to discover who we truly are. Fortunately, there is a universal guide map for those of us who dare to answer this summons into the unknown.

Transitions

What Universal Journey Are You Traveling?

Massive life upheavals strike us at the core of who we are. They create identity storms, in which we feel helpless, overwhelmed, and lost. Transitions are how we reorient and find our way.

A transition extends an invitation to experience something new. But suppose we don't stop, pay attention, and perhaps create a ceremony or ritual that gives a conscious ending and a new beginning. In that case, we miss the potential growth of the invitation. In our mid-life and late-life transitions, most of us travel without a map or the counsel of wise guides. Without assistance, how can we find and salvage the treasures of these stages? That is why *The Quest* and this book were created and, specifically, why this waypoint was written.

A transition is a pathway to the next stage of life. Significant changes may be voluntary (an affair, losing confidence in one's religion and moral ideals) or involuntary (a relaxation in life's requirements). They are also external (retirement party) and internal (feeling old and useless). But the choice to *navigate* a transition is optional.

Traditionally, humanity created sacred rites to mark the passages. But rituals to commemorate the turbulent transitions to the third and fourth stages of life are rare, if non-existent.

Suppose our lives are motivated by a search for identity. In that case, few experiences reveal the challenges of this *Quest*— with its ups and downs—like our transitions. They embody, however tumultuously, an understanding of what life might be about, outside the constraints of what we once perceived as usual. The first half of life inundates us with advice on *what* we should *do*, but we hear little about *who* we should *be*.

A closer look at life's transitions helps us understand what the Greek philosophers beautifully termed *enantiodromia* or the principle in which everything eventually changes into its opposite. Jung describes it as "the principle which governs all natural life cycles, from the smallest to the greatest."[71]

At mid-life, we struggle with polarities such as young and old, light and dark, love and hate, male and female, good and evil, power and vulnerability, triumph and tragedy, life and death. A primary task is to integrate the opposites—to transcend dualities. Ironically, the wounds of transition provide the opportunity for transformation and insight. There will be more about this in the Enlightenment waypoint.

The Greeks recognized that all is flux and nothing stays still. Nothing endures but change. However, change does not have to be devastating. It can take a particular form, and in *The Quest*, those forms are *universal journeys*. They are the treasure maps (templates) to help navigate life's transitions.

The Stages and Transitions waypoints are where the meaning of the phrase "all stories are different, yet all stories are the same" converges. The stages of our life are as unique as the people, places, memories, and events that influence us. *The*

Quest proposes that we can better navigate the tumult of life's transitions by applying the truths of the universal journeys to the significant changes in our lives.

Major Life Transitions

Let's explore four (a quaternity) challenging life changes.

First, around age twenty to thirty, is the transition from childhood to first adulthood. The classic novel *The Magic Mountain* by Thomas Mann beautifully recounts this transition. This life change precedes the scope of this book.

Second, at around age thirty-five to fifty, is the transition to second adulthood, also known as second life or the second half of life. At this point, we may find we have engaged with life blindly and therefore suffer a cataclysm. So much of what we took for truth seems bogus, and we must acknowledge that we are in pieces.

This brokenness is where *The Quest* can begin. The second transition provides the opportunity for a universal journey into the innermost depths of who we are. At this pivotal time, the holy grail of wholeness awaits discovery. Two recent movies about mid-life transition are *The Wrestler* and *Lost In Translation.*

Third, somewhere around age seventy to eighty is the transition to elderhood. A popular Netflix™ series, *Grace and Frankie*, attempts to portray this transition, albeit myopic. Likewise, the movie *Fried Green Tomatoes* does a superb job portraying a positive and nuanced elder. Again, however, it is unusual to find art forms that depict the real-life psychological tasks that one finds in late life.

Fortunately for us, psychiatrist Allan B. Chinen has compiled a book *In The Ever After* containing rare fairy tales that address the second half of life issues. Two of my favorites are "Fortune and the Woodcutter," a story of loss and the return of magic, and "The Old Man Who Lost His Wen," a story of breaking free of culture's expectations. Reading these timeless stories may help clarify your personal myth and universal journey.

Fourth, age unknown is the transition to death, the final door, rebeginning, or afterlife. Some may feel more comfortable calling it heaven, paradise, nirvana, hereafter, beyond, bliss, empyrean, afterworld, or utopia.

In her ground-breaking book, *Deathing*,[72] Anya Foos-Graber believes that death, like birth, should be a light-filled, conscious moment. Death is not a disease. Instead, it is the most natural passage we will make since inception. She writes that looking at death before the time comes is like learning about natural childbirth before having a baby.

Just as mothers now choose to be conscious participants in the birth process, Foos-Graber feels that all of us should be conscious of our eventual death. She believes we should prepare for it the way the Tibetan Buddhists and American Indians used to do. The book is a thoughtful treatise that guides this transition to mortality. We will explore this idea further in the Enlightenment waypoint.

These are the four major life transitions of *The Quest*. We do not have to attempt to navigate them alone.

****

One of the primary motivations to create *The Quest* experience and this book was the utter frustration at the lack of knowledge required to navigate my second significant life change at age forty-two. I had no resources to help survive the transition to second adulthood. It was a frightening and devastating time. Repeatedly I sought advice from respected elders and yet was inevitably met with embarrassment, confusion, or cliches.

However, I am insatiably curious; perhaps I should say desperate, and I began to scour writings and respected thought leaders for a recurring theme. Joseph Campbell and the *Hero's Journey* repeatedly surfaced with the idea of a universal journey.

I determined to read everything written by Campbell and was encouraged when I found the Hero's Journey had been inspired in part by Carl Jung. His psychology and philosophy focused on the transition to the second half of life. It was then I realized I had discovered a universal waypoint (a template, a map, a narrative arc) for the significant transitions of life. The Heroine's Journey, a subsequent discovery, outlined a feminine perspective. The steps of these journeys are listed later in this waypoint.

While the stages of life are unique and composed of the many facets of our individual lives, the transitions of life benefited from a universal story. If the components of the universal journeys had worked for countless humans before, why not now? Why not me and you?

A crucial eureka moment occurred when I understood that the universal journey does not require a hero or heroine like Ulysses, Circe, Luke Skywalker, or Wonder Woman. Instead, to be a hero or heroine in real life requires a journey (*a Quest*) inward to what Campbell calls the "Special World" of the mind: the self, the conscious, and the unconscious.

Recalling the first significant life change into my first adulthood, I compared the pivotal events of that transition. To my surprise, they aligned with the Heroine's Journey steps. One example, my "Separation," came at the age of twenty-four when I was offered a job in Stuart, Florida. It was a thousand miles apart geographically, demographically, psychographically, and ideologically from my "Ordinary World" in the Tennessee Appalachians. Yet, my "New Understanding" was an enlarged perceptual view.

I then compared the events of my second significant life change into second adulthood. This time, they mirrored the steps of the Hero's Journey. My "Call to Adventure" was to leave my identity as an evangelical minister and stage performer in the bible belt to "The Special World" of shamanism and solitude in the wilderness. I felt called to pursue the inner masculine while exploring my essentials—the aspects of my being. My elixir, my boon, is the knowledge contained in this book and *The Quest*.

Now, I am finally (Yes!) able to *anticipate* the third significant life change to stage four of enlightenment. I can better navigate the transition by utilizing the narrative arcs of the universal journeys. Although more than a decade away, my intuition is that my next "Call to Adventure" may be to leave my calling as a shaman, to "Accept the Call" to enlightenment as a sage.

Michel Montaigne, Wendell Berry, Louise Aronson, Sharon Kaufman, David Plath, Roy Baumeister, Connie Zweig, Rabbi Zalman Schachter-Shalomi, and others have written profoundly about the fourth transition to elderhood, and ultimately death, or the final door. But, of course, we have no concept of when that ultimate transition will occur or what it entails. Still, we can determine to be fully prepared and to live every day to its fullest until it comes. Suppose the fates allow us to live long into the fourth stage of life. In that case, we trust that we will be able to face our mortality and answer the "Call to Adventure" with courage and few regrets.

What about you? Can you compare the pivotal events of your first significant life change and transition to first adulthood and see how they mirror the steps of one of the universal journeys? And how about your considerable life change and transition to second adulthood? If you compare personal life events at this moment to the components of one or more of the universal journeys, which step are you currently on?

The idea of these universal journeys as narrative arcs is appropriate for our mandalas, our circles. My understanding of these arcs includes a quaternity: hero, heroine, elder, and healing. So, let's explore each of them further. Look for similarities as you review your life's journey.

The Hero's Journey

At first, I recoiled from the idea of being a hero. The lyrics to Tina Turner's iconic song, "We Don't Need Another Hero," come to mind. But as I studied this concept formulated during a lifetime of research by sociologist Joseph Campbell, I understood that there are true heroes among us. They are the ones who are courageous enough to risk a journey to their innermost being. Please note that the Hero's Journey is different from the hero myth in the Symbols waypoint.

What about you and me? Restless and approaching young adulthood, mid-life, or old age, we timidly attempt (voluntary or involuntary) a brief foray inside the deep recesses of our self. It is dark and scary, a vast unexplored sea, with memories, events, places, and people we would prefer to forget. Then the moment approaches to answer the "Call to Adventure" and confront these voyages of the past, with the chance to unearth buried treasure. Yet many of us are overcome with exhaustion.

We think how tiring it would be to venture into the unconscious. It would require confronting our dark side and fighting to understand the pain, feeling the pain and enduring uncomfortable emotions, expending valuable time, experiencing guilt and shame, and stirring up nightmares that psychological movie thrillers tersely describe. It would spoil our good-enough life.

What is the benefit of a taxing journey inward when a person can travel sitting in one's easy chair mindlessly surfing the internet? Am I not already in my dream home, where familiar smells, comfort food, an easy job, and kith and kin are all about me? What more could I expect to find while getting to know myself except fresh disappointments?

Settled into our overstuffed recliner, we reflect. I must have been suffering from some temporary mental breakdown to have rejected the reality of my normal life. And to have believed—like some aging sentimental fool—that it is necessary, interesting, and useful to muster the courage to answer this invitation to adventure.

We ignore the call to finally grow up and find out who we truly are. We suppress the longings once again. And stumble to bed, get up, go to work, do the same predictable things— much like Bill Murray in the movie *Groundhog Day*—over and over. Our deepest childhood dreams and hopes fade slowly away.

And many never pay attention to their inner self again. We have completed the outer Hero's Journey of first life, which is good enough. We have accomplished many things and feel no need to take an arduous journey to the unfamiliar—our tenuous interior.

But then there are those brave ones who resonate with Luke Skywalker in the movie *Star Wars.* Who somehow cannot be content to ignore the "Call to Adventure." Something inside relates to Luke's gradual, often treacherous journey from a humble farmer on Tatooine to a Jedi warrior.

Every compelling tale of adventure, every *Quest,* needs a call to action—a protagonist who's willing and courageous enough to embark on the Hero's Journey far from their comfort zone. Luke, the farmer who finds himself stuck in his mundane life, gets this push after stormtroopers destroy his home and murder his aunt and uncle. And, unfortunately, for some, it takes a catastrophe to propel us into our essence.

His proclamation to Obi-Wan, "I want to learn the ways of the force," marks the first significant milestone in the narrative. It launches Luke's journey to becoming a Jedi. These universal aspects of the Hero's Journey have established *Star Wars* as a modern and ubiquitous transition story.

The journey begins when a "hero" finds themself experiencing upheaval. And discover the solution lies in finding and retrieving an elixir or treasure deep inside, then taking it on themselves to undergo the perilous journey into the unknown.

It's *Star Wars, Green Knight, Lord of the Rings,* and *The Princess Bride.* And suppose you transplant it from fantasy into something a little more earthbound. In that case, it's *Master and Commander, Saving Private Ryan, Guns of Navarone,* and *Apocalypse Now.* Finally, if you look back through history, you find *Dionysus, Jesus Christ, Don Quixote, Faust, and Joan of Arc.*

Sociologist Joseph Campbell spent a lifetime identifying twelve significant components of these stories throughout history. He called this narrative arc the Monomyth, more commonly known as the Hero's Journey.

The twelve stages are:

1. Ordinary World—The hero's everyday world before the story begins.

2. Call to Adventure—The hero is presented with a problem, challenge, or adventure.

3. Refusal of the Call—The hero refuses the challenge or journey, usually because he's scared.

4. Meeting with the Mentor—The hero meets a mentor to gain advice or training for the adventure.

5. Crossing the First Threshold—The hero leaves the ordinary world and goes into the special world.

6. Tests, Allies, Enemies—The hero faces trials, meets allies, confronts enemies, and learns the rules of the "Special World."

7. Approach—The hero has hit setbacks during tests and may need to try a new idea.

8. Ordeal—The most significant life or death crisis. Also known as the inmost cave, or descent into the ashes.

9. Reward—The hero has survived death, overcomes his fear, and now earns the reward.

10. The Road Back—The hero must return to the "Ordinary World."

11. **Resurrection Hero**—Another test where the hero faces death—he has to use everything he's learned.

12. **Return with Elixir**—The hero returns from the journey with the elixir, also known as treasure or boon, and uses it to help everyone in the "Ordinary World."

Campbell emphasizes that the order is not concrete and that every hero may not encounter all twelve steps. That is true for the other journeys as well. He believed that a life well-lived involves a series of universal journeys. Over and over, adventure calls us to new horizons. Each time there is the same challenge—do I dare?

The Heroine's Journey

As I read Joseph Campbell and Carl Jung, patriarchal influences of an earlier and outdated world heavily influenced their views of the universal journey. While this certainly does not discredit the importance and relevance of the Hero's Journey, it does demand a new narrative arc. A journey that provides a template for those who do not fit neatly into the masculine construct.

As a long-time protégé of Campbell's, Maureen Murdock came to think that the Hero's Journey model did not adequately address the journey of the feminine. She was the first to chart an alternative. Murdock believes the Heroine's Journey is more appropriate for those less patriarchal.

She developed the model based on her work with females in therapy. It is described in her book *The Heroine's Journey: Woman's Quest for Wholeness* and contains ten stages.

Nearing the third transition of life, I was surprised to find my journey has encompassed not one but three different narrative arcs, including the Heroine's Journey. Furthermore, I learned that each universal narrative arc could be compatible with anyone, no matter their gender. The following is my paraphrase of this journey.

1. **Heroine Separates From the Feminine**—The "feminine" is often a mother or mentor figure.

2. **Identification with the Masculine and Gathering of Allies**—The heroine embraces a new way of life. This often involves choosing a different path from the prescribed feminine cultural role. They may enter some masculine or dominant identity-defined sphere and gear up to "fight" anyone or anything that limits their life options.

3. **Road of Trials and Meeting Ogres and Dragons**—The heroine encounters trials and meets people who try to dissuade them from pursuing their chosen path. Adversaries who try to "destroy" the heroine.

4. **Experiencing the Boon of Success**—The heroine overcomes the obstacles in their way. (This is typically where the Hero's Journey ends.)

5. **Heroine Awakens to Feelings of Spiritual Dryness or Death**—The heroine finds the new way of life (attempting the masculine and dominant identity) is too limited. They realize success in this new way of life is either temporary, illusory, shallow, or requires a betrayal of self over time.

6. **Initiation and Descent to the Goddess**—The heroine faces a crisis of some sort in which the new way of life is insufficient and falls into despair. The masculine and dominant strategies failed them.

7. **Heroine Urgently Yearns to Reconnect with the Feminine**—The heroine longs to return to their initial "limited" state or role.

8. **Heroine Heals the Mother-Daughter Split**—The heroine reclaims some initial values, skills, or attributes but now views these feminine traits from a new perspective.

9. **Heroine Heals the Wounded Masculine Within**—The heroine seeks to understand and make peace with the "masculine" approach to the world as it applies to them.

10. **Heroine Integrates the Masculine and Feminine**—The heroine integrates "masculine" and "feminine" qualities and perspectives. They face the future with a new understanding of themselves. This permits the heroine to interact with a complex, blended world, that is larger and more harmonious than their old way of life.

The Elder's Journey (From Hero to Sage)

I constructed the Elder's Journey primarily from the insightful thoughts of Allan B. Chinen. The elder-sage cultivates consciousness, illuminating the foundations of human existence. Chinen says that if a youth is considered the flower of humanity, the elder is its root. They embody the noblest and most splendid virtues of humanity's spirit.

The aging yet resilient hero and heroine have salvaged the treasures of the unconscious—personified by shipwrecks. They have integrated the conscious with the unconscious. Elders and sages cultivate their strengths and essentials—qualities such as serenity, equanimity (composure), and transcendence (spiritual growth).

Here are the stages of the Elder's Journey.

1. **The Call to Maturity**—This call is based on self-knowledge, self-awareness, and the transcendence of the personal ego. And the willingness to serve culture as a mentor and teacher to the young.

2. **Break Free of Ambitions and Dreams**—Unlike the hero or heroine whose first life task is to establish a self, an identity—the elder's second life task is to dissolve self and identity by cultivating wholeness.

3. **Replace Personal Self**—As the personal self dissolves as the guiding force in life, it is replaced by a higher self. This could be humanity or a god. The elder turns away from a preoccupation with status and wealth and learns to heed the soul's dictates.

4. **Seeks Transformation Through Painful Insight (Life Review) and Authentic Reformation (Life Repair).**

5. **Seeks Emancipation from the World**—Where the hero or heroine seeks victory in the institution of culture, elderhood is based on freedom from social convention.

6. **Moves from Prominence into Obscurity**—Opposite of the hero or heroine, the elder moves toward a more profound and more fundamental layer of human experience.

7. **Rediscovers and Lives the Universal Beliefs and Truths**—Elder's counsel and inspire youth, helping them balance their unique idealistic aspirations with the universal needs of the culture.

8. **Deepens Consciousness**—By integrating and cultivating consciousness, the elder illuminates the foundations and treasures of human experience.

9. **Serve as Wisdom Keepers**—They help connect the spirit to the natural world to heal the earth. Because elders are in touch with the traditions and stories of the past, they can transmit a spark, a living flame of wisdom, to help young people meet present and future challenges. When they hand down a tradition or myth, they communicate something timeless in its truth and universal in its beauty. Elders recognize that traditions constantly must evolve to avoid stagnation. They know an excessive veneration of the past destroys creativity and intellectual curiosity.

10. **Possess an Inner Authority**—An elder doesn't need to bolster personal power through self-assertion. Unlike traditional stereotypes of the conventional older adult, they are flexible, unattached to outcomes, tolerant and patient, and willing to teach when asked. And because of this, they can evoke a questing spirit in younger people.

11. **Dwell at the Intersection of Time**—The elder expands our idea of time beyond the current sound-bite and quarterly-report mentality. Their vantage point at the intersection of the vast panorama of life and coming mortality provides a long view that can redirect humanity's values from shortsightedness and mistaken materialism. They can provide wisdom and inspiration to begin the reclamation of our endangered planet.

The Healing Journey

The Healing Journey is the fourth narrative arc. It includes elements from the hero and heroine journeys. A healing journey focuses on a paradigm shift that enables the protagonist to accept their circumstances and view themselves with compassion.

The steps of the healing narrative arc are similar regardless of whether the abuse, injury, or illness is physical, mental, emotional, spiritual, or some combination. And irrespective of whether the source of the damage is natural, inflicted by another, or self-inflicted. Although there are several healing arc versions, this journey derives from the Buddhist Library website.[73]

There are eleven stages in the Healing Journey.

1. Hurt—The person gets hurt, ill, betrayed, injured, or receives a diagnosis of illness. The hurt is life-changing, and their expectations are disappointed.

2. Fear or Anger—The person feels the urge to flee, deny the situation, or play the victim. They are afraid or react with anger at self, illness, others, or gods or fate. May feel that the situation is unjust or there has been a mistake. Or feel that someone ought to fix it.

3. Fear and Anger Give Rise to Conflicts—The person experiences anxiety, develops obsessions (as if activity or information is all that is needed to change the situation), excessive grief, guilt or false guilt, shame, resentment, envy, jealousy, remorse for one's role or depression.

4. Loss of Love for Self and Others—As conflict intensifies and coping strategies fail to work, they lose initial faith. They lose the urge to keep up the fight and lose love for themselves and others. The person no

longer feels the joy of life and may become indifferent to others and the future.

5. **Activation of the Death or Illness Wish**—The person hits bottom and consciously or unconsciously may wish for things to be "over." They may try to give in to the illness or addiction. Either death follows, or the body, mind, soul, spirit isn't ready for the end.

6. **Lift in Life Energy**—The person experiences a slight lift in energy, if only because giving up isn't an option. May feel others' love and concern or a glimmer of self-caring.

7. **The Decision to Get Well Whatever that Means, Whatever it Takes**—They decide to get well even if it isn't according to their terms. The person also decides to do whatever it takes to get better. They choose not to bargain with the gods or doctors. They refuse to put limits on what they are willing to do to get better.

8. **The Decision to Forgive-Forgiveness Process**—Even if primarily physical, The Healing Journey always involves self-transformation and forgiveness. This includes letting go of blame for the source of the illness or someone's inability to treat, prevent, or respond optimally. The person usually has to forgive themself.

9. **Unconditional Love**—Whether the person recovers, partially recovers, or is going to die, they must let go of grievances to reach a culmination of suffering.

10. **Healing and Understanding**—The person resolves internal conflict, leading to an experience of restoration, acceptance, and understanding of self and the world. They now know themself far better than when the journey began.

11. **Wholeness and Health-Being True to One's Self**—The person is neither in denial nor passive. They have come to terms with their strengths and limitations and now know something about the future. They understand there will be unknowns. The person brings themselves fully to self, others, the world, and the future, whatever that is. No matter what, it is not the world they imagined or experienced before the hurt.

****

The universal journeys provide us with priceless and time-proven maps and templates for navigating the stormy transitions of life. They help outline a clear path while giving room for the uniqueness of who we are. Likewise, narrative arcs can help us shorten our learning curve and endure less pain and suffering as we navigate the stages and transitions of *The Quest*.

The mandala on page 323 portrays the four common aspects of the universal journeys: the call, descent, fulfillments, and magic flight. The mandala on page 322 outlines four common mid-life crises. I was shocked to realize I experienced all four at the same time. The more knowledge we have preceding a transition, the better prepared we can be. Now, let's continue the journey to discover our unique way to the holy grail.

Emotions

What Are Your Healthy and Unhealthy Affects?

The waypoints of our journey all lead to the holy grail of wholeness. *The Quest* is a reconciliation (an integration) of opposites. Our task is to integrate the adapted persona with the natural persona, feminine with the masculine, dark and light of the shadow, and unconscious with the conscious. As these diverse and competing aspects of our being reconcile, we form an intimate relationship with our true selves. The uniqueness and beauty of who we are (from the inside out) emerges. Perhaps at the heart of this integration is knowing and regulating our healthy and unhealthy emotions.

Two theories repeatedly emerged during my years of research. The first is attachment theory, as discussed in the Stages waypoint. The second is Affect theory which we will explore here. (Note: I capitalize Affect throughout the book to distinguish it from the verbal form.)

It is not too bold to say that Affect theory changes virtually everything we know about emotion. This theory posits there are nine innate emotions with distinct physical manifestations. There are two "positives," one neutral, and six "negative" Affects.

The same and different, unique yet universal principle again comes into play. While the nine biological Affects are universal, the way they are "triggered" in each of us is unique. Once the Affect is triggered, an emotion or feeling emerges, followed by a script and a mood. Thus, the Affect quaternity is trigger, emotion, script, and mood. There are two mandalas for this waypoint on pages 325 and 326.

Affect theory explains human emotion, motivation, behavior, and personality—elegantly, thoroughly, and convincingly.[74] The creator of this concept is Silvan Tomkins. We owe it to his legacy to test, retest, and apply his theory in our life. We can then unlock the good it can do and the truth it exposes.

We will look at each of the nine Affects and the Affect quaternity in more detail. But, first, let's explore why most of us have not heard of this innovative and far-reaching theory.

A Complex Theory that Refuted Freud

Silvan Tomkins was born in 1911 in Philadelphia and died in 1991. At age twenty-five, he began a postdoctoral study in philosophy at Harvard University. He became fascinated by the pioneering work on personality emerging from the Harvard Psychological Clinic. The thread connecting all of his scholarly interests was this question, "What do human beings want?"

In 1947 he began an eighteen-year tenure in Princeton University's Department of Psychology. It was there he developed an interest in the biological relationship of emotion. He called them Affects (pronounced 'a-ˌfekts). The term has a short "a" sound and the first syllable is emphasized. Thus, personality formation became the defining theme of his career. In 1962 and 1963, he released the first two volumes of his masterpiece, *Affect Imagery Consciousness* (AIC).

The world is only now hearing about this fascinating theory because Tomkins broke with mainstream psychology to declare the priority of the Affect system as the motivating force in human life. He did this in an era dominated by Freudian drive theory, which many psychoanalysts still accept to this day.

Furthermore, this theory is relatively unknown because he waited thirty years before releasing the final two volumes of *AIC* before his death in 1991. Only then was there a glossary for all four volumes. His books are notoriously dense and academic. Even with a dictionary, it has taken years for experts to begin unraveling this complex theory. He has often been called America's Einstein.[75]

The Affect quaternity attempts to simplify this multi-layered theory for *The Quest*. I will do my best to be true to Tomkin's original intent. My research comes directly from his writings and those of his collaborators. I've found that much of the material online regarding Affect Theory has been obtained through secondary sources and does not represent Tomkin's work accurately.

For those curious and who desire to explore this fascinating theory in greater detail, I recommend *Exploring Affect*, edited by E. Virginia Demos and *Shame and Pride: Affect, Sex, and the Birth of the Self* by Donald L. Nathanson, M.D. Be forewarned;

these books (and the nuances of this theory) are daunting. However, the hard work of close examination will produce many treasures.

A Brief Introduction to the Affects

First, Affects are life processes. They act to trigger the drives, memories, events, places, ideas, and people to which emotions are linked. When an Affect has been triggered, it releases a known pattern of biological events.[76] This reaction has enormous implications for our life journey.

To illustrate, whatever causes an increase in brain activity will trigger the *interest* Affect. It does not matter if the brain is an infant or an adult. When the proper conditions are met, the specific Affect is triggered. (Note: I italicize the nine Affects throughout the book.)

The stimulus for the infant may be the bright colors and movement of a mobile hanging over the crib. The older the child, the more memory can be "brought to mind" when *interest* is triggered.[77] This becomes exponentially true for the adult.

Second, Affects can be mixed. When an event triggers the *rage* Affect, the resulting feelings and emotions may trigger *shame* Affect, which may trigger *disgust* Affect. Thus, the term "conflicting emotions."

Third, Affects are contagious. Being around someone with an intense Affect will cause others to share a part of their experience. We can positively see this while doing the wave at a sporting event and negatively by a lynch mob. This infectious aspect is why Tomkins says Affect makes good things better and bad things worse.[78]

Fourth, Affects are physical. The affective reaction is seen best in the face and affects the circulatory system and verbal expressions. You will find a list of Affect descriptions and their physical manifestations later in this waypoint.

Finally, it is crucial to understand that some types of negative Affect can be an essential part of our *healthy* emotional makeup. Although negative Affect can be tumultuous, unpleasant, and sometimes problematic, these negative emotions can also be beneficial. For example, it is healthy to feel the tingling of *fear* in situations where physical harm is possible. And it is helpful to feel the thrust of *anger* when you need to defend your children. The "negative" emotions signal that something isn't going right and needs immediate attention. (Note: The hyphenated Affects indicate the range from low to high intensity.)

The Nine Affects

Positive

1. Contentment-Enjoyment—This Affect ranges from the *contentment* of the "all-is-right-in-the-world" feeling (afterglow) immediately after sex to the jubilant face of *joy* at the end of a rollercoaster ride. Dr. Nathanson explains it this way, "The reduction of stimulus level accompanying the relief of any high-density experience will trigger the Affect *contentment-enjoyment*."[79]

    The next time you coast to the end of a rollercoaster ride, pay attention to the faces of your fellow riders. You will notice that the affective response to the *decrease in the stimulus* of fright triggers physical reactions, feelings, and emotions: shrieking laughter, uplifted and pumping arms, and explosive sounds of glee. These reactions result in scripts of interaction recalling past rides, comments about the scariest part, and a mood of euphoria.

2. **Interest-Excitement**—An optimal increase in the intensity and rate of activity of anything going on in the brain will trigger the Affect *interest-excitement*.[80] It ranges from the *interest* in a good story and may also be triggered by a hunger pang barely discerned. *Interest* can make us feel nostalgic or hungry.

    As we grow older, our vast array of memories provides layers of Affect-experience connections. Any artist can tell you about the timeless *excitement* generated by experiencing a flow of ideas that constantly trigger the *interest-excitement* Affect as they create.

The two positive Affects are a vital pursuit of *The Quest* and a key to the enjoyment of self, others, and our world during the second half of life. We will explore them further in the Enjoyment waypoint.

Neutral

3. **Surprise-Startle**—The function of the Affect *surprise-startle* is to clear the mind so that one can refocus attention to whatever startled it. It is common to forget about the Affect and only remember what caused it—a clap of thunder, a scream, or a loud noise.

    The Affect *surprise-startle* deletes or refreshes whatever Affect, emotion or feeling, mood, or script presently occupies our being and prepares us to take on new Affect. It then triggers other appropriate Affects such as *fear* or feelings of *helplessness*. Finally, it shocks us into awareness.

Our reaction to this Affect depends on our biography. We probably do not enjoy surprises if we had a parent who was always jumping out and yelling "Boo!" when we least expected it. Or one who had unpredictable acts of *rage*. This reaction is particularly true in post-traumatic stress disorder (once called shell shock). Particularly for soldiers exposed to bursts of gunfire, the detonation of bombs, or sniper attacks. Then, this Affect can trigger *terror* and *helplessness* scripts, even when the Affect occurs in harmless situations.

Negative

4. Fear-Terror—This Affect triggers memories of frightening events. They invade our consciousness and produce ever-increasing amounts of *fear*, feelings of discomfort and *anxiety*, and emotions of *dread* and *horror*. These feelings and emotions result in an ominous mood. As we grow and develop, we accumulate many fearful memories and triggers.

Nathanson says when *startle* Affect precedes *fear* Affect, we say we were "scared by" whatever surprised us. However, when *fear* Affect mixes with *shame* Affect, we are "caught unawares."[81] We have many descriptive words and phrases for the emotions triggered by *fear* Affect. For example, we can be "frightened stiff," "scared to death," filled with "doom and gloom," hysterical, panic-stricken, horrified, apprehensive, or "spooked." It also can affect the body physically with "cotton-mouth," diarrhea, nausea, shaking, shivering, or sweating.

Some events in life build up so much negative Affect that a fleeting memory will evoke unpleasant emotion. Therefore we suppress or repress it, and force it out of awareness. By the second half of life, most of us have relegated countless unpleasant emotions to the vast sea of forgetfulness we call the unconscious. These hidden memories create *anxiety* and other problems. We talk more about this in the Unconscious waypoint.

5. **Anger-Rage**—We express *anger* Affect in different ways. Some of us are rarely angry, while others always seethe. Some erupt at the drop of a hat but calm down immediately; others have a long fuse, yet it is catastrophic when they finally explode. *Anger* Affect makes some scream, and others clam up; some hit, and others cry. Some never forgive, and others rarely hold a grudge.

    We all experience the identical Affect biologically, but our biography (how our family, neighborhood, and culture handled *anger*) magnifies or impedes it. Same but different. Each of us compiles patterns of events that make us angry. Those memories make up our understanding of this Affect and form our unique version.

    Paying attention to someone angry tells us a lot about what is happening inside. Life institutions have taught many of us to disguise it, but close observation reveals clues such as a clenching jaw, a flushed neck, or closed fists.

144

As with the other negative Affects, we bury many of these unpleasant emotions in our unconscious.

6. **Distress-Anguish**—Any unpleasant stimulus by a drive, memory, or experience can trigger the Affect *distress-anguish*. If life mixes in a small amount of *fear* Affect, the result is "stress" or being "stressed out." If the Affect *distress* is triggered by the hunger drive and combined with *anger* Affect, we say we are "hangry." When triggered by the thirst drive, we are "thirsting to death" or "dying of thirst."

   An essential characteristic of *distress-anguish* is the way we handle our tears. As we grow up, we have been taught to regulate or avoid our Affects at some level. As a result, some of us cry at the drop of a hat, and others cannot remember the last time they had tears. The way we describe this emotion is revealing—"tears of joy" (*enjoyment*) or "reduced to tears" (*shame*).

   Cultural norms alter and suppress how we express biological Affect. Many of us were humiliated and called "crybabies." We were admonished not to be "childish," commanded to keep a "stiff upper lip." Life's institutions taught us not to cry in public. Even in the darkened privacy of a movie, an unexpected verklempt or tear will cause many of us to look around in *shame* to make sure no one sees.

   If we have a past filled with sadness—distressing feelings and emotions can dominate our moods and, ultimately, our life. Memory is capable of overloading our being. One of the benefits of exploring our unconscious is the gift of healing tears and deep emotion as we encounter positive and negative memories, experiences, and events.

7. Dissmell—The term for this Affect describes an impediment with the physical act of smelling. The drive that correlates best with *dissmell* Affect is hunger. Evolution has taught us to determine the quality of food by its odor. It is a mechanism that protects and keeps track of the hunger drive and our food intake.

    The physical reaction to lousy odor is to wrinkle our nose, raise the upper lip, and retreat. We have the same biological response for people that trigger our *disgust* Affect. When I did something my parents did not like, they would call me a "stinker."

    A smell can instantaneously stimulate recollection of memories in time and space. They can elicit nostalgic thoughts of a former lover. Still, they can also transport us to the horrendous odors and poverty of third-world slums. Dr. Nathanson makes this stunning observation. "I have never seen a marriage, a business partnership, or any working relationship survive once *dissmell* Affect has entered the picture in therapy."[82] He also notes the lifelong debilitating effects to those raised by mothers who expressed *dissmell* Affect at whatever displeased them.

    Much of our concept of *shame* comes from our history of response to the Affects of *dissmell* and *disgust*. This pair of Affects always encompass racism. When these two Affect's physical manifestations are combined, they form the sneer of contempt.

8. **Disgust**—*Disgust* Affect causes us to react to people, places, memories, or events in our life as if they were lousy food. Memories associated with *disgust* Affect, such as food poisoning, can trigger a lifelong aversion to the food or taste that caused it.

    Many Americans develop a belief that certain foreign foods such as snails, cockroaches, and insects are contaminated and therefore trigger a feeling of repulsion. In addition, bodily substances such as saliva (spit), urine (pee), excrement (shit), and phlegm (snot) have descriptive names, and they tend to trigger *disgust* Affect in most people. It is no coincidence that many of these words are considered slang or curse words.

    Author Justin Cronin in *City of Mirrors* says, "Behind every great hatred is a love story."[83] The ironic and heartbreaking fact is that the extreme loathing and endurance of much family hatred is directly related to the previous strength of the familial bond—of the "drive" to be close, of the need for each other, of the warmth once given the other, and of the degree of nurturance each represented in the other.[84] Once loving families now treat the one they have determined as the "offending" partner with *disgust*.

9. **Shame-Humiliation**—*Dissmell* and *disgust* Affects limit our drives; yet *shame* Affect interferes with other Affects at their height.[85] *Shame* is the most social of the negative Affects because it modulates, regulates, and impedes the *interest* and *enjoyment* that power all interaction.[86] *Shame* Affect is probably at the root of

the trauma, frustrations, and conflicts that most people and institutions carry.

The Affect *shame* is triggered when there is a hindrance to the positive Affects. We all experience *shame* differently. One person's source of *shame* can be another person's fulfillment, satisfaction, or indifference. We see these differences in the porn and sexual fantasies we prefer.

As was stated earlier, this Affect can be confusing because there is a difference between the Affect *shame* (a noun), and the action of shame (a verb). An excellent way to understand this delineation is that Affect *shame* is biological (universal), and the verb shame is biographical (unique).

We can better understand this Affect by the terms "hurt feelings," "shyness," "embarrassment," "humiliation," and "discouragement." How these words apply to us depends on our life experiences of *shame* Affect.

This Affect may be the most significant interference to the enjoyment of everyday life. *Shame* Affect has the power to render us joyless when there is every reason for *joy* Affect to continue. It is a painful experience that limits intimacy and empathy. Nathanson says that *shame* is by far the more commanding Affective experience in the life of mature, successful people. It is the fall from grace, the loss of face, and the forfeiture of social position accompanying exposure that we fear most.[87]

****

A significant portion of this book intends to help us bring *shame* Affect to consciousness and regulate and reconcile these unhealthy feelings instead of repressing them. A way to enjoy *Quest* and the second life is to maximize positive (healthy) Affects and regulate negative (unhealthy) ones.

It is worth repeating; although negative emotions can be chaotic, unpleasant, and sometimes challenging, they can also prove beneficial. They signal that something isn't going right and needs your immediate attention. Not all negative Affects are unhealthy in certain situations.

The Quaternity of Affect

Here is Affect Theory in an incredibly encapsulated form: Something or someone *triggers* an *affect* that activates a *script* that produces a *mood*. Now, let's expand this process. A drive or source *triggers* an Affect, and it lasts but a few seconds. Likewise, a feeling lasts only long enough for us to make the flash of recognition; an *emotion* as long as we keep finding drives or sources that trigger that Affect. A *script* is like a play, a drama, with sequences of experiences that help connect our past and present to determine the next affective response. Often an emotion lasts for a while and produces a *mood*—a persistent state of emotion in which we can be stuck for hours or days.

The following summary of the four foundational elements will help illustrate the profound consequences Affect theory can have on emotional health during the second half of life. They are presented in order of biological occurrence.

Triggers

Drives maintain our physical health and normal functioning. We should have studied them in high school. These internal mechanisms inform us about various needs and how to satisfy them. Examples of drives are breathing, thirst, hunger, and sex. They have the power to *trigger* one or more of the nine innate Affects.

For example, when the hunger drive assembles with the *interest* Affect, it prompts the nice foreshadowing of a good meal. However, when it combines with the *distress* Affect, it creates the sobbing hunger of early childhood. A hungry and fearful person may eat furtively or not at all. At the same time, one whose memories trigger *shame* Affect may avoid food entirely.

Various sources also have the power to trigger Affect. They come from our history and include memories, events, places, ideas, and people.

Feelings and Emotions

Feelings indicate the levels of awareness that an Affect has been triggered. Since the first stage of life (development), we have experienced patterns of muscular contraction, circulatory changes, odors, postures, and noises associated with innate Affect. We have learned to associate certain feelings with those patterns.

Tomkins says that "feelings are like swords; they are only as good or evil as the end to which they are used."[88] For example, consider the relationship between a flushed face and the feeling of embarrassment; masturbation and *shame*; feelings of nausea caused by an exotic food; or lust caused by an unclothed body. These feelings and how we view them (healthy or unhealthy) say a lot about our history.

The following statement is crucial to our journey. *The level to which we are conscious determines the awareness of the Affect and the strength of the feeling.* It is possible to be so inattentive that we are unaware an Affect has been triggered. We may have been influenced in our development stage by an institution that denies or condemns the existence of certain feelings.

Therefore, one will use defense mechanisms such as repression to relegate them to the unconscious. It smothers the ability to perceive the feeling. We describe such people as insensitive, dull, or spiritless. We may say they have no self-awareness. When one lacks sensation or feeling, they feel "numb." The character Spock in the story of *Star Trek* is a good illustration of someone without feelings.

Learning to share and understand the feelings of others is called empathy. We summon a lifetime of remembered emotional experience in an attempt to appreciate the world of the other person. Tomkins calls this affective resonance or empathic relatedness. Captain Kirk illustrates a person with empathic relatedness to continue the *Star Trek* analogy.

As we enlarge our consciousness and begin the work to empty our unconscious during *The Quest,* our awareness of Affect intensity may increase. We may become more outwardly emotional and experience stronger internal feelings. As long as this increase occurs in Affects (positive or negative) that we have determined are healthy for us, this is a sign of growing whole. That is why it is crucial to identify our healthy and unhealthy Affect processes. We need to examine unhealthy triggers and regulate unhealthy Affect. Furthermore, we will need to rewrite unhealthy scripts.

Emotion is biographical. Affect can trigger personal memories. Consider the Affect *anger-rage*. When the Affect *anger-rage* is triggered—the biological Affect and facial expressions are the same in all of us. The difference in our reaction is the personalized (biographical) way we remember experiences of anger. Therefore, we must ask: How did we get angry in my family as a child? How was anger handled in the culture in which I grew up? What specific events trigger *anger* Affect in me currently?

To properly understand *anger* Affect, and determine if it is healthy or unhealthy, we must access our history—our trigger points. Furthermore, the way we react to our memories can trigger other Affects. For example, suppose the reaction to the Affect *anger* is **dysregulated**. We "fly off the handle." In that case, the response can trigger different Affects such as *disgust* and *shame*. Emotional dysregulation is the inability to manage the intensity and duration of negative Affects such as *fear, sadness*, or *anger*.

Anger as Affect can be the fleeting tension of a moment or recognized as an angry feeling. Too many angry thoughts about too many issues left long-unsolved can produce an unhealthy mood capable of lasting until something brings relief. If one can find no relief, or if the Affect is continually Triggered, *anger-rage* can become a disorder.

Like symbols, Affects (emotions) are like onions. They have layers.

Scripts

While the nine Affects are universal, the way we play them out in our lives is intensely personal. So again, every story is different, yet each story is the same.

We all construct scripts to undo childhood traumas, conflicts, and frustrations. As we grow older, our memory bank fills with events triggered by Affects. Tomkins believed these memories are grouped and stored as bundles, which he calls scripts. They work unconsciously to make a quick summary of repeated experiences. Think of how a person having a heart attack reports a rapid review of many scenes of their past life. The phrase, "my life flashed before my eyes," provides a simplistic understanding of how scripts work.

A script is like a play, a drama, with sequences of experiences that help connect our past and present to determine the subsequent affective response. Affect Theory teaches that people act toward one another according to social scripts. Therefore, we can better enjoy life by understanding how our scripts work and rewriting unhealthy ones.

Dr. Nathanson recounts working with a client whose life experiences had made her extremely sensitive to *shame*. She would constantly apologize for things beyond her control and not her fault and say "I'm sorry" every five minutes. A random event would trigger the Affect *shame*, and a progression of experiences would bundle together as a script and prompt her to apologize.[89]

There are many types of standard scripts. For example, when the Affect *shame* is triggered, scripts include avoidance, withdrawal, attack self, and attack others. Other script examples include narcissism, self-deprecation, resentment, depression, low self-esteem, passivity, and rage.

Think of when a long-time friend dies. We do not have the mental or emotional capacity to remember every experience we have shared with them. Instead, the Affect *anguish* triggers a feeling (an awareness) of loss. As we recall how we have handled the Affect of *anguish* in the past, we experience emotions. For example, the emotion of loss may trigger additional Affects such as *anxiety* or *anger*, which may result in even more feelings and emotions.

These lead to a mood that we call a period of mourning. We then review—with ourselves and others—a "movie" of life together with that departed friend that is much like a highlight reel of shared experiences.

An essential part of *The Quest* is rewriting our unhealthy scripts. This "script work" is complex and tedious but necessary. Examples may include editing clinging away from love, boyish bravado away from manly firmness, passive-aggression away from fierceness, and rage away from passion.

Moods

Moods have social implications. No one wants to be around someone in a bad mood. But, conversely, everyone wants to socialize with someone who is perpetually happy.

One of the aspects of *The Quest* is to identify links between our moods at mid-life and experiences from the first half of life. We attempt to remember scenes from our history that have been placed in hidden compartments of our memory. Verbalizing and letting them go can relieve anxiety and depression.

Moods are persistent states of emotion in which we can remain stuck for various periods—from hours to days. There are times when a mood will not disappear—when nothing we can do will make it go away. We all know what it's like to have troubled feelings and emotions resulting in "bad moods."

Persistent instances of mood can be a reason for psychotherapy. Dr. Nathanson recommends techniques such as *cognitive therapy* to help. Cognitive-behavioral therapy

(CBT) is a common type of talk therapy that increases awareness of inaccurate or negative thinking. It helps to view challenging situations more clearly and respond to them more effectively.

It can be a beneficial tool in treating mental health disorders, such as depression, post-traumatic stress disorder (PTSD), or eating disorders. CBT can also be an effective tool to help anyone learn to manage stressful life situations better.[90]

Physical Manifestations of Affect

The physical manifestations are essential because they help us recognize and identify the specific Affect. Our body provides ample clues to discern Affect in ourselves and others. Most of these take place in the face. For example, well-trained psychologists and members of law enforcement take classes emphasizing the importance of identifying facial expressions.

Tomkins calls the face the display board for the Affect system.[91] He believed that internal bodily responses are secondary to external facial expressions. As humans have evolved, the human face has become much more expressive.

However, our facial expression remains the same throughout life, and some facial muscles have no physical function other than expressing Affect. Being conscious and paying close attention to the face reveals clues needed to determine specific feelings, emotions, and moods. I have included vocal expressions that Nathanson and Tomkins link to the biological Affects.[92]

1. **Contentment-Enjoyment**—A smile, with the lips slightly opened and widened, smiling eyes (circular wrinkles), and a calm spirit. *Vocal expression:* Whew!

2. **Interest-Excitement**—Eyebrows lower, eyes track, look, listen, flushing, fast breath, the face pays full attention. In a child, the entire body seems to be tracking something. *Vocal expressions:* Yaayyy! Yippee!

3. **Surprise-Startle**—Eyes blink, eyes open wide, eyebrows raise, sudden burst of laughter, sudden intake of breath, mouth opened. *Vocal expressions:* Scream, OH! Yikes! Wow!

4. **Fear-Terror**—Individual hairs stand on end, frozen stare, the face becomes cold, pale, sweaty, shiver, facial trembling, pulse, and respiration will speed up, suspended breath, nearer the upper range of terror there may be a gripping sensation in the chest. *Vocal expressions:* Scream, shriek.

5. **Anger-Rage**—Frown, clenched jaw, red face. *Vocal expressions:* Growl, Roar, Arrgh!

6. **Distress-Anguish**—Tears, rhythmic sobbing, arched eyebrows, mouth down. *Vocal expressions:* Cry, Whine, Weep, Whimper, Gulp.

7. **Dissmell**—Upper lip raised, head pulled back, looking down our nose. *Vocal expressions:* Uggh! Ewwww! Yucchh! Shoo!

8. **Disgust**—Bottom lip lowered and protruded, upper lip up, sneer, head forward and down. *Vocal expressions:* Yucky, Icky, Puke.

9. **Shame-Humiliation**—Eyes down, head down and averted, blush, confusion, briefly incapable of speech. *Vocal expression:* Wince.

Once you understand the physical manifestations of Affect, it is fascinating to see the great writers utilize them effectively as literary symbols. Affect provides powerful communication tools and is a significant reason the classic works endure. They speak a universal language that is somehow unique to each one of us. Consider these passages.

"She tucked her head in shame." Delia Owens in *Where The Crawdads Sing.*

"Franz threw up his chin, his eyebrows, the transient wrinkles of his forehead…." F. Scott Fitzgerald in *Tender Is The Night.*

"He twisted his mouth into an expression of disgust that was as unlike him as the shoulder-shrug." Thomas Mann in *The Magic Mountain.*

"Her still face, with the mouth closed tight from suffering and disillusion and self-denial, and her nose the smallest bit on one side, and her blue eyes so young, quick, and warm, made his heart contract with love." D.H. Lawrence in *Sons and Lovers.*

"But still smiling, for she was so humble and so sweet that her gentleness towards others, and her continual subordination of herself and of her own troubles, appeared on her face blended in a smile which, unlike those seen on the majority of human faces, had no trace in it of irony, save for herself, while for all of us kisses seemed to spring from her eyes, which could not look upon those she loved without yearning to bestow upon them passionate caresses." Marcel Proust in *Swann's Way.*

Affect In Everyday Life

As I wrote this chapter, three affective events of *interest* captured my attention. First, please know that I have determined in my second-life *Quest* to share the gift of a smile with everyone I encounter during my exercise times.

Recently, I saw a baby carriage about four miles into my usual run on the Pinellas Trail. It is usually a senior adult strolling with their puppy. But that day, the frantic screaming of a baby pierced the air. Drawing closer, it was apparent the baby was past the *anger* stage and into a heightened *rage*. Shrieks were interrupted only by gags brought on by the intensity of the furor.

The mother was casually strolling as if nothing was happening. Then, as I drew to about twenty yards, she gently lifted the baby out of the carriage. The baby had contorted its face into a scowl, jaw clenched, swollen red face, tears streaming, and gasping for air between wails. She placed the child—a little boy with long black curly hair who looked about two years old—on the trail and let him walk beside her.

The Affect was striking and immediate. The cries instantly stopped as the escape from the stroller triggered a relaxed smile of *contentment*. The relief transformed the child's features as if by a miracle. As I passed, they walked together peacefully, hand in hand. The only clue of the emotional storm raging a few seconds before was a pink flush quickly receding from the face.

The fact struck me that the child's *rage* had not triggered *anger* Affect in the mother throughout the entire adventure. On the contrary, it seemed to trigger her parental instinct to impede or minimize the event causing her child discomfort. I smiled at the mother and gave her a thumbs up. She returned the smile, shook her head, and said, "It's been an *exciting* morning." I replied as I resumed my running, "Yes, I've been there twice." She gave me an empathic look.

Affect theory helps us understand why some parents react with *anxiety, disgust, shame,* or *rage* during an event like this—while others respond calmly and methodically like this mom. Both types of reactions are scripts. The former examples recall childhood traumas, conflicts, and frustrations, and the latter from the healthy way *anger* Affect was handled in her past.

As I approached our whimsical Main Street about a mile later, a short, full-bodied Hispanic lady jogged near me at the crossing lane with her head down. She sensed my presence as I passed and tentatively glanced up. I smiled at her, and after a millisecond pause, she shyly returned it. I glimpsed a smile on her face and in her eyes.

The affective exchange lasted only a few seconds. After that, I couldn't help thinking of the many Hispanic people who pass me on the trail, many on bicycles heading to work, head down, shoulders slumped, unseeing.

I wonder how often they encounter faces of *disgust* Affect instead of a warm smile because of their ethnicity and skin color. Looks of *disgust* are affective responses from *angry, fearful, anxious,* or *shame-*filled people.

The third encounter was a mile later at another crossing. I approached a homeless man organizing his rusty grocery cart of belongings. He was slumping his shoulders, head down and averted, and his feet pointed away from the trail. Body odor was distinct as I grew closer, and I gladly gave him the courtesy of a six-foot distance. This was during the 2020 Covid pandemic. I tried to catch his eye, but he would not (or could not) raise his face.

As my pace separated us, he cursed loudly but not at me. Instead, he was swearing at something needed for his cart. It seemed my attempt to engage triggered his *anger, fear, anxiety, or shame*—it was obvious he wanted me to stay away from him. He probably has discovered the best deterrent to proximity with other people: avoiding eye contact, talking loudly to himself, smelling bad, and loudly peppering his language with curse words.

The various emotional Affects one can encounter over a short six-mile run enthrall me. These examples illustrate that a life without Affect would be sterile, boring, and meaningless. It is incredible how a simple action (a smile) can trigger varied emotional responses. Paying attention to Affect and how it is triggered and expressed provides *enjoyment* that I am only now beginning to understand.

Affect matters. Tomkin's idea that the positive and negative Affects are the basis of human motivation has enormous implications for *The Quest*. During childhood, our behavior is drilled into us by the institutions of life (religion, family, culture, and education) with precise rules for displaying and controlling the nine innate Affects.

We must ask ourselves questions. What are my triggers? Why do I react the way I do? We must pay attention to our everyday lives, retrieve these answers from the unconscious, and move them to consciousness. We must learn to read our physical responses and those of others.

What are our levels of awareness? What are the scripts we fall back on? When the Affect *shame-humiliation* is triggered, do we withdraw, avoid, attack ourselves, or attack others? Our roles (our personas) are shaped and limited by *shame*, which impedes *interest-excitement* and *contentment-enjoyment* Affects.

Suppose we could make our life into a movie with actors to represent our unique response to the Affects. In that case, I wonder how the storyline and characters would play out. As adults, there are expectations and requirements to play various roles. All of the parts we assume, the characters, and the personalities we exhibit to others converge and are known as our conscious.

Conscious

Are You Awake and Aware?

It is a miracle that we are conscious at all—that we are aware. And somehow, aware that we are aware. Consciousness is an elusive thing. Vladimir Nabokov described it as "that sudden window swinging open on a sunlit landscape amidst the night of non-being."

We can grow our consciousness; one might call it strengthening our mind. When we increase our capacity for being aware, our enjoyment is enhanced. Research reveals that we would correctly describe it as integrating the brain. Assimilating the conscious and the unconscious is the crux of *The Quest*. This synthesis entails cultivating the brain's ability to regulate Affect, focus attention, open awareness, and practice kind intentions.

This growth is a way to the holy grail, to the treasures within us. If we are not enlarging our consciousness, it is contracting. With a thousand pardons to the band *U2*, there is no such thing as being stuck in a moment. We can never stay the same.

Most of us directly experienced an enlarged consciousness— as a child. We need to remember what we've forgotten and perhaps, repair and re-form much of what we've learned. This work is hard. Our adult self fills up with memories and traits, and we speak to ourselves with a lot of deeply embedded language.

Perhaps that is what the teacher Jesus Christ was alluding to when he said, "unless you return to square one and start over like children."[93] *The Quest* is a call to experience each present moment with wide-eyed wonder.

Psychologist Alison Gopnik says, "being inexperienced in the way of the world, the mind of the young child has few preconceptions, to guide their perceptions down predictable tracks. Instead, the child approaches reality with the astonishment of an adult on psychedelics."[94]

In their search to make sense of things, she believes that a young child's mind explores not only the usual mundane paths but "the entire space of possibilities." We will focus on psychedelics as a communication vehicle between the conscious and the unconscious in the next waypoint.

We have talked about how life institutions have methodically chipped away at our actual being. Gopnik continues, "consciousness narrows as we get older." The people who ridicule child-like magic are the ones who are heart-sad about what they've allowed to wither within. However, there is no question that children are willing to embrace new pathways and ideas.

She says, "if you want to understand what an enlarged consciousness looks like, all you have to do is have tea with a four-year-old." Or swallow a few grams of magic mushrooms. The summary is that children are basically tripping all the time.

It suddenly makes sense why the world-renowned Carl Jung would interrupt his psychotherapy sessions to play with stones in the field by his office. So, maybe we do need to return to square one and become like children again. Not to be childish, but to become child-*like*.

Is it possible to shake ourselves out of our usual pathways of thought in ways that might enlarge our well-being? To make us more open and help us pay attention to the "sunlit landscapes" of life? As children, we were far more conscious (aware) than today. Children have no problem being who they are and enjoying life.

This waypoint intends to help those approaching the second half of life remember what we've forgotten. As we continue our *Quest*, we realize that our mind (our consciousness) can be much more significant and the world much more alive than we ever dreamed. A taste of consciousness can be as addictive as alcohol, drugs, or sex.

Let's explore four (a quaternity) aspects of consciousness.

1) Open Awareness

The four (quaternity) aspects of open awareness are self, others, ideas, and the world. First, let's talk about openness. One of the traits psychologists use to assess personality is an openness to experience. Unfortunately, pronounced and lasting changes in nature are rare in adults. We are "set in our ways."

Still, studies show that cultivating openness increases aesthetic appreciation and sensitivity, fantasy and imagination, and tolerance of others' viewpoints and values. It also predicts creativity in both the arts and sciences.[95]

Open Awareness of Self

At the height of the devastation of my mid-life transition, a friend urged me to be kind to myself. He told me he was afraid that I was not treating myself with the compassion and kindness I afforded others. He felt I was too hard on myself.

I had never heard that phrase, "be kind to yourself." My religious upbringing taught me the opposite. To be holy, they commanded that I *deny* myself. To me, this kind of openness and self-awareness was counter-intuitive. But he was right. How do we expect others to extend kindness if we are not kind to ourselves?

Cultivating open awareness of ourselves is foundational to expanding consciousness. Self-awareness signifies we are finally growing up. Let's summarize what we have learned about our self so far in *The Quest*. Being openly aware of oneself, of who we are, means:

1. Finding the symbols that best represent our essence.
2. Knowing our essentials, learning all we can about them, and applying them to everyday life.
3. Understanding the stage of life and transition we are in currently. Empathizing and being kind to ourselves if we are in crisis mode.
4. Actively seeking out mentors, friends, and allies to walk alongside us during our universal journeys.
5. Knowing our healthy and unhealthy Affects. An open awareness of self means understanding how unhealthy Affect contracts us and healthy Affect enlarges us. It means knowing our triggers.

Open Awareness of Others

Our mentors, friends, and allies are a priceless aspect of our journey. Here are several ways to show an open awareness of others.

First, practice empathy. Enhance the ability to recognize, understand, and share the thoughts and feelings of others. Developing empathy is crucial for establishing relationships and behaving compassionately. It involves experiencing another person's point of view in addition to one's own.

Empathy enables us to establish rapport with another person and help them understand that we hear and see them. In addition, we can understand and reflect (or mirror) their emotions through words, facial expressions, and body language by knowing the physical manifestations of the nine Affects.

Second, practice the lost art of listening. The essence of good listening is empathy. So instead of listening to state your agenda better, listen to understand and feel the needs of others.

Everyone wants to be heard. We all have a yearning to be understood. But in this frantic world of radical discontinuity, people who practice the open awareness of listening are rare. Few things hurt more than when we sense that people close to us aren't listening to what we say.

The gift of open awareness makes others feel validated and valued. And effective listening is one of the best ways to enjoy others and learn from them. In short, it helps us to grow our consciousness.

Third, practice becoming a good conversationalist. The speed of life has eroded the leisure time required for a proper conversation. Yet, we define and sustain ourselves in conversation with others. Our character, history, ideas, and approach to life emerge through dialogue.

There is a vast difference between honest dialogue and taking turns talking. Authentic conversation involves appreciating the other's perspective and, at times, asking questions to clarify what remains unsaid. It is the mark of a generous spirit.

The context of a good conversation is the setting. The time, place, participants, and expectations add to the experience. My wife Gina often says that some of our best and most meaningful conversations have been during coffee and cocktail hours.

At our home, those two "hours" each day are sacred. They have become a cathartic part of the ritual of our lives. We establish the setting (the back porch or gathering room) and during the day, we file away tidbits of information for dialogue. Often, these times are the most enjoyable parts of the day for us both.

Fourth, practice sensitivity. People who cultivate sensitivity often pick up on things other people miss. Journalist Andrea Bartz writes in *Psychology Today*, "For people who are sensitive, emotional experience is at such a constant intensity that it shapes their personality and lives."[96] This awareness is particularly true of one's social life and intimate relationships.

Sensitivity triggers the positive Affect *interest*, which inevitably activates a script of caring deeply about the experiences of others. This open awareness allows us to see others in a new light. And as the practice grows, it gives us sympathy for the helpless and the hurting.

Open Awareness of Ideas

An open awareness of ideas enhances our *perceptual view*—our perception of the world around us. For example, travel (experiencing different cultures and places) enhances our perceptual view. Following are a few ways to be conscious of (to be aware of) new ideas. They are drawn from a fascinating book by Scott Kaufman and Carolyn Gregoire, called *Wired To Create*.

First, practice imaginative play. We talk about our playstyles as a child in the Stages waypoint. Remembering our favorite childhood play experiences can bring more enjoyment to our adult activities. For example, my habit of doodling grew into painting watercolors. The little books I read became big books.

It doesn't necessarily need to be toys, but it does need to be something that supports having fun. In second life, we often utilize a different set of materials. Personal memories, fantasy, and emotions can all be objects of play. Activities that encourage imaginative play as adults help us approach life with childlike open-eyed wonder. And this approach intuitively embraces new ideas.

We tend to lose the wonder of play and fun as we grow older. And our lives become dominated by more serious business such as work and religion. George Bernard Shaw wrote: "We don't stop playing because we grow old; we grow old because we stop playing." The evidence supports it. Allocating time for curiosity and play enhances enjoyment in life.

Second, practice an openness to experience. We need new and unusual encounters to enjoy life better. I have challenged myself to do one new thing every day. For example, the day I wrote this, I had enchiladas for breakfast for the first time in my life.

A desire and motivation to engage with new people, places, and activities enhance our ability to savor the second half of life. In his memoir *A Movable Feast*, Hemingway beautifully describes the process of savoring life.

Look for ways to get yourself out of the rut of first life. Perhaps try a new creative outlet. A minor rearranging of "normality" can provide an unexpected jolt of insight into new ideas.

Third, practice solitude. It sounds counter-intuitive that isolation cultivates open awareness of ideas. But when we are alone, there is no place to hide from our thoughts. Being alone gives us the space to observe the whole spectrum of our emotions—our healthy and unhealthy Affects. And we can turn these thoughts, feelings, scripts, and moods into ideas.

In the words of writer Marcel Proust, "solitude is a way to redeem our sense of time lost." This mantra became the subject of his masterpiece *Remembrance of Things Past*. Intimacy with oneself can yield insight into new ideas. Solitude provides time to savor and enjoy parts of ourselves we do not usually take the time to examine.

We take pride when introducing people whom we know will mutually benefit from a new relationship. Similarly, one benefits when allocating alone time to meet unfamiliar aspects of oneself. We become more integrated, and we feel a growing sense of wholeness. It is invaluable to quiet down enough to hear our ideas, the good and the not as good ones.

Fourth, to cultivate our awareness of ideas, *practice turning adversity into advantage.* Francis Bacon once said, "An artist must be nourished by his passions and by his despairs." Inevitably, by the time mid-life comes around, the ups and downs of life will have led most of us to several deep caves of despair. (See Transitions waypoint).

Ideas born of adversity are an almost universal theme throughout history. Many symbols we find in music, theater, paintings, and literature ascribe meaning to suffering. Research has found that up to seventy percent of trauma survivors report psychological growth.[97]

The crises that occur at mid-life deeply challenge our beliefs of first life. Transition into the second half of life often shatters our world views, ideals, morals, and identities. It can be like an earthquake. The more seismic the transition, the more we must let go of our former selves and assumptions and begin to rebuild our sense of self from the ground up.

And when a transition causes us to conceive new possibilities and ideas in our life, we will grow. It is inevitable. This growth illustrates the principle of *enantiodromia* (the play of opposites in the course of events) that we discover in the Transitions waypoint.

What we might think of as bad may turn out for our benefit. Jung advises, "… be cautious and patient waiting to see how things will finally turn out." Practicing open awareness means treating all of life's moments—the good and the bad—as potential sources for new ideas and growth. In short, when you go through shit, you can learn things.

Open Awareness of Our World

My wife Gina and I often walk at a neighborhood park with our dog Remy. One morning, a mom and her daughter strolled by. We heard the child ask if it was okay to pet the dog. Her Mom agreed on the condition that she ask permission. She did, and we assented. Our little morkie Remy is tactile, brimming with Affect, and loves attention. The little girl looked up at us as she stroked her head and said, "I have puppies and kittens in my brain all the time."

As we resumed our walk, on a whim, I turned back and asked the mom the age of the little girl. She was four. I commented about the wide-eyed wonder of a child. And that I was writing a book containing the analogy that having tea with a four-year-old gives one an idea of how it would be to take psychedelics. Young children are basically tripping all the time.

She laughed and nodded vigorously in agreement. I said, "I'm not telling you anything you don't already know. You are living with a human being that is openly aware of the world around her. Enjoy."

Most of us worked inside a sterile, temperature-controlled office in our first life. Only in rare moments did we get to interact with nature. Second life, if we have planned well, allows us to get out into the world and savor it.

During his time at Walden Pond, Henry David Thoreau explained his reasons for leaving civilization in his journal. He wrote, "I went to the woods because I wished to live deliberately, to front only the essentials of life, and see if I could not learn what it had to teach, and not, when I came to die, discover that I had not lived."[98]

A crucial aspect of *The Quest* is living with an open awareness of the world, deliberately reducing life to its essence to learn what it has to teach. That is why we identify our essentials in the Essentials waypoint. For me, that means encountering the world with sensuality, curiosity, communion, and freedom. What about you?

In the second half of life, if we are lucky, we get to leave the time clocks, the pages of our calendars, and the sterile cubicles behind. Thoreau wrote, "I wanted to live deep and suck all the marrow out of life."

We don't necessarily need to go out into the woods like Thoreau. But, we can go into the world. Over the past twenty years, the words of Ken Gire have inspired me to cultivate an open awareness of this extraordinary planet we inhabit. He created a journal called *Reflections on Your Life* that has been my constant companion. It is battered, dog-eared, and filled with unique reflections—in short, it is priceless to me.

In it, he says we need to embark on an experience similar to Thoreau's. And we can do this even if we are still in the throes of the ordinary world. When an alarm starts the day, we have to keep track of time, and at the end of the day, we have to set the alarm and do it all over again tomorrow. It is a world where we not only have to make a living but somehow make a life.[99]

How? We do it in our world the same way Thoreau did it at Walden. Deliberately.

We have to make deliberate decisions to slow down on the roads we're traveling, stop at the intersections, and look and listen. Then, if we are lucky, we can take a side road somewhere off the beaten path and spend some time enlarging our essentials.

What we encounter may whisper as subtly as the aroma of a flower blossom, or it may startle as suddenly as the glimpse of a lightning bolt. But unless we are there breathing, open, aware, we won't smell. And unless we are there looking, we won't see.

Seeing the world is a process that replaces our lack of consciousness with an open awareness. When we engage with beauty, it fills the abyss of our emptiness, and we begin to see treasures previously hidden or forgotten.

We grow more significant and more conscious, practicing a life of open awareness of ourselves, others, ideas, and the world. And in doing, we begin to discover the holy grail of *The Quest*. We find ourselves becoming increasingly whole and wonder of wonders, thoroughly enjoying the second half of life.

Consider the words of Mary Oliver.[100]

INSTRUCTIONS FOR LIVING A LIFE.

PAY ATTENTION.

BE ASTONISHED.

TELL ABOUT IT.

2) Focused Attention

The second aspect of consciousness is *focused attention*. There is a reason our parents and teachers would ask us to "pay attention." It costs something to focus our attention. The cost becomes clear as we look at the quaternity for this second aspect. Each one seems like a simple task, yet we rarely are willing to pay the price to practice them.

Meditation

The first aspect of focused attention is meditation. More people are growing irritated, outraged, and frightened by the world outside: the climate crisis, uprisings of racism and hate, global pandemics, and rampant misinformation. Therefore, we need a daily refuge from the noise. In finding this calm center, we can recover and rejuvenate.[101]

Meditation is trendy to talk about but difficult to do. Most of us know we need to meditate, some of us may be aware of the benefits, but still, we never seem to get to it. I have dedicated this portion of the Conscious waypoint to dispelling obstacles that keep us from this life-changing practice. The roadblocks include religious taboos, time constraints, not knowing practical steps, or which meditation style best suits our personality.

Christianity (particularly evangelicalism) has always had a problem with meditation. They teach it is from the pagan practices of the Far East. They brand it "New Age" and thus unacceptable. Religion trained me as a child that a daily prayer life was better than the questionable practice of self-examination. They taught that to deny oneself was holy and to examine oneself could lead to doubts and questions, which was a slippery slope best avoided.

Even today, Christian authors are wary of using the "M" word. Instead, they refer to the "reflective life" or "contemplative living." Somehow meditation smacks of Hinduism, Buddhism, or Zen. To utter the word seems like sacrilege.

But in actuality, meditation need not be religious at all. For example, neuroscientist, philosopher, and popular podcaster Sam Harris (an atheist) is a devout practitioner and advocate of a version of meditation called mindfulness. He considers it so necessary that recently, he wrote the book, *Waking Up*, and launched a podcast, training series, and website.

These tools aim to serve (in his words) as guides to understanding the mind and living a more balanced and fulfilling life. Utilizing these resources, Harris explores the practice of meditation and examines the theory behind it.

We have not only religious taboos but time constraints as well. The tyranny of the urgent often supersedes our desire for the ultimate. Our watches and calendars are demanding masters. There is little time, and practices like meditation are relegated to day's end, if at all.

The *only* notification allowed on my phone is a regular reminder to meditate. And my universal need for rhythm and ritual has proven the practice invaluable. Yet, it takes every ounce of self-discipline to meditate regularly.

This reluctance makes no sense considering the ultimate benefits received. As a tactile and highly sensitive person, I love therapeutic massage. And meditation is like a massage not only for the body—but for the mind, soul, and spirit. When finishing my allotted time, it is hard to describe the feelings of serenity, contentment, and wholeness that permeate my being.

For many of us, meditation is a fuzzy word that connotes uncomfortable yoga poses, humming, and some sort of mind control. But in reality, meditation can be efficient and customized to your preferences. The most crucial requirement is not *how* you do meditation; it is *doing* it.

1. Designate a time and place. At approximately 3 pm each Tuesday and Thursday, I go to the privacy of my art studio. I sit in my favorite chair with good posture and bare feet flat on the floor, eyes closed, with the lights dimmed. If I prepare well, there is incense burning. At this writing, my session lasts twenty minutes. I began with ten minutes and am now gradually increasing my time.

2. Create a playlist of rain showers, nature sounds, and brown noise. Some people prefer no music, but for me, it helps drown out distracting external sounds.

3. Through trial and error, discover the meditation style that works best for you—more on that in a moment.

4. Choose a mantra. A mantra is a sound, word, or phrase repeated by someone who meditates.[102] For me, the personal mantra, the "Serenity Prayer," that a popular

meditation writer suggested brought up past religious trauma. Therefore, I developed one based on my essentials and personal intentions. (See Resources p. 350. Feel free to adapt and use as needed.)

5. Set the timer on the phone to not worry about duration. Next, let everyone know that you are meditating, and activate the "do not disturb" setting on the phone.

6. Suppose you become distracted, or your mind wanders. In that case, a characteristic of Transcendental Meditation is not to criticize oneself but gently return to the beginning of the mantra and begin again. Thus, each time distraction comes, gently start over, being kind to yourself.

7. Instead of immediately getting up when the timer alarm sounds, sit still and purposefully take a few minutes to savor the blissful feelings and breathe deeply.

It is that simple. Meditation boosts our enjoyment of the external world and helps us tap into and nourish our inner worlds. When the body is tired, mind cluttered, soul hungry, and spirit depleted, a minor event triggers one's unhealthy emotions. Meditation then serves like a replenishing massage for the entire self.

Styles of Meditation

There are at least seven kinds of meditation practiced throughout the world. Be sure to explore them all to find the style best suited for you. We will explore four techniques.

First, let's look at transcendental meditation. Transcendental meditation doesn't focus on breathing or chanting, like other forms of meditation. Instead, it encourages a restful state of mind beyond thinking. A 2009 study by the highly-respected

175

Cleveland Clinic found that transcendental meditation helped alleviate stress in college students. While another found it helped reduce blood pressure, anxiety, depression, and anger.[103]

The website *TM.org* describes it as a technique for inner peace and wellness. Anyone can do it—even if you "can't meditate." Maybe that's why I enjoy it. And it's evidence-based with hundreds of published research studies. Over five million followers practice it every day.

If you've tried to meditate in the past but couldn't stick to it long enough to experience its benefits, perhaps this simple method will help. All one needs to do is keep the eyes closed and silently recite a mantra. The beauty of this style is that it doesn't have to be in a solitary place. It can be on the train ride home or sitting at your desk.

For those with creative and artistic minds, this style of meditation may seem more conducive to a peaceful state. Yet, ideally, the goal in transcendental meditation is not to free the mind of thoughts but to deal flexibly and kindly with them as they inevitably arise.

Second, walking meditation. I first encountered this style of meditation in the delightful book *Man Seeks God: My Flirtations With the Divine* by Eric Weiner. In his travels, Weiner learns that this style of meditation is part Buddhist and part Jewish.

The task is simple. Find a peaceful and private pathway, perhaps in the woods or on the beach, wherever you prefer. Then slowly stroll. Simply be aware. Pay attention. Then take one breath for each step. One breath, one step. Let go.

It is about taking an everyday activity—walking—raising it, elevating it from the physical realm to the spiritual. It is about transcending earth for a few moments. I love this style of meditation.

The sights and sounds of the landscape come alive. Weiner makes the excellent point that we miss many sounds not because we fail to listen but because we're too busy talking to ourselves.

Breath, step. Breath, step. Weiner says a Sufi master Pir Zia once told him that he imagines himself "making love to the earth" whenever he walks. Once you do a meditation walk, chances are, you will understand what he means.[104]

Third, **mindfulness meditation**. Sam Harris has much to say about this method. He writes that the purpose of meditation isn't merely to reduce stress or to make you feel better in the moment—it's to make fundamental discoveries in the laboratory of your mind.[105]

Harris says much of our thinking about ourselves and the world is either pointless or actively harmful. *Anxiety, envy, self-hatred*, or other negative emotions produce these thoughts. In turn, it perpetuates those states of mind. Mindfulness allows one to experience life in the present without ruminating about what should have happened, what almost happened, or what might yet happen. The connection to happiness is straightforward. At the bottom, mindfulness is the ability to pay attention to what matters.

When asked why making meditation part of our routine seems challenging, he replies that it's not the hardest step. Instead, it's simply the first. The next step is to turn these periods of meditation into significant experiences of non-distraction—then you can notice what consciousness is like previous to thought.

When you genuinely know how to meditate, you discover that it isn't a practice at all. The freedom you feel isn't the result of something you are doing; it's the result of something you have stopped doing. "Practice" is nothing more than enjoying what the mind is like when it is no longer distracted.

The website *mindful.org* provides a practical guide to mindfulness meditation.[106] It says:

1. Settle into your private place.

2. Feel your breath—or some say "follow it"—as it goes out and as it goes in. Next, pay attention to the physical sensation of breathing: the air moving through your nose or mouth, the rising and falling of your belly or your chest. Choose your focal point, and with each breath, you can mentally note "breathing in" and "breathing out."

3. Inevitably, your attention will leave the breath and wander to other places. Don't worry. There's no need to block or eliminate thinking. Instead, when you notice your mind wandering—in a few seconds, a minute, five minutes—gently return your attention to the breath.

4. Practice pausing before making any physical adjustments, such as moving your body or scratching an itch. With intention, shift at a moment you choose, allowing space between what you experience and what you decide to do.

5. You may find your mind constantly wandering—that's normal, too. Practice observing without reacting instead of wrestling with or engaging with those thoughts. Simply sit and pay attention. As hard as it is to maintain, that's all there is. Come back over and over again without judgment or expectation.

6. When you're ready, gently lift your gaze (if your eyes are closed, open them). Take a moment and notice any sounds in the environment. Notice how your body feels right now. Notice your thoughts and emotions. Then, pausing for a moment, decide how you'd like to continue with your day.

That's it. That's the style. Practitioners often say it's effortless, but it's not necessarily easy. The work is to keep doing it. Results will accrue.

Fourth, a look at **metta meditation** sometimes called loving-kindness meditation. The website *healthline.com*[107] tells us this style of meditation is used to strengthen feelings of compassion, kindness, and acceptance toward oneself and others. It typically involves opening the mind to receive love from others and then sending a series of well-wishes to loved ones, friends, acquaintances, and all living beings.

This type of meditation promotes compassion and kindness. It may be ideal for those holding feelings of *anger* or resentment.

You don't need any special equipment or gear to start metta meditation. Another bonus is that you can do it anywhere you like—in a quiet corner of your home, outdoors in a yard, or even at your desk. Try to choose a spot where you're least likely to be distracted, then follow these steps:

1. Sit in a comfortable position. Close your eyes. Take a slow, deep breath through your nose and continue breathing deeply.

2. Focus on your breathing. Imagine your breath traveling through your body. Then focus on your heart.

3. Choose a kind, positive phrase. Silently recite the words, directing them toward yourself. You can say, "May I be happy. May I be safe. May I find peace."

4. Slowly repeat the phrase. Acknowledge its meaning and how it makes you feel. If you get distracted, avoid judging yourself. Simply return to the words and keep repeating them.

5. Now, think about your friends and family. You can think about a specific person or a group of people. Recite the phrase toward them, "May you be happy. May you be safe. May you find peace." Again, recognize the meaning and how you feel.

6. Continue reciting the phrase toward others, including neighbors, acquaintances, and challenging individuals. Recognize your emotions, even if they're negative. Repeat the words until you experience compassionate feelings.

Some people use visual imagery while reciting each phrase. For example, you can imagine light emitting from your heart or the person you're thinking of. You can also change the words throughout the practice.

****

The crucial thing is finding a style of meditation that feels comfortable, which will encourage you to begin and continue this ancient and time-honored tradition of focused attention. Consider Taoist wisdom from the 6th century BC. It teaches that it is wise to busy oneself with doing nothing.

WHOEVER PRACTICES NON-ACTION
OCCUPIES THEMSELVES WITH NOT BEING OCCUPIED.
—LAO TZU

The Quest's goal is being not doing, and not only *being*, but *becoming*, and not *becoming perfect* but *becoming whole*. Wholeness is what the contemplative life helps give us.

Thinking

The second aspect of focused attention is thinking. It is precisely to prevent us from *overthinking* that life institutions create rules, dogma, busywork, and amusement. Terrance McKenna, a radical philosopher and drugs researcher, when asked why culture doesn't allow us to be idlers, said this: "Institutions fear idle populations because an Idler is a thinker, and thinkers are not a welcome addition to most social situations. Thinkers become malcontents. Essentially, we're all kept swamped; under no circumstances are you to inspect the contents of your mind quietly."[108]

Thinking could lead to that terrible thing; a vision of the truth, a clear image of the horror of our fractured, dissonant world. But, because thinkers refuse to be held hostage by the customs and expectations of others, their minds are curious, their spirits are free, and their eyes are open.

As a patron of the Nashville Public Library, I had the opportunity to hear one of my favorite authors, David McCullough (*Truman, 1776, John Adams)*, speak about writing. He is the two-time recipient of the Pulitzer Prize and the National Book Award.

During his talk, he made these observations, "Writing is thinking. To write well is to think clearly. That's why it's hard. People always ask me, 'how much time do you spend researching, and how much time do you spend writing?' That's a good question," he said. "But what they don't ask me is 'how much time do you spend thinking?'"

McCullough said he spends days thinking before writing a word in his studio. He does not put much stock in speed. "If anything, I would prefer to go slower," he said. "The part of writing that takes the most time is not typing, but thinking." And he does some of his best thinking on early morning walks.

We have been taught that humanity was created to work, not to think, feel, or dream—that every idle moment is treason. It is our patriotic and religious duty to work hard. To *do* not to *be*. I've often said, "Americans suck at thinking."

Busyness is yet another weapon in the armory of the capitalist and the evangelist. It is vital to keep the working classes ignorant of how wickedly the institutions exploit them. The government and the church teach us to work much and use our minds little. They demand that we think exactly like them should we have a spare minute to think.

But to paraphrase the 1997 media campaign of Apple Computer™, "Here's to the crazy ones. The misfits. The rebels. The troublemakers. The round pegs in the square holes. The ones who *think* differently."

To think differently, one must take time to think. Thinking is an essential aspect of focused attention. It expands the mind. In other words, it is a vehicle of growth, of *becoming*. When was the last time you allocated a whole day for thinking? In today's frenetic world, the question smacks of sanctimony.

I have the enviable gift of an early "retirement." Somehow the entrepreneurial planets aligned and endowed me with the freedom to do anything I desired at age forty-seven. But the indoctrination of work and busyness permeated my being. As a result, it has only been the last few years (around age sixty) that I have honestly allocated time to think. Yet, I still find myself fighting feelings of guilt if I do not produce a tangible artifact of my labors. But the sheer enjoyment I experience at the end of a "thinking" day helps me know that *guilt* (at least in this case) is an unhealthy emotion.

All of us can think; therefore, it is a universal phenomenon. Yet, again, we encounter the same but different principle. The transitions of life are universal, but the people, places, events, and memories from our stages of life make our thoughts unique.

Thinking covers all the nuances of human accomplishment and can create something new or reimagine something old. Thinking focuses our attention, enlarges us, and has the power to move us toward wholeness.

Active Imagination

The third aspect of focused attention is *active imagination.* Carl Jung developed this meditation technique. It utilizes dreams, fantasy, and focused attention to strengthen the mind. It helps the conscious confront the unconscious.

The conscious part of our minds is what makes us feel *awake, aware, and attentive* of what we are doing right at this moment, which in your case is reading these words. The conscious self is composed of our ego and persona.

The subconscious part of our minds is much more vast, dealing with background processes and sensations, like keeping our heart beating. And the unconscious stores the people, places, events, and memories of our lives. These things are unconscious because they distract the ego from concentrating on the present moment.

Active imagination works by encouraging the conscious and unconscious mind to *communicate* through using focused attention to explore the unconscious mind. Author Charles

Foster writes, "one may call this 'wakeful dreaming,' and it is an important spiritual discipline in many religions. It's a powerful lens for the examination of your own consciousness."[109]

A Way to Practice Active Imagination. The method Jung taught is relatively straightforward. Choose a recent dream or fantasy to examine, grab a writing instrument, find a quiet place to sit down, meditate, and follow the steps.

Everyone is different, but an ideal time for Active Imagination is during the *hypnopompic* state. This state is the transition from sleep to wakefulness. For Jung, it often happened at his desk. As you begin this practice, your best setting will become evident—it may be simply relaxing in bed.

Step One—Focus Your Attention

When starting any style of meditation, the mind is usually active and unfocused; first, calm the mind and focus attention. Then, as the mind gains clarity, become aware of thoughts and surroundings. But unlike other styles of meditation in which we seek to remove all thoughts and clear the mind, in Active Imagination, we engage our thoughts.

Step Two — Focus on the Dream or Fantasy

When the mind has focused and is present, move attention to an image from the chosen dream or fantasy.

It is essential to focus attention on the image as long as it takes. Be patient. The mind may wander but gently move attention back to the visual if that happens.

Step Three — Allow the Unconscious to Speak

When focusing on the dream or fantasy image, we are peering into the unconscious mind. To understand what the unconscious wants to communicate, we need to allow it to speak through the symbol's image.

Loosen the focus so the unconscious can activate the image. But not too much, or we may become passive and begin to wander or return to sleep.

Then comes a crucial aspect. As we allow our unconscious to speak, we can enter into the dream or fantasy. And attempt to talk to one of the characters or talk to one's self-image.

This action may seem weird or dark, especially if it is highly emotional or a nightmare, but it will be okay. It's simply something we may have avoided or refused to accept. Now is an excellent time to face our emotions and view them as treasures.

Jung's words remind us that there is no coming to consciousness without pain. People will do anything, no matter how absurd, to avoid facing their souls. However, one becomes enlightened by making the darkness conscious.

Whatever form this image or symbol takes—actively engage with it. As with sleeping dreams, for masculines, feminine images may represent a guide or mentor, and masculine images represent one's shadow. Conversely, for feminines, masculine images may represent a guide or mentor, and feminine images represent one's shadow.

It could be a feeling or an emotion. Whatever it is, speak to it. Ask the image something like, "Now what are you up to? What do you see? I should like to know." Remember to imprint the image or symbol into your memory because you will *make it art next.*

Step Four—Create an Artifact

Now channel the inner artist by finding a writing instrument, pencil, paintbrush, clay—whatever works best for you. Write, draw, paint, or sculpt whatever you experienced in your Active Imagination.

The goal is not to create a masterpiece but merely to make that unconscious image into an artifact which we then attempt to decipher in the next step. Jung would first record it in his journal and later, when time allowed, create the artifact.

Step Five—Become an Analyst

Now take a break. It's time to take the mind out of the imagination and back into ordinary consciousness. Then, at the next opportunity, return to the artifact, and see if you can find the layers within the symbolic artwork you created.

Allow these unconscious elements to move along the pathways of the active imagination and integrate into the conscious. As Jung himself said: "Until you make the unconscious conscious, it will direct your life, and you will call it fate."[110]

Presence

The fourth aspect of focused attention is presence. Presence is a heightened awareness of our momentary bodily sensations, feelings, and thoughts. It can expand outward for others and empathize with their feelings and thoughts. It can reach out even further to connect us to all living things.[111]

As your physical self moves throughout your day, does your mental and emotional self keep up? Being present means all of your being is focused and engaged in the here and now and not distracted or mentally and emotionally absent. I call people who are consistently not present: sleepwalkers or time travelers. Many are too occupied with the residue of the past or anxieties about the future. And never fully awake. The whole self never entirely comes together at the same time and place.

I recently heard an interesting definition of a boor. It is someone who deprives our solitude without providing companionship. We all know people who fit that description. Several people probably immediately came to mind. If we are honest, this describes most of civilization.

Consider America, where a staggering sixty-six percent check their phones up to 160 times daily. We are addicted to being somewhere other than where we are. Boston Globe Consulting asked folks what they would give up to keep their cell phones. More than three in ten would stop seeing their friends in person. Almost a third of Americans replied they would give up sex for a year.

Living in a beach community brings this to life even more. Travel journals consistently vote our seashore as one of the most beautiful in the world. Yet, stroll down the beach awake and aware. You will see that most people relaxing on the sparkling sand are not looking at the emerald-blue waves and cerulean sky. Instead, they are squinting at a tiny digital screen. Their body is tanning, but their mind and emotions are elsewhere. Most of us sleepwalk or time travel through life.

That is why the rare person who is fully present seems like a breath of fresh air. Being more present with those around you positively impacts relationship satisfaction. Instead of letting our minds wander elsewhere, try focusing on the moment-to-moment experience of your relationships. This focus will make it easier to enjoy the many things you appreciate about your friends and family and authentically address problems or concerns as they happen.

The Quaternity of Presence

Here is a simple color code for levels of presence. It is a valuable tool to gauge your level of engagement and that of others. The four states (quaternity) of presence are based loosely on a traffic light. They are:

Red—unaware, not paying attention.
(Ideal level for relaxing or sleeping at home.)
Orange—passive attention, relaxed.
(Ideal level for watching television.)
Yellow—moderately attentive, focusing.
(Ideal level for casual conversations, small talk.)
Green—actively attentive, aware, focused.
(Ideal level for interaction with friends and family.)

This simple color code clearly illustrates that we are often at the red level when we should be at yellow or green. *Ultimately, the more present we are, the more people want to be around us.* Practice using the color codes daily with family and friends and integrate them into your focused attention.

Phenomenology

To sum up thoughts on focused attention, let's talk about phenomenology. This daunting multi-syllable word has become one of my favorites. It comes from the root "phenomena," a Greek word that means "things that appear." Dr. Roger Walsh tells us that phenomenology is the careful description of raw experience. In the East, traditions such as yoga and Buddhism have used phenomenology to classify states of consciousness for over 2,000 years.[112]

The phenomenologist Martin Heidegger added a different spin. He said the most critical question is that of *being*. He recommended this method: disregard intellectual clutter, pay attention to things, and let them reveal themselves to you.

Simone de Beauvoir was Jean Claude Sartre's part-time lover and muse. They were both extraordinary thinkers and helped make *existentialist* a household word. She recounts a conversation between Sartre and fellow philosopher Raymond Aron at a bar in Paris.

Aron said, "You see, *mon petit camarade*, my little comrade, if you are a phenomenologist, you can talk about this cocktail and make philosophy out of it." Beauvoir wrote that Sartre turned pale upon hearing this. He realized the implications of this simple statement were enormous.[113]

To paraphrase Aron, if you practice being fully present with yourself and others and paying attention, your conversation about the most common thing will trigger positive Affect. These feelings of *interest, excitement, contentment*, and *enjoyment* will activate pleasant facial and verbal reactions and one's healthy scripts to produce moods of transcendence and wholeness. In other words, you will be fully present—body, mind, soul, and spirit—awake, aware, and attentive.

The ritual of mealtime provides an opportunity for phenomenology. For example, my wife has taught me to take a bite and then place my fork or spoon on the plate until the food is chewed thoroughly and swallowed. Then pick up the utensil again and continue. Sound simple? I dare you to try it. Somehow this little technique transforms food into something communal for every sense.

It not only feeds the physical being, but it engages and enhances the sensory experience in our mental, emotional, and spiritual aspects. So often, mealtime in our frenetic world is much like driving. We arrive at our destination, we finish our meal, but we cannot remember the journey. Instead, conscious people enjoy the journey.

Another way to pay attention during meals is by asking the person who prepared the food to talk about the recipe, techniques, and ingredients. It is no coincidence that we have four (a quaternity) food groups.

Suppliers have begun to understand the growing desire to know more about the food we buy, including its origin and production aspects. For example, Cento has a "find my field" website, bringing traceability to their tomato products. Using the code found on each can and Google Earth, one can view the field where the tomatoes were grown.

One can raise a simple meal to another level by taking a few moments to source the ingredients and selecting a wine from the same region. When the wine and the food come from the same dirt and climate, the same terroir, it elevates the sensory experience to new heights. Something mysterious, almost philosophical, can happen as you pay attention and wholly enjoy the meal. It transforms into phenomenology, a communal celebration, a mystical union with oneself, others, and the food.

3.) Kind Intention

We don't talk about kindness often. The word itself, "kind," has a foreign ring when verbalized. In the institution of modern culture—traits such as gratitude, gentleness, well wishes, and compassion do not mix well with the "succeed at all costs" mentality of western civilization. But the way we relate to ourselves and others has profound effects on our entire being. Research has repeatedly shown that our sphere of relationships enhances the enjoyment of life and promotes longer life.

Making his way to the pulpit of St. Paul's Cathedral in 1642, I wonder if John Donne had any clue the words he would speak that day would echo throughout the world for all time. Ironically, one of our greatest poet's most famous lines came not from a poem but a sermon.

> "No man is an island entire of itself; every man is a piece of the continent, a part of the main; if the sea washes away a clod, Europe is the less, as well as if a promontory were, as well as any manner of thy friends or thine own, were; any man's death diminishes me because I am involved in mankind. And therefore never send to know for whom the bell tolls; it tolls for thee."[114]

Donne embedded the words "No man is an island" in a message about how human beings connect and how important that connection is for the well-being and survival of any individual. When one hears the church bell tolling for someone who has died, don't ask who it is. Donne says that it's tolling for you as well. You are part of the same culture. The death of anyone takes a part of one's own life away.

Incidentally, this sermon is famous, not only for the words "no man is an island," but also for the phrase "for whom the bell tolls." The terminology used by Ernest Hemingway as the title of his timeless novel about relationships. Both Donne and Hemingway's enduring works portray the universal yet unique principle that all stories are the same, yet somehow different.

To be all that we are to be on *The Quest*—to enjoy life to its fullest—we must embrace the interconnectedness of our self, our companions, our community, and our world. All the universe comprises a collective consciousness. When we understand this connectedness, the need to show kind intention becomes obvious. Here are four ways to pay attention to kindness.

Gratitude

The act of being grateful activates the positive Affect *contentment* within one's self and affords pleasure to others. Another apt definition says the act of gratefulness is pleasing because of comfort supplied or discomfort alleviated.

While teaching a course on positive psychology, Dr. Martin Seligman created an exercise called "gratitude night." The idea triggered my *interest-excitement* Affect while reading about the assignment in his influential book, *Authentic Happiness*. It was instantly apparent that I should apply this act of gratitude to the most significant people in my life.

Seligman asked his students to write a brief one or two-page handwritten letter to a person of profound influence. One requirement was to invite that person to physically (not virtually) attend the class gathering and then read them the letter. Afterward, gift them with the note. Simple enough.

Most of the students later reported that the time was one of the most profound moments of their life. It was a tearful and joyous event. Dr. Seligman implemented the assignment and gathering as an integral part of the positive psychology curriculum. He writes that the annual gratitude night class is a high point of the year.[115]

After some thought, I decided to handwrite a personal letter of gratitude to three people who have profoundly influenced my life. Two of them lived out of state and required planning to meet face to face. I'm fortunate that I live with the other. It took over six months to get with the other two physically, but it was worth it.

Via email I told them it was vital that we get together (I decided to do it individually and privately) and reassured them that it was good. The readings were positive, enjoyable, meaningful, and emotional times.

I followed Seligman's instructions by reading the testimonial aloud slowly, with expression and eye contact. Then let the person react unhurriedly. We then spontaneously reminisced. The subsequent discussions were mutually life-giving and memories to treasure for a lifetime. I had previously snapped a digital photo of each letter for a personal artifact. Furthermore, I laminated the handwritten original for the recipient to keep.

William Arthur Ward says, Feeling gratitude and not expressing it is like wrapping a present and not giving it.[116]

Gentleness

In our culture, we conflate gentleness with the concept of meekness. The definition of gentle has reference primarily to disposition and behavior and often suggests a deliberate or voluntary kindness or forbearance in dealing with others: *as in a gentle pat; gentle with children.*[117] Meek, however, is a different word. It implies a submissive spirit and may even indicate undue submission in the face of insult or injustice: *meek and even servile or weak.*[118]

The strongest of us can be gentle. This concept makes me think of the movie *The Princess Bride* and the character Fezzik, played by André the Giant. In particular, the beautiful scene at the end of the film, when he holds out his arms to catch

Princess Buttercup as she jumps from the window. His face is beaming with joy as she lands *gently* in his massive arms.

André the Giant (André René Roussimoff) was a French professional wrestler and actor. He stood over seven feet tall and weighed over 500 pounds.[119] Called the *Eighth Wonder of the World,* Roussimoff dominated the rough and tumble world of wrestling for years. Yet Carey Elwes (who played the character Westley) writes in his delightful memoir *As You Wish* that André the Giant was the most beloved actor on the set.[120]

Because of his size, many people got the wrong impression of him. They believed him to be cold and rude. However, those close to the wrestler would tell you that he was a gentleman at heart.

The actress Robin Wright (Princess Buttercup) recounts that it was frigid cold during the movie's filming, and she would ask the giant to keep her warm. To do this, he would gently place his hand on top of her head. She was astounded to discover that his whole hand covered her entire head, and the body heat of his hand would warm her in no time.

Wholeness and enjoyment have a lot to do with how people behave toward themselves, others, animals, and the world. In the words of Leo Buscaglia, "Only the weak are cruel. Gentleness can only be expected from the strong."[121] An essential nuance of gentleness is *courtesy* in the old sense of the word—politeness of the heart, kindness, and tenderness of the spirit.

Well-Wishes

Well-wishes are kind intentions, either spoken or written, that express a desire for another to have good health and possessions.

They also show encouragement. In today's culture, ways to give well-wishes include greeting cards, social media posts, written letters, and verbal expressions. But whether one speaks or writes them, the critical thing is personally sharing positive thoughts for someone.

One might consider giving well-wishes to a friend or family member if they are going through a difficult time, transition, illness, death of a loved one, or divorce. They are also appropriate to let someone know you care about them.

The first historical record of well-wishes comes from around 1595. It combines *well*, meaning "satisfactory, pleasing, or good" and *wish*, meaning "an instance of desiring or hoping for something." Thus, you hope they have a better life when you wish someone well.

Today, we often express these wishes utilizing technology such as email, social media posts, comments, or direct messages. But all too often, our best intentions are never spoken. Instead, they live unsaid in our minds. A fully conscious person pays attention to those promptings and verbalizes kind intentions. These expressions are always mutually beneficial, offering joy and comfort to all involved.

For example, people rarely express how proud they are of someone. There is power in this simple yet sincere well-wish. However, our culture does not tend to acknowledge pride. A religious background makes us suspicious of anything that smacks of it. After all, scripture says, "pride goeth before a fall."[122] Therefore, we are hesitant to puff someone up.

But pride can be a healthy outgrowth of the Affect *contentment–enjoyment*. It is a normal emotion that follows a purposeful, goal-directed activity. The effort expended and the subsequent achievement of the goal naturally trigger the Affect *enjoyment*. One can witness this in the end zone celebration of a football game after a touchdown.

During my career, one of the inevitable warnings from my boss after our team would work hard and accomplish a successful outcome was "okay, but that was yesterday. What are we going to do tomorrow?" Those words still haunt me. He allocated no time for a natural release of joy and emotion. He felt it was wrong to pat someone on the back and express pride.

Healthy pride involves "competence pleasure," a phrase coined by Francis Broucek in his book *Shame and the Self.*[123] It's the excitement experienced in the successful accomplishment of a pursuit that has been purposely and doggedly striven for.

One can see this expression of competence pleasure in people of all ages. For example, observe a baby's face as they accomplish a task such as a first step. You can watch the child as it beams with *pride*. It is an innately triggered Affect, which in turn physically triggers our *enjoyment* as we watch. We do not hesitate to clap and exclaim, "Yay, that was good!"

We should do the same for adults. A sincere acknowledgment (a verbal expression of a well-wish) of another's accomplishment triggers *joy* for all involved.

Compassion

The definition from the *Merriam-Webster* dictionary assists in this context. Compassion is the sympathetic consciousness of others' distress together with a desire to alleviate it. It is interesting to note the difference between empathy and compassion. Compassion is the broader word: it refers to understanding another's pain and the desire to mitigate that pain somehow.[124]

It is an expression of kindness that we can apply to ourselves, our companions, our community, and the world. And yet, in the hectic pace of life, we rarely take time to express it. The act of compassion provides a vital way to enjoy life. We apply this while under the influence of the Affect *interest-excitement*. When this biological emotion is released and expressed, it triggers the Affect *contentment-enjoyment*.

Here is a practical example of this somewhat technical explanation. As I look back over the stories of my life after six decades, one vividly comes to mind.

A friend told me about the small third-world nation of Kyrgystan. Because the extremist Muslim influence was waning, there was an opportunity to teach students about the myriad ways art can enrich life. But unfortunately, most of the artists in the impoverished country created utilitarian works. Because they desperately needed money.

My friend managed to trigger my *interest-excitement* Affect and convince me to get out of my comfort zone and travel to this far-away and hard-to-reach country. One of the highlights of my life was teaching these students free enterprise and the possibility of earning more money by making art one loves.

As I addressed these young people growing up in a lonely and impoverished country, their faces beamed as the teaching triggered their *interest-excitement* Affect. And as we talked further, it mutually triggered the Affect *enjoyment*. Writing these words almost two decades later still triggers my *contentment* Affect. The act of compassion activates healthy emotion.

As with most aspects of consciousness, we must be kind to ourselves. It is easier to understand another's pain than our own for some reason. However, if we do not show compassion to ourselves, how can we expect others to do so.

The older I get, the more I'm convinced that the Beatles had it right. "All You Need Is Love" for self, for others, and our world.

Much like many people around the globe, our natural world has been abused and neglected. As this fact becomes more evident with the catastrophic events caused by climate change, we can do no less than show compassion to nature. We can do our part by conserving water, saving our trees, preserving rain forests, and lessening our carbon footprint.

There is much to be said here. However, I hope these few words serve as a reminder to be openly aware, focus our attention, and demonstrate a kind intention to this planet we call home.

4. Continued Growth

We are either growing larger or smaller. In *The Quest*, we believe one of the supreme tasks is to gradually move the contents of the unconscious to the conscious. This continued growth results in wholeness. It should occur in all aspects of our being—physical, mental, emotional, and spiritual.

As we conclude this discussion of the Conscious waypoint and prepare to look at the unconscious, the holy grail should begin to come into focus. The treasure we are questing for is wholeness. Enjoyment is simply a natural outgrowth of that state of being.

We are all unique. My way to wholeness is not your way. Still, we are universal, so we have pathways of growth that have stood the test of time and some that are extremely practical.

Physical Growth

Good health embodies our goal of wholeness. But the individual methods we use to attain that objective are unique. What we eat and drink, how we exercise, where we live, and the stress inside us are significant aspects of a healthy body. Moderation and the acceptance of personal responsibility for good health help us experience the many rewards of second life.

Again, I should mention the position one holds in the world, good luck, and where one lives influences health. Enjoyment of life sometimes stems as much from a position, social expectations, and environment as ability. These cultural factors matter as we age. They increase our chances of living well and meaningfully throughout our second life.

For me, an essential aspect of physically becoming who I am, being whole, means the expansion of my sensuality. It was denied and suppressed most of my life. My wife's physical essential is fitness. It plays a vital and enjoyable role in who she is. What is your physical essential?

The Essentials waypoint provides an opportunity to identify your physical requisites. The practical value in determining the four essential aspects is that it becomes easier to recognize, grow, and integrate them once one knows them.

Mental Growth

There is a crucial difference between an older person who can serve on the Supreme Court and one who can no longer work the remote or remember their family.

Mental health forces us to think about what makes us human. Yet, behind cancer, dementia is the most feared disease.

Fortunately, medical breakthroughs provide ways to not only protect but expand our mental health.

These are a few words of encouragement from Dr. Louise Aronson in her Pulitzer Prize-nominated book *Elderhood*.[125] First, dementia and aging are not synonymous. Only fourteen percent of adults in their seventies or older have dementia on average.

She says that the traits of dementia: slowed processing, delayed recall, and greater sensitivity to distraction are inconveniences but not significant impairments. They are fundamentally different from not being able to roughly copy a simple drawing or name more than a few animals when given a minute to think about it.

An older person with a healthy brain may do things more slowly or differently for reasons that have more to do with their hands, their eyes, or their aging brain, but they can still do them. It is important to note that one can delay dementia by minimizing the same risk factors associated with heart disease, stroke, and certain cancers. We can mitigate these factors by regular exercise, healthy eating, avoiding obesity, and shunning cigarettes.

However, she gives a word of caution. Mental health in second life is harder to maintain and expand if you live in an impoverished community for a long time. And developed traditions, including favorite foods and family customs, that are deeply meaningful but unhealthy.

Here we see the vital importance of integrating the physical self with the mental, becoming whole. The Essentials waypoint provides an opportunity to identify your mental requisites.

Emotional Growth

We take for granted that our emotions exist, for better or worse, and that we have to live with them. As a result, there is little thought given to emotional growth. Yet, once again, we see the vital importance of integration in all four aspects of our being.

Our physical, mental, and emotional health are interdependent. Experts say we learned ninety-five percent of what we know about the human brain in the past two decades. [126]For example, neuroscientists have found that events trigger emotions. Whatever resides in our memory is stored with its accompanying emotion; thus, each of us has a highly personal "information bank" of emotion-related data.

As we investigate this information bank, the vast realm of our unconscious, we can study and enjoy ourselves in a new way. Grow emotionally and take pride in our whole being, and disavow the shame that hides our private secret thoughts and desires from view.

Emotionally, we grow when we move our shame from the unconscious to the conscious. Dr. Nathanson poses a powerful question in his book *Shame and Pride*. How will *shame* change when it is no longer secret?[127]

How will *you* change when the unhealthy emotions (Affects), painful memories, events, places, and people, are identified and expressed and not suppressed, denied, or repressed? The paths to our emotions, both healthy and unhealthy, are the way to a new understanding of our human condition. In short, they are pathways of growth and wholeness.

Knowing the nine Affects (biological emotions) and how they trigger our feelings, reactions (scripts), and moods is the way to expand emotional intelligence. So this group of nine "actors"—who put on the "dramas" that make up our entire emotional life—becomes an internal repertory theater.

As a result, we understand more fully the words of Shakespeare in the play *As You Like It.* "All the world's a stage, And all the men and women merely players; They have their exits and their entrances, And we each in our time play many parts."

We explore these nine innate universal emotions and the unique way we react to them in great depth in the Emotions waypoint. We see the crucial importance of integrating the physical self with the mental and the emotional self, becoming whole. The Essentials waypoint provides an opportunity to identify your emotional requisites.

Spiritual Growth

There are now four major spiritual life stances on earth, Christianity, Islam, Hinduism, and Humanism. Christians believe in Yahweh, Muslims in Allah, Hindus in Brahman, and Humanists in Humans.

Many writings chronicle the first three religions, but few tell about Humanism. It may surprise you to know that nonbelievers can be spiritual, too. Those who don't choose to worship an invisible being or spend life fretting about eternal punishment in Hell still want to be able to share values we hold universal.

Greg Epstein, the chaplain at *Harvard University,* says, "consciousness is an incredibly mysterious thing. Many theologians and religious thinkers have argued that it must have been given to us by God. But our minds are highly complicated and not because God said they should be so. But because, in the words of Carl Sagan, our brains have ten to the eleventh power of neurons and ten to the fourteenth power of synapses. Do the math."[128]

The gods don't create values. But humans can, and we must do it wisely. I have come to believe our spiritual ethics should come from human needs and interests. As the "Humanist Manifesto" puts it, "ethical values are derived from human need and interest as tested by experience."

Values provide a spiritual roadmap for human beings to flourish, enjoy life, and become whole. Yet, ironically, millions of people who say they believe in God also live by Humanistic ideals. But, unfortunately, craving an emotional connection to the past, they convince themselves that modern morality springs from the ancient religion of their ancestors.

Whatever your beliefs, it is essential to note that firmly convinced nonbelievers and strongly convinced believers are the least depressed people on earth. They enjoy life. This satisfaction makes the case to explore the depths of your spiritual being.

In the words of Felix Adler, freedom of thought is a sacred right of every individual. Following the way of *The Quest* means exercising one's freedom. Regardless of our beliefs, we must all act together for our good and the greater good. Doing this will lead to spiritual growth.

Hopefully, we can visualize the potential when integrating the physical, mental, emotional, and spiritual selves. We see what transcendent moments can happen when we become fully conscious, in short, whole. The most crucial point is that human life, for all its diversity, imperfections, and disappointments, is well worth integrating.

Again, as a reminder, the Essentials waypoint provides an opportunity to identify your spiritual requisites.

Becoming Fully Conscious

Consciousness *is* a marvelous thing. However, in today's world, it is also a rarity. Most people sleepwalk their way through life. They are "time travelers." They are never truly present in the moment, minds racing through time and the unconscious—reliving or regretting the past and assessing or worrying about the future.

Furthermore, we have finally invented the time machine of science fiction lore. It is called the cell phone and it's virtually impossible to find a time traveler without one. They constantly peruse the past and the future via search portals and social media streams. Not realizing that even though they posted only a few moments ago, it is already a mostly forgotten artifact of the past.

When Nabakov wrote about the sudden window swinging open on a sunlit landscape amidst the night of non-being, he was not talking about digital devices. If we manage to put them away for a few minutes, we may find time to grow our consciousness. For some, I realize that may prove impossible. But for those who desire to walk the path of *The Quest*, it is essential.

As we cultivate open awareness, focused attention, kind intention, and continued growth, it becomes more than a philosophy of life—it becomes phenomenology. If an apricot cocktail can overflow with meaning, imagine what could happen if a few of us wake up, pay attention to ourselves and others, and start living in the present—free and clear.

To summarize, symbols are communication tools between the conscious and the unconscious and reveal who we are inside. A primary goal of our journey is to begin to think as we dream

—symbolically. Essentials identify words for *who* we are. Stages and transitions help us locate *where* we are in life. And consciousness grows *when* we pay attention to ourselves and begin to empty the unconscious. Yet, paradoxically, one must become "unconscious to do consciousness properly."

To discover and salvage the healthy and unhealthy contents of our unconscious and move them to consciousness, we need **vehicles** of communication. So let's now turn to the Unconscious waypoint and explore a fascinating quaternity of these modes of transport.

Unconscious

Are You Emptying Your Unconscious?

The Quest is an effort to heal the split in consciousness. It is a journey that integrates body, mind, soul, and spirit into one enlightened being. The end goal is to dissolve the ego, unmask the persona, embrace the feminine and the masculine within (gender), and reconcile the darkness and the light (shadow).

When we were young and in the development stage of life, our conscious ego functioned much like a warship—its cannon blasting at the slightest danger to stability. The ego defended against any feelings, thoughts, behaviors that brought disapproval or loss of love or respect (anger, tears, lust, neediness, laziness, and more). As a result, these actions were attacked and sunk into the oblivion of the unconscious.

Even before we got to church and school, the vast sea of our unconscious was awash with shipwrecks. At most of these institutions, aspects such as self-identity, gender issues, spontaneity, divergent opinions, and "abnormal" desires garnered disapproval from our teachers, preachers, and peers. The ego doomed these perceived "weaknesses" to the dark and stormy deep.

During the first stage of life, the ego functioned as master and commander of the vessel of our being. It was defending and condemning threatening ships to the subliminal regions of our mind—the location of our shadow and gender. And we are destined to spend a large portion of our lives attempting to salvage them.

And let it be said, this journey is a noble and necessary pursuit because these regions contain the hidden treasures of our life. For example, one may discover a creative dream or an unfulfilled fantasy sacrificed for adulthood's responsibilities. Those aspirations and longings, lying dormant in the deep, await our discovery in second life.

The unconscious is like a vast ocean. Oceanographers tell us that as one dives deeper into the sea, less and less sunlight shines through, and about 200 meters beneath the surface, there is an area called the "twilight zone." Daylight fades almost entirely out of view, and knowledge about these dark depths fades too. "It's almost easier to define it by what we don't know than what we do know," says Andone Lavery of the Woods Hole Oceanographic Institution.

Yet this region of the ocean is critical. More fish may live in the twilight zone than the rest of the ocean combined, and the dark sea creatures play a significant role in regulating the climate.[129]

The similarities are eerie. Most of us have little if any knowledge about our unconscious's "twilight zone." Unfortunately, it is far easier to define ourselves by what we don't know than what we do know. There are probably more contents (people, places, memories, and events) in our unconscious than in our conscious. Moreover, the vast sea of our unconscious plays a disproportionately large part in regulating the climate of our emotions and our being.

We now come to our most extraordinary adventure yet, exploring the unconscious. To become whole—to reach the holy grail—we must become seasoned explorers. However, we have almost no training in plumbing our depths. This process of slowly bringing the shipwrecks to the surface into awareness, back into the light of day, and remembering what we've forgotten, is a primary focus of the following four waypoints.

The most uncharted expanse of the unconscious is where we encounter the mysteries of *The Quest*. And they are reclaimed at the confluence of the conscious and the unconscious.

Each week, I hop on my bicycle and escape the routine of life at Honeymoon Island for a few magical hours. At the north end lies over two miles of natural unspoiled beach that time has not touched. On the east side of the barrier island, there is a three-mile trail through one of the last remaining virgin slash pine forests.

My five-mile roundtrip along the sugar-sand beach features rocks, dunes, and private nooks. Sea oats, sea rockets, and beach elders grow and spread their roots in the dunes. Exposed to wind and sea spray, these plants face the harsh reality of living close to the ocean.

Like *The Quest*, it is the same path, yet it is different every week. As in life, the changing tides and weather create a unique experience each time. My goal is always the northernmost tip of the island. Farther north is uninhabited Three Rooker Island. Between the two islands is where the protected waters of St. Joseph Sound to the east meet the open waters of the Gulf of Mexico to the west.

It is always turbulent there. Choppy, churning waves spray seafoam and mist. Looking to the right, one sees the far away waterfront towns of Ozona and Crystal Beach. And to the left is the vast ocean basin of the Gulf of Mexico, a "marginal" sea of the Atlantic Ocean.

The water currents are powerful, some of the world's most robust and most colorful. The Gulf Stream is a system of dynamic, fast-running, and clockwise-rotating warm ocean currents. Many metaphors are possible here.

It transports water at an astonishing rate of about 39 million cubic yards per second. At Cape Hatteras, North Carolina, the cold meets the warm, resulting in some of the world's most significant and most severe storms.

The Gulf is the ninth-largest body of water in the world. It contains 615,000 square miles of majesty, mystery, beauty, and wonders. In comparison, the ocean surface area is 139 million square miles with an average depth of over 12,000 feet. Yet, only a fraction of the world's watery vast depths, about 20%, have been explored.[130]

The planet earth is a planet of oceans, as the human being is a being of unconsciousness. And as the oceans' tremendous presence causes them to have a considerable effect on the planet and our civilization, the unconscious has a significant impact on our quality of life. For example, the ocean is greatly responsible for the climate of the earth. It regulates air temperature and supplies moisture for rainfall. The sea also provides us with food, energy, minerals, and a cheap method of transportation. Without the ocean, the earth wouldn't be able to sustain life, and so it is with the unconscious.

It is greatly responsible for our emotional climate, regulates our mental health, and controls the action of breathing. The unconscious also relieves stress and provides storage for our memories, people, events, and places. It contains everything that has ever happened to us since the moment we drew our first breath.

Without the unconscious, human beings would be unable to sustain life. It is a virtually untapped resource for growth and enjoyment in life. But inexplicably, most of us slog on through life, neither conscious nor unconscious, waiting for something to happen, yet excluded from the adventure.

What if (like explorers of old) we gather courage and organize an expedition into the inner regions of this waypoint. We will not only need communication tools; we will need *vehicles* of communication. Many of these transportation methods are available, and surprisingly, with a few exceptions, the only cost is time and effort.

In this waypoint, we will consider four (quaternity) vehicles. We will organize them in correlation with the four aspects of being: body, mind, soul, and spirit. First is the physical movement of *ritual,* second is the mental movement of *psychedelics,* third is the emotional movement of *therapy,* and fourth is the spiritual movement of *dreams.*

The concepts of movement and transportation are essential to any explorer. The Knights of the Round Table rode horses; for Don Quixote, it was a donkey. For those in the modern era, canoes, ships, planes, trains, automobiles, and rocket ships provide a way to discover new domains.

Beneath the vast and mysterious sea of our unconscious lies the shipwrecks our ego has repressed, denied, projected, and forgotten. And many things we do not know or have never acknowledged. So, one may rightly ask, why should we then dredge up these painful memories, places, events, and people? And that is an excellent question.

Dr. James Hollis provides an answer. He says the power of our earliest unconscious messages from childhood and first adulthood are challenging to confront. Yet, what we do not know does indeed hurt us—and others—and has the potential to guide our choices in directions different from those our soul desires.[131]

Many of us unconsciously live the unlived lives of our parents. We repress sexual desire, suppress religious trauma, deny childhood wounds, avoid the pain of the past, or find ourselves unable to rely on the world to meet our needs. These are a few of the many ways our ego defends against the turbulence of our emotional history. These places, memories, events, and people dominate how we do business in our daily life.

At the risk of oversimplification, they are the shipwrecks scattered about the vast seafloor of our unconscious. However, a word of encouragement is appropriate here. Where there are shipwrecks, untold treasure lurks.

The journey of *The Quest*, for the most part on land, now takes us to the "sea." To reach the waypoint of the unconscious and ultimately the holy grail, we must gather sea vehicles and blaze "underwater" trails. Creating new pathways is the crux of the matter. To grow more significant, to become whole, we must salvage the wrecks (and the treasure) and raise them to the surface of the conscious. Only then can we live free and clear in open awareness.

Ritual

Ritual provides our first vehicle of communication with the unconscious. It provides a way to affirm life, the good, the bad, and the ugly. These traditions help us center ourselves to reconcile the conscious with the unconscious. And do it with gratitude, love, and recognition. As a result, we can be confident that we will discover the joy of treasure within the shipwrecks of our lives.

Joseph Campbell tells us that ritual helps us understand that the primary experience at the core of life is a sweet, wonderful thing wrought through bitterness and pain. This affirmative view comes pouring through the various rites and myths of culture and nature.

He continues, the ritual also presents an image of the cosmos, a picture of the universe that will maintain and elicit this experience of awe. This understanding of wonder gives one a context to reconcile life, existence, consciousness, and expectation of meaning.[132]

These discoveries are why humanity needs the timeless and universal stories of myth. They are tools of communication. It also answers why humans cling to a religion, whether archaic or flimsy. We all need universal symbols to help us maintain a sense of mystical awe and explain everything (the good and the bad) that we encounter within the universe around us.

Rituals can help us make sense of difficult transitions. Whether found in tribal groups or modern culture, the ceremony invariably insists upon a rite of death and rebirth. It provides the participant with a "rite of passage" from one life stage to the next. These transitions occur from childhood to youth, youth to first adulthood, first adulthood to second adulthood, second adulthood to elderhood, and finally, elderhood to the afterlife.

Carl Jung tells us that every new phase of development throughout an individual's life features a repetition of the original conflict between the self and the claims of the ego. However, he believed that the battle is perhaps most potent at the mid-life transition.

The universality of the initiation rite (since ancient times) tells us that it has long offered a spiritually satisfying means to help bridge the complex and vital transitions of life. For example, consider the ceremonies surrounding birth, marriage, and death. Conspicuous in its absence is a rite of passage for divorce. But that is for another book.

The purpose for the rituals performed during the problematic transitions always remains the same. It creates the symbolic mood of death from which may spring the extended spirit of rebirth. Therefore, the rite of passage brings the creative breath of resurrection (for more, see Catharsis waypoint) to any new stage of life.

You may also recall the universal journeys of the Transitions waypoint. The quaternity for the universal journey always contains a call, departure, initiation, and magic flight. In *The Quest*, I list these steps as a quaternity: pre-liminal, liminal, sub-liminal, and post-liminal.

The word liminal is intriguing. Liminality (literally, "a threshold") is the confusion in the middle of a rite of passage. It occurs when participants no longer hold their previous status and have not yet transitioned to the position they will hold when the ritual is complete. During a rite's liminal stage, participants "stand at the threshold" between their previous identity and new ways of life, which begins when they complete the ceremony.

During the live experience of *The Quest*, a secret rite of passage (the sub-liminal time) takes place on the second night. It is a time to pay attention to the anxious period between identities. The times we feel lost and filled with despair. This period in the rite of passage is like a chrysalis—no longer a caterpillar but not yet a butterfly. It may include a time of deep grieving for all one has lost in the first half of life.

The guide swears each participant to secrecy about the details of the ceremony. It has become a part of the mystique and myth surrounding *The Quest*. Each person who completes the initiation rite is encouraged to create a symbol that immortalizes the time.

One purchased a samurai sword and engraved the *Quest* symbol into the sheath. It rests on the mantle of his fireplace. I decided to create a mark on my body to commemorate the life-changing ritual forever.

No, I was not circumcised or mutilated. But I was pierced— by a tattooists' needle. I got my first (and most likely, my only) tattoo at age fifty-four. *The Quest* symbol portrays the death of my first life and the resurrection of the second life that occurred. Every time I glance down at my right calf, it beautifully reminds me of that once-in-a-lifetime event.

My rite of passage caught me by surprise. It was the first *Quest*, and as with all initial attempts at something crucial and new, the organization and leadership demanded my focused attention. After leading the ceremony and instructing and situating everyone, exhausted, I settled into my private time of the ceremony. I expected little.

It was high on a mountain top in the wilderness of Angel Fire, New Mexico. The sky was ablaze with stars, and elks filled the air with their calls. Then, finally, I laid my head back and let go. As I began to review my life, the universal power of the ritual did its work, and mother nature helped me make the arduous journey to my unconscious. I began life repair as I discovered shipwrecks (i.e., unforgiveness, repression, wounds, and trauma). The rest, as they say, is history. It was one of the most significant, life-changing times of my life.

One of the central puzzles of creating this written version of the live experience was handling this *Quest* ritual *most meaningfully* in a book setting. However, I have realized the details are out of my control. It is much bigger than me and too large to preserve in secrecy.

I feel there is no substitute for the sensory impact of the live experience. But for those of you who are reading these words, I hope the Catharsis waypoint ceremony outline will guide you in creating a personal sub-liminal *Quest* rite of passage.

A rite of passage provides a template for liberation from any state of being that is too immature, rigid, or final. It celebrates one's release from—or transcendence of—any confining pattern of existence as we move toward a superior or more mature stage of development.

We achieve catharsis and a growing sense of wholeness through a confluence of the conscious and unconscious contents (shipwrecks and treasures). The purpose of ritual is not perfection; it is completeness. Which is indeed a worthy goal, yet another step on the pathway to the holy grail.

Symbols can help us in this arduous task. Jung calls them "symbols of transcendence." They tell us how the unconscious contents can be salvaged and moved to the conscious mind.

The symbols can also be an active expression of those contents. For example, what is an animal that represents your transcendence? I have learned to pay attention to any occurrence in my unconsciousness of a phoenix. The symbolism of rising from the ashes is significant in my journey on many levels.

The lonely journey or pilgrimage theme is another symbol in ritual, psychedelic trips, therapy, and dreams. Also, make a note of flights of birds, airplanes, rockets, wilderness journeys, release from confinement, the underworld, rodents, lizards, snakes, and fish.

Notably, author Sam Harris writes about being raped by a panther during a psychedelic trip. And I've come to understand that the phallus symbol represents not only power, confidence, animus, and biological fertility but also mental, emotional, and spiritual intercourse.

I cannot overemphasize the significance of the symbols that appear to us from our past and in times of ritual, psychedelic trips, therapy, and dreams. These communication vehicles can facilitate meeting points and pathways between the conscious and the unconscious. They make it possible to integrate opposing forces within ourselves and reconcile conflicting elements.

But unless they are correctly understood and translated into a new way of life, the liminal moment of transcendence can pass. We must not let that happen. The power of ritual is that it helps us balance what makes us truly human and truly the master of our self.

Psychedelics

Psychedelics have been used as a vehicle to explore the unconscious for thousands of years. Specifically, indigenous tribes in Central America utilized a little brown mushroom, also called LBM, magic mushroom, or psilocybin, as a sacrament. The Aztecs called it the "flesh of the gods."

But as usually happens, an institution, this time the Roman Catholic Church, brutally suppressed (in the name of Christian love) the practice and drove it underground. This pattern of accessible usage and subsequent suppression by an institution would repeat itself over the years.

In 1957, R. Gordon Wasson wrote a lengthy article for *Life* magazine recounting his experience with "mushrooms that cause strange visions." And word about a new form of consciousness reached the general public. For the next ten years, many psychiatrists regarded psilocybin and LSD (also a psychedelic) as miracle drugs treating various disorders, including alcoholism, anxiety, and depression.

But again, it was suppressed, outlawed, and driven underground—this time by the United States government. Then, the propaganda machine of Richard Nixon and his band of authoritarian white men began widely distributing publicity about the dark side (bad trips, psychosis, and suicides) of psychedelics.

The government was afraid they were losing the youth of America to experiences beyond their control. After all, they had better uses for the young, to send them to die in the rice fields of Vietnam.

But once again, after fifty years underground, psychedelics are back. And we who wonder what it means to be fully human with a free and clear consciousness are fortunate to have several fantastic travel guides producing invaluable resources.

Michael Pollan's book *How To Change Your Mind*, the podcasts of neuroscientist Sam Harris, the maps.org website, the research of Dr. Roland Griffiths at Johns Hopkins University School of Medicine, and the documentary film *Fantastic Fungi*, provide invaluable information about these "mind manifesting" compounds.

Be warned; these little brown mushrooms have the power to alter our consciousness. To travel safely and effectively into the vast sea of the unconscious with these fantastic vehicles, one should be familiar with a few terms. And be aware the words can be daunting when dealing with neuroscience.

I will attempt to explain some of what I have learned. But to fully understand the context of these substances, and before trying them, please fully utilize the resources mentioned previously. They provide brilliant guidance and insight into this renaissance of consciousness expansion.

The knowledge we have available about the human brain has increased exponentially over the past few years. One of the most exciting findings is identifying the "default mode network" (DMN).

Neurologists noticed that several brain areas exhibited heightened activity when their subjects did nothing. In other words, they had discovered the place where our minds go to wander—to daydream, meditate, travel in time, reflect on ourselves, and worry. It may be through these structures that the stream of our consciousness flows.

A pioneer in psilocybin and default mode network research describes the DMN as the brain's "orchestra director."[133] He initially thought that a dose of psilocybin would increase brain activity in the emotion centers, similar to dreaming. But instead, he found that psilocybin *reduces* brain activity in these areas and *heightens* it in the default mode network when the subject is doing nothing mentally.

The experts feel that the DMN can lead to intense self-reflection, transcendence, and ego-dissolution. This engagement of the DMN then creates the possibility of a mystical exploration, openness, moments of oneness, and ecstasy.

Another vast implication is the integration of synaptic connections or lines of communication when taking psilocybin. Experts tell us that the brain is more flexible and interconnected under the influence of hallucinogens.

One of the most eye-opening illustrations is the graphics of a scanned brain on a placebo compared to one on psilocybin. You must see it to believe it. Find the link in the endnote.[134]

My Psychedelic Journey

After reading Pollan's compelling book, I listened to a Sam Harris podcast interview of Dr. Roland Griffiths. I also had a trusted friend who is a behavioral psychologist offer to be my underground guide. Therefore, I decided to take a trip to my unconscious. To realize the momentousness of this decision, you should know throughout life, if at all possible, I have abstained from drugs (including prescribed medications and over-the-counter) of any kind.

I rigorously researched various websites about precautions and prerequisites to a safe and beneficial experience. For example, they stressed the importance of having a peaceful, cozy place that feels safe. Another suggestion was to set an intention —something one wants to accomplish during the trip. Next was the importance of having a trusted guide throughout the time, someone that feels comfortable holding one's hand or body if the trip becomes scary or difficult.

Also suggested was choosing a playlist conducive to a psychedelic trip (i.e., Boards of Canada) and headphones to block out ambient noise. Finally, a requirement—one mustn't have schizophrenia or mental illness in oneself or a close relative.

After extensive research and preparation and taking care to follow the advice of experts, the day arrived. I decided to begin the trip around noon, and to prepare, I took an extended walk on my favorite beach. It is isolated, so I could meditate on the people who have been instrumental in my growth throughout each decade of my life.

I went back to childhood, remembering the first ten years of my life. Then I progressed a decade at a time (a life review of sorts), identifying specific people and how they had impacted me. For each one, I breathed words of gratefulness. It was an emotional time.

After an hour or more, I came to the northernmost part of the island, confirmed I was alone, and I removed my bathing suit and stretched out spread-eagle on the sand. It was a perfect day, cerulean blue skies, puffy white clouds moving slowly by, a slight breeze from the sea. The sand felt damp and grainy, soft and comforting.

I lay there a few minutes, melding with the earth, a part of nature, and at peace with the world. There was a feeling of tranquility and weightlessness as I cleared my mind in preparation for the afternoon adventure. Then, after a while, I got up, brushed off, donned my swimsuit, stood at the surf, and felt the tide wash over my skin, the sand subtly shifting beneath my feet.

On the way back, I continued the journey through my life (life repair) and whispered words of forgiveness to myself and to those who had wounded and wronged me. The entire experience felt like a "full being" massage. The afterglow was as intense as the "all is right in the world" euphoria felt after sex.

I mixed the psilocybin mushrooms with peanut butter and honey to digest them better. Next, I took them as a sacrament from the ornate wine glass we used for our wedding. My wife Gina and I then strolled hand in hand around our neighborhood pond as the compound began to take effect.

She helped me settle comfortably on our couch, closed the blinds, dimmed lights, and played music softly. The following six hours are hard to put into words. But, as many people have said, it indeed was one of the most significant mystical and spiritual experiences of my life.

Highlights include traveling through time via a swirling vortex with hieroglyphics and symbols into the collective unconscious. Tears were streaming down my face, cleansing and full of joy. Gina later told me I was repeatedly saying, "It's okay, everything is okay." I had an intense feeling of understanding why my mom loved me. It was because I came from her body. It's why Gina loves her two sons; they are a part of her flesh.

As the experience climaxed and began to ebb slightly, we went outside to our back porch and sat. I am at a loss to adequately describe how the leaves of the trees were shimmering like diamonds; the air felt visceral, the sky was the bluest of my memory. For the next 24 hours, I felt as if I was in an 8K video game. The entire world was vivid, pulsing with life, and filled with intense color.

I wrote seventeen handwritten pages journaling the experience. Much of it is only meaningful to me. Still, all of it is profoundly important to my understanding and reconciliation of the past, present, and future. Equanimity permeated my being.

My primary intention was to understand what would happen upon death. Religious baggage, fear of hell, and uncertainty about the existence of heaven fill my past. Afterward, I felt that I had salvaged shipwrecks and treasures from my unconscious and moved them to the clarity of the conscious. I had sensed an afterlife, a collective unconscious, that I had no reason to fear. Thus, the words, "it's okay, everything is okay."

The trauma of my past, the shame, guilt, and fear caused by the institutions of my life, while not alleviated, seem more manageable. I feel more able to recognize unhealthy Affect and rewrite the negative scripts of my life. And to understand and reconcile the light side and the dark side of my life. I believe the temporary dissolution of my ego helped me better integrate my emotions and my shadow.

Psilocybin is a powerful and mysterious compound. I struggle to understand how a naturally occurring little brown mushroom plucked from the earth elicits profound mystical experiences. For me, it was overwhelmingly positive, but I do realize that not every trip is a good one. People have bad trips. One should not lightly decide to ingest a psychedelic.

For me, having a psychologist serve as the shaman, a trusted guide (my wife) with me in a safe, comfortable place, a purposeful intention, and getting away from everyday routine became the best way to experience psilocybin. Pollan explains that the guides not only create a setting to feel safe enough to surrender to the experience, but they also help make sense of it afterward. Importantly, they help us see something worth making sense of.

My shaman guide and I scheduled a follow-up breakfast to debrief and discuss the trip at length. It proved a crucial part of the experience. The dialogue helped ensure those new pathways remained open and that I would not easily forget them.

****

Pollan writes that the images and narratives and the insights don't come from nowhere, and they certainly don't come from a chemical. They come from inside our minds. If dreams and fantasies and active imagination are worth interpreting, then indeed so is the vivid and detailed material with which the psychedelic journey presents us. It opens a new door to one's mind.[135]

These psychedelics, which include peyote, LSD, and ayahuasca, carve new pathways from the unconscious to the conscious. This integration and subsequent growth to wholeness are what *The Quest* is all about. I still do not understand all that happened that day during my psychedelic experience. Still, I know the unconscious sea is vaster, and my conscious world is much more alive and enjoyable than when I began the journey. To echo the words of musician Bruce Cockburn, "you can't tell me there is no mystery."[136]

Therapy

There are many types of therapy. We will explore a quaternity: psychotherapy, art therapy, positive psychology, and attachment-based therapy.

The first method is *psychotherapy*. I write extensively about the importance of psychotherapy in my book *The Loss of*

Belonging. The book contains practical advice about choosing the right therapist and explains the danger of utilizing someone who is not qualified, mainly the hazards of selecting a "Christian" counselor.

I would urge anyone who had a highly dysfunctional first stage of life to seek professional help. These wounds include a lack of physical attachment from mother or caregiver, abuse of any kind, a cultish religious background, or any severe cultural abnormality. Psychologists function as empathic guides as you together plumb the vast implications of your past.

The second method of therapy is *art therapy*. When I first began painting with watercolors, it was to find a hobby that would fill the vacuum created when I retired at an early age. Several years later, the suggestion came from a life coach that my art could also serve as therapy during the difficult transition from the first half of life to the second. He suggested I paint my feelings, my emotions.

And it was not until a decade later, while researching for this book, that I began to truly understand the ramifications and layers of the symbols I was creating. From the outset, when painting, time would cease to exist. I would paint for eight hours, which seemed like a few moments. Later, I would learn the concept of "flow" from an artist friend. The flow process was discovered and coined by psychologist and author Mihaly Csikszentmihalyi.

In the 1960s, Csikszentmihalyi studied the creative process and found that, when an artist was in the course of flow, they persisted at their task relentlessly, regardless of hunger or fatigue. Flow is the joy of doing something for the sake of doing it.

It is a conscious state of complete immersion in an activity —from painting and writing to meditation and hiking. It involves intense focus, creative engagement, and the loss of time and self-awareness.

A disturbing aspect of this state of flow was a flood of what I felt were negative memories, places, people, and events that would surface. But now, I understand this was the therapeutic power of art. During the flow state, the loss of self helped my unconscious bring shipwrecks of my life to the conscious. This dissolution of self enabled me to deal with them instead of letting the ego defend against them.

These intense feelings and emotions invariably found their way to my canvas creating evocative and provocative paintings. The shipwrecks became treasures to me as the beauty and power of the watercolor translated to catharsis and clarity. Viewing these paintings (which at times seemed to paint themselves) elicited freedom from the shame and guilt of my past.

Another aspect of my art was the subject matter. No matter how often I tried to paint a male figure, a landscape, or a still life, inevitably, I was drawn back to the female figure. To be specific, the nude female figure. And even more to the point, because of personal physical characteristics that evoked *shame* throughout life, the well-endowed female figure. I allude to this in the Symbols waypoint, but the story bears elaboration in the context of therapy.

At first, I thought this was a pathway to sensual freedom after a lifetime of censorship. But it was only recently that I had a eureka moment while reading about gender: the anima (feminine) and the animus (masculine.) The paintings of nude females were *self-portraits*.

The nudes were therapeutic pathways between my unconscious and consciousness. They served as visual representations of the growing integration of my masculine and feminine aspects. Finally, they symbolized the struggle for freedom from the shame and guilt surrounding my body.

The third method of therapy is *positive psychology*. For some people, being joyful comes naturally and easily. Others need to work at it. So how does one go about becoming more joyful?

This relatively new field of research has been exploring how people and institutions can support the quest for increased *contentment* and meaning. It has uncovered several routes to enjoyment:

- Feeling *Joy*: seeking pleasurable emotions and sensations.
- Engaging Fully: pursuing goals and activities that engage you fully.
- Doing Good: searching for meaning outside yourself.
- Gratitude: expressing appreciation for what you have in life.
- Savoring Pleasure: placing your attention on pleasure as it occurs and consciously enjoying the experience as it unfolds.
- Being Mindful: focusing your attention on what is happening at the moment and accepting it without judgment.
- Self-Compassion: consoling yourself as needed, taking the time to nurture yourself, and building the motivation to try again.

In the Enlightenment waypoint, we will explore further the fascinating implications of positive psychology.

The fourth method of therapy is *attachment-based therapy (ABFT)*. The client-therapist relationship develops or rebuilds trust and focuses on expressing Affect (emotion). John Bowlby's attachment theory heavily influences this method of therapy which posits that humans have an inherent, biological desire for meaningful relationships.[137]

An attachment-based approach to treatment looks at the connection between a child's early attachment experiences with primary caregivers, usually with parents, and the ability to develop normally and ultimately form healthy emotional and physical relationships as an adult.

However, when abandonment, neglect, criticism, or detachment occur, the child's trust in the relationship is likely damaged, and insecure attachments may result. ABFT helps increase the security of the attachment between a parent or caregiver and child so the relationship can provide a supportive foundation for an enjoyable life.

Individual, family, couple, and group therapy, with both children and adults, utilize ABFT to help mend or recover from fractured family relationships. Those who may benefit from attachment-based treatment include adoptees, children in foster care, and children of depressed mothers. In addition, victims of trauma (children of divorce or children who have been sexually abused or otherwise mistreated, particularly at the hands of a caregiver) may also find it helpful.

Please note that attachment-based therapy as described here should not be confused with the unconventional and potentially harmful treatments referred to as "attachment therapy." These unproven methods involve physical manipulation, restraint, deprivation, boot camp-like activities, or physical discomfort of any kind.[138]

There is growing evidence that attachment-based therapy and Affect theory (see Emotions waypoint) have traveled along separate paths for too long. There seems to be an apparent correlation between "attachment behaviors" and the nine innate Affects. The psychological community is making some fascinating attempts to heal this rift. The implications are exciting when combining the findings of attachment theory and the physical manifestations of emotion and Affect theory.

As a child learns to build pathways between the unconscious and conscious, secure attachment with a parent or caregiver dramatically influences the growth of positive Affect (*pride, contentment, love*). Conversely, when a child is ignored or abused, their ego employs defense mechanisms to repress or deny the lack of attachment resulting in negative Affects such as *shame* and *guilt*.

When qualified therapists combine these theories, they can build new integration pathways and healthy Affect. Here we find yet another exciting way to explore the vast sea of our unconscious and salvage treasure from within the shipwrecks of our lives. These new pathways can lead to positive and healthy outcomes.

****

Not all therapy treatments are comparable in terms of results. While it's no simple fix, therapy can often bring clarity and peace of mind to those distressed by complex events, people, places, and memories in their lives. Salvaging negative (unhealthy) thoughts and emotions through various therapy methods and understanding the positive (healthy) emotional impacts on our consciousness can lead to freedom, clarity, and, ultimately, enjoyment and wholeness.

Dreams

Each night offers the priceless opportunity to explore the vast sea of our unconscious. Sleep comprises almost one-third of our lives—the average person spends nearly twenty-five years of their life sleeping. Yet, most of us have never acknowledged, recorded, or benefited from the many adventures in our dreams. When surfing the internet, one finds many New Age, mystical, and fantastical interpretations and methods to explain this oft-misunderstood aspect of life.

However, in exploring this extraordinary and virtually untapped communication vehicle for the unconscious, we will attempt to remain grounded while delving into this ethereal world of symbols. Specifically, our dreams speak the language of the unconscious.

Over fifteen years ago, when beginning research for *The Quest*, I read *Modern Man In Search of a Soul* by Carl Jung for the first time. After turning to page one of this classic work, considered one of the essential books in psychology, I promptly skipped the first chapter and moved to the second.

Only after several years did I realize that I could no longer reasonably ignore a theme that came up repeatedly in my explorations. It was the subject of Jung's first chapter and a large portion of his lifework. The title is "Dream Analysis In Its Practical Application."

This classic book has been in existence for almost ninety years. Yet, despite the fantastic progress in science and technology, not much has changed in understanding dreams.

In the first paragraph of the chapter, Jung writes that dream analysis in psychotherapy is still a much-debated question. However, many practitioners find it indispensable to treat neuroses and ascribe as much importance to the psychic activity manifested in dreams as to consciousness itself. Others, on the contrary, dispute the value of dream analysis and regard dreams as a negligible by-product of the psyche.

I thought that I had occasional yet infrequent dreams that were rarely detailed and vivid. But throughout life, like most people, I did not pay much attention to them. Indeed, I did not ascribe as much importance to my dreams as to my conscious life. Most of us tend to ignore and even deny the message of our dreams because our ego-consciousness naturally resists anything unconscious or unknown.

However, Jung urges us to teach ourselves to be receptive to dreams. And once again, synchronicity struck. The same yet different, universal yet unique principle appeared. Dreams are not only a direct, personal, and meaningful vehicle of communication, but they employ universal symbols common to all humanity.

It soon became apparent that I could no longer ignore this topic if I were to have integrity while leading *The Quest* live experience and writing this book. So, on June 24, 2020, as the Covid pandemic spread throughout the world, I decided to journal the details of every dream for six months.

Captain Jack Sparrow (the iconic hero of the *Pirates of the Caribbean* films) would be proud. It was a rollicking, eye-opening, and sensual adventure into the depths of the vast sea of my unconscious. The recurring dreams included falling elevators, airplane crashes, huge waves and tsunamis, weird flights, bathrooms, excrement, urine, religious trauma, lack of preparation, family reunions, hatred, breasts, penises, and sex.

The frequency and sheer magnitude of my dreams were a stunning revelation. During the six months, I filled a massive journal with handwritten entries. In all, I had 692 dreams in one hundred and eighty nights—*an average of four per night.*

I previously mentioned this was during the Covid pandemic. Because my wife is high-risk, we self-quarantined for almost two years, including the six months I recorded my dreams. We had physical encounters with less than twenty people during that time.

Yet, in my nightly dreams, in the same six-month period, I encountered 1252 different people. Astonishingly, I was able to identify most of them, and the majority were named. And this did not include groups over three, of which there were many. The total number of people in my dreams during those one hundred and eighty nights would be in the thousands.

Another revealing exercise was listing the people who reappeared numerous times. My current wife, former wife, daughters, and son-in-law were the most frequent. But there were also surprise return guests that helped make sense of several hidden or forgotten shipwrecks that my ego had repressed, suppressed, or denied. These people's past actions were causing distress and trauma in my conscious life. They were like festering splinters in my soul.

Jung says that dreams give information about the secrets of inner life and reveal hidden factors of one's personality to the dreamer. As long as they are undiscovered, they disturb our waking life and betray themselves only in the form of symptoms. In other words, what we don't know can and will hurt us. Our consciousness can be overwhelmed by the unconscious when repressions are excluded from life or misunderstood and depreciated.

Knowing my dreams triggered catharsis. They acted as purification instruments to purge unhealthy emotions and release tension, much of which I was unaware of. And once brought to light, the trauma began to heal. Amid the shipwrecks of my life, I discovered hidden treasure.

The six-month exercise revealed many valuable bits of help in recording dreams. After perusing various websites purporting expertise about the dream world, I found many seemed never to have journaled their dreams. The advice was impractical, useless, and at times ludicrous.

Following are a few guidelines for those who wish to pay attention to conscious life and the unconscious. Please know this requires dedication and effort, but the rewards are priceless.

- Determine to record your dreams in an organized manner suited to your style.
- Set a specific time frame, i.e., four weeks, six months, etc.
- Have a device next to the bed to write down significant points of dreams when you awake during the night, so as not to interrupt sleep any more than possible. You will be surprised how much you will remember the following day if you record the outline of a dream.
- Each morning upon waking, immediately go to a private place, where undisturbed you can meticulously write down your dreams. This journaling requires time, be sure to allow enough. Often, I spent over an hour recalling and writing dreams.
- Do nothing else first. I found that even taking time to brush my teeth, wash my face, or brew a cup of coffee caused me to forget important details, and at times, entire dreams. Go immediately to your private place before speaking to anyone and begin writing.

- If a family member or friend acts disinterested or bored, when you are recounting a dream, do not be disappointed. Dreams are highly individualized and often make little sense to others. It is nearly impossible to understand somebody else's dream well enough to interpret it correctly.

- Elements often occur in dreams that the dreamer cannot derive from personal experience. Freud called these "archaic remnants." Jung calls them archetypes. (See Symbols waypoint). They occur universally and come from the primitive mind and its mythological motifs— collective thought patterns of the human mind that are innate and inherited. Their names and labels mean little, but how they are *related* to you is all-important.

Recent events, people, places, and memories float slightly below the surface of our consciousness. And some of our dreams tend to reflect current thinking. That is why a long-term journal can help us take a deeper dive into the unconscious and aids in identifying recurring symbols and motifs (regular ideas, subjects, and themes.)

Universal (common) motifs include falling, flying, being persecuted by dangerous animals or hostile people, and being insufficiently or absurdly clothed in public places. Other motifs include being in a hurry or lost in a milling crowd, fighting with useless weapons, being wholly defenseless, and running hard yet getting nowhere. The motifs must be considered not on their own but in the dream context.

A journal helps gain insight into complex dreams such as lucid dreams (where one becomes aware they are dreaming and may even have some control). Other examples include nightmares, "supernatural," creative problem solving, and fantasy. In addition, the exercise of expressing these dreams in written form often proves illuminating and provides context.

Dreams are an integral and personal expression of our unconscious. And symbols are the language of dreams; so it behooves us to know as much about them as possible. Moreover, the knowledge of symbols will help us fluently interpret our dreams.

That is why a deep and broad understanding of symbols' past and present is vital. The dream language of symbols has much emotional energy, forcing us to pay attention to it. Furthermore, symbols always stand for more than their obvious and immediate meaning.

Jung felt that dreams are an invaluable source of information. He also believed that dreams are our most frequent and practical pathways to inner growth. Marsha Norman writes that "dreams are illustrations from the book your soul is writing about you."[139] If so, then how is one to interpret those pictures?

By far, the best interpreter of your dreams is you. A therapist, family member, or trusted friend cannot possibly know the contents and context of every event, person, place, or memory of your life. Therefore, one can not overemphasize the contextual aspect of dreams.

For me, reading through six months of dreams in one sitting was eye-opening. It provided an invaluable perspective of my unconscious. It also revealed several stunning surprises. It was like playing the role of detective in my private mystery novel, working to find clues to the secret and forgotten shipwrecks and treasures of my life.

There are many discoveries too personal to mention here. But one eureka-type finding was recognizing the correlation between several of my watercolor paintings and various dreams. I also felt compelled to paint several of the most vivid fantasies, nightmares, lucid, creative, and recurring images.

If this subject grips you—treasure awaits those who explore the many writings, mandalas, and drawings of Carl Jung. Here are a few final observations I gained from several careful readings of *Man and His Symbols*. It is difficult not to take dreams literally when they contain painful and personal subject matter. However, there is a huge benefit to other types of analysis.

It is unwise to believe in ready-made systematic guides to dream interpretation. Nevertheless, there are two fundamental points in dealing with dreams. First, the dream should be treated as a fact, about which one must make no previous assumption except that it somehow makes sense. Second, the dream is a specific expression of the unconscious.[140]

Unlike a waking story, a dream does not usually have a solid structure—beginning, development, and ending. Its dimensions in time and space are much different. To understand these types of dreams, one must examine them from every aspect. It is like taking an unknown object in your hands and turning it over and over until you are familiar with every detail of its shape.

Images that seem contradictory and ridiculous crowd in on the dreamer, the usual sense of time is lost, and commonplace things can assume a fascinating or threatening aspect. This confusion is one of the main reasons ordinary people find dreams hard to understand. In addition, we all have widely different social, political, religious, or psychological experiences, which compounds the difficulty of analysis.

Another factor is that we have stripped many ideas of their emotional energy in our modern civilized life. As a result, we do not recognize or respond to them anymore.

Thunder is no longer the voice of an angry god, nor is lightning his avenging missile. No river contains a spirit; no tree is the life principle of humanity, no snake the embodiment of wisdom, no mountain cave the home of a great demon. No voices now speak to humans from stones, plants, and animals, nor do humans talk to them, believing they can hear. Our contact with nature is gone and with it the profound emotional energy that this symbolic connection supplied.[141]

The symbols of our dreams compensate for this enormous loss. But unfortunately, when they express their contents in the language of nature, it is strange and incomprehensible to most of us. Therefore, we must reacquaint ourselves with natural phenomena—the phenomenology of things.

We are captivated and entangled with the frantic pace of life, and we have forgotten the age-old fact that the gods speak chiefly through dreams and visions. Jung says the Buddhist discards the world of unconscious fantasies as useless illusions. The Christian puts their church and their Bible between themself and the unconscious. And the rational intellectual does not yet know that their consciousness is not their total psyche.[142]

Therefore, this complex and unfamiliar part of our mind, which produces symbols, is still virtually unexplored. It seems incredible that though we receive signals from it every night, it seems too tedious for most people to decipher those communications.

If we are to complete our *Quest* and attain the holy grail, each of us must explore our unconscious and heal the split between it and the conscious. Only when we boldly travel the pathways between them and salvage the shipwrecks and treasure will the fragments become whole, and we will be able to enjoy life fully.

*****

The unconscious produces symbols—light and dark, beautiful and ugly, good and evil, profound and silly—which are meaningful to the individual. The *way they are related* to that person is all-important.

Rituals, therapy, psychedelics, and dreams function to restore psychological integration, or in a word, wholeness. Catharsis will come by recognizing that we cannot ignore our unconscious; it is as natural, as limitless, and as powerful as the stars.

Catharsis

Have You Completed Life Review and Repair?

Symbols of catharsis abound in mythology, nature, and dreams. Examples include the phoenix, dragon, winged horse, bird, two entwined serpents, and butterfly.

Pop culture gives us a powerful story of catharsis filled with symbolism in the television series *Game of Thrones*. Daenerys Targaryen places her wedding gift of three dragon eggs onto her husband Drogo's funeral pyre. Someone lights the wood when the first star, a red fire comet, is seen in the sky. Once it is entirely ablaze, Daenerys walks into the flames. The following day, when the fire dissipates, she is found naked and unharmed, kneeling amidst the ashes and holding three freshly-hatched dragons. She inherits a new name, "the Unburnt."

Mythology gives us yet another vivid symbol. The Egyptian phoenix was the size of an eagle, with brilliant scarlet, gold plumage, and a musical cry. As its death approached, the phoenix fashioned a nest of aromatic boughs and spices. Then, it lit a fire, and the flames consumed it. From the pyre miraculously sprang a new phoenix. After embalming its father's ashes in an egg of myrrh, it flew with the ashes to Heliopolis ("City of the Sun") in Egypt. It then deposited them on the altar in the temple of the Egyptian god of the sun, Re.

Catharsis (initiation) is both a unique process and a universal journey. Uniquely, it begins with a personal ritual of *submission* followed by a period of *containment, liberation, and transcendence.* Universally, as we see in the Transitions waypoint, the journey consists of a call to adventure, departure, initiation, and magic flight.

In *The Quest*, catharsis recognizes one's need for liberation from the shipwrecks of the first half of life. It concerns a moving beyond—or transcendence of—any confining pattern of existence as one progresses toward a superior or more enjoyable stage in life. It is a time of metamorphosis, a union of the consciousness with the unconscious contents of the mind. Out of this union, one can reach their highest goal; wholeness, the full realization of the potential of self.

To symbolize catharsis in the live experience of *The Quest*, we have a rite of initiation called the "circle of life." It begins with a fire ceremony at sunset, culminating in an extended silence until the next sunrise (submission). Then, in darkness, a shaman transports the initiate to an isolated place in the woods or on a mountaintop. Next, the participants create a circle with stones found on the land.

They enter the circle (a mandala) and must not leave it for any reason until the tip of the sun rises (containment). During the night, the initiate is encouraged to recall and relive the first two stages of life, the shipwrecks and the treasures, the healthy and unhealthy people, places, events, and memories. These moments will stay repressed unless they are adequately understood, dealt with, and translated into a new way of life.

The "circle of life" is a subliminal ritual time, and the central task is a life review. We will discover a practical tool to help conduct a review later in this waypoint. Reviewing our lives may include the struggle between constraint and freedom, the feminine and masculine, the dark and light, establishment and enjoyment, childishness and childlikeness, family and friends, others and self, excitement and contentment, fragmentation and integration, the past and the future, and goodness and wholeness. They are lifelong struggles that trouble us—yet we never take time to pay attention or reconcile them.

But there are answers. The initiation rites help us find solutions during the subliminal time between containment and liberation. Catharsis can make it possible for us to unite the opposing forces within us and achieve equilibrium, enjoyment, and wholeness in our lives.

But the rites do not offer this opportunity automatically. Only you can make the personal decision to begin, sustain, endure, and complete *The Quest* by following the template (map) of the universal arcs bequeathed by those who have preceded us.

When the tip of the sun appears, the initiate may step out of the circle (liberation). Often, they take a stone with them to commemorate the time. Discussion and assimilation follow while enjoying a hearty breakfast together.

The participant then departs into the post-liminal world and returns home, symbolically transitioning from the first half of life to the second. Then, ideally, they begin creating a new pattern of life (transcendence) by moving out of the Establishment stage into the Enjoyment stage.

The Enjoyment stage is a pivotal time when one decides what to do in the next stage of life—whether to work or play, stay home or travel, live in a new place, find a new companion, and more.

Suppose excitement, adventure, insecurity, or change filled one's first life. In that case, one may desire a second life of contentment and stability. But suppose one spent the first life conforming to institutional (family, church, social) demands. In that case, one may desperately need a liberating change.

This need may be filled temporarily by an affair, a trip around the world, or something as simple as downsizing. But these external changes will be temporary unless there is an inner transcendence, a moving beyond old values. Change comes from creating, not only beginning, a new pattern of life. The emphasis must focus on becoming a new person, not simply doing new things. This waypoint is yet another integral adventure along the epic journey of *The Quest*.

Catharsis is an emotional release that helps as we salvage unconscious conflicts. The term means "purification" or "cleansing." In psychology, catharsis involves a kind of emotional purge to restore our psychological balance.

It is an intense and intimate process that is often liberating. We *express* content that the ego has repressed and give it new meaning. We raise these shipwrecks, find any hidden treasure, incorporate them into our lives, and then transcend them. Freud defined catharsis as "the process by which we reduce or eliminate a conflict by activating it in the consciousness and allowing it to express itself."[143]

Practically, catharsis is an awareness of damaging people, places, memories, and events that operate below the surface of consciousness. Catharsis is the discharge of emotions (Affect) triggered by repressed traumatic events. We then relive our past (the purpose of the ritual during *The Quest*) and return the traumas to the consciousness to re-experience them and repair their negative or limiting influence.

Further, emotional catharsis helps us feel better by releasing unhealthy thoughts and feelings. It also leads to positive change in our self. Finally, emotional catharsis allows us to salvage, express, and integrate forgotten wounds (shipwrecks). These may include traumatic people, places, events, and memories that the ego buried deep in the unconscious using defense mechanisms such as repression, suppression, and denial.

We can experience catharsis in all four aspects of our being. For example, it contains a robust *physical* component such as crying, shivering, laughing. Next, the *mental* feature allows us to ask questions and acquire new knowledge or perspectives that help us leave behind emotional wounds. Then, there is a powerful *emotional* component as we express long-held repressed emotions.

Finally, there is a *spiritual* component as we experience freedom from the festering wounds of shipwrecks. Transcendence is a vital aspect of the catharsis quaternity. It takes place when lasting positive change occurs. How?

First, it occurs by accepting and expressing your feelings. We should welcome all emotions and feelings during catharsis. Avoid the idea that there are "negative" emotions one should not experience. It is vital to understand that all feelings are valid, and no matter how turbulent, they do not make you a weak person.

Therefore, do not try to repress or fight against those emotions. Instead, express them and connect with them so you can understand the message they convey. For example, sometimes behind anger lies deep sadness or the feeling of helplessness. Remember, you cannot resolve the conflict and experience catharsis if you disconnect from your emotions.

Second, find the methods of catharsis that work for you. For example, Dr. Thomas Scheff believes that the formula for triumphant catharsis is when the technique reawakens unresolved distress in everyday life. And the reawakening must occur in a sufficiently safe context so that the pain is not overwhelming.[144]

The Quest ritual, ceremony, and circle of life have proven transformative for most participants throughout the years. However, there have been three outside their comfort zone, and the distress was too much. These experiences helped me do a better job creating safe and individualized aspects of the ritual.

We are all unique. What can be cathartic for some is not for others. Therefore, one must find the emotional outlet that works best individually.

Despite popular thought, it is not always necessary or advisable to hit a pillow, throw a tantrum, get naked in a sweat lodge, or suffer extreme hardship. Instead, for some, keeping a therapeutic diary, utilizing art therapy, or any of the methods mentioned in the Unconscious waypoint can be ways to salvage your shipwrecks.

One technique that is vital to catharsis is a life review. Renowned gerontologist Robert Butler suggested that the purpose of life review is to recall unresolved conflicts and reconcile them through seeing a larger picture or reframing the events. It enables us to see the narrative arc of our lifetime. This review naturally leads to life repair—reconciliation with estranged loved ones, making amends and forgiving them, or forgiving ourselves. In the best case, it leads us to give up denial or blame and become accountable for the life we've lived.[145]

Connie Zweig provides invaluable advice on how to begin in her book *The Inner Work of Age*. First, find a private and quiet place. Then, draw a circular or horizontal line on ten different pages to represent ten decades of life. Next, recall the key events and people of those years for each decade. Finally, write them down above the arc of the circle or line, representing the realm of conscious awareness. To jog your memory, it may help to note the numbered years, beginning with your birth year.

For instance, from birth to age ten, what do you know of critical events, transitions, gains, and losses for your first decade? Who were the central people in your story, families, romances, and mentors? How did they influence you?

Taking your time, continue through each decade, remembering as much as you can about the forces that shaped you. What were your significant transitions in each decade? What insights did you gain coming out of the transitions? How did you grow, open your heart, and develop new awareness?

A key event may be a beginning or end, a gain or loss, success or failure, a birth or death, a rite of passage, a gift or trauma, reading a book, or a meeting with a remarkable person.

It is possible to do a life review for each aspect of your body, mind, soul, and spirit. Charting a physical timeline can open up new perspectives on affection, abuse, and health. A mental review can reveal seasons of curiosity and learning, a tendency for black and white thinking, receptivity, and close-mindedness.

An emotional review can uncover periods of deep grief and anxiety and times of contentment, satisfaction, and happiness. Finally, a spiritual review can show the transformation of your beliefs, values, and virtues. Other possible aspects include work-life, creative life, and romantic life.

The life review helps uncover our personal myth—as we look at the narrative arc of our life and compare it to mythic tales and universal journeys (see Transitions waypoint). It is fascinating to examine the life review and see which universal journey appears. It also helps one see recurring patterns or motifs.

In *The Inner Work of Age*, Ms. Zweig offers detailed guidance for conducting many life reviews, including a shadow review. One can write the dark sides below the arc of the circle or line. The ego and shadow typically develop opposite qualities. For example, your family may have discouraged dependency if they value independence. Linking the ego's story to the shadow's story in each decade can prove cathartic. It may be helpful to name the shadow character. A life review can be a portal to the holy grail.

Third, do not forget the four elements of catharsis. There is a *physical* release that generally has a solid bodily component. There is also a *cognitive* factor that involves mindful reflection on what happened. Furthermore, the *emotional* release has a powerful affective component. Finally, the *spiritual* release is one of freedom, euphoria, and afterglow. It is vital to experience all four aspects of catharsis.

Fourth, do not force your healing rhythm. Sometimes contents are hidden in the unconscious because we do not have the necessary psychological tools to face them. Bringing them to consciousness can prove extremely difficult. Again, Connie Zweig comes to our aid by practically outlining a life repair sequence. She provides insightful context for this practice in her book *The Inner Work of Age*.[146]

Life repair can help us salvage what has been repressed and banished in the unconscious. It helps us take responsibility for our choices, speak our truths, forgive ourselves and others, realign our values, and make meaning for the present.

Find a private and quiet place. Then choose an adult wound that you suffered at the hands of a parent, teacher, spouse, friend, child, mentor, or spiritual teacher and write down that story. Next, return to your life review and set this painful moment in the context of what followed. How did your life direction change from this event? Which doors opened, and which closed? Which people appeared, and which disappeared? What did you learn about yourself and others? How did it change you?

Contemplate these questions for emotional repair. Have your journal nearby.

- Do you have unfinished business with your parents? Siblings? Children? Partners or ex-partners? Friends?
- What goes unspoken or undone that will lead to regret?
- Which shadow character (small child, angry teen, disappointed young adult) stops you from forgiving others? What does it gain from holding on?
- Which shadow character prevents you from forgiving yourself?

With the closure of unfinished business to release the past, we can feel profound gratitude for how our lives unfolded with life repair. We can forgive, bless, and free people, memories, and feelings so that we can enjoy the second half of life and continue our *Quest*.[147]

Experiencing catharsis as therapeutic self-healing and self-acceptance means taking small steps each day. However, if the method proves overwhelming, don't hesitate to find professional help. A wise guide can accompany you and help safely process the information. In addition, trained and empathic psychologists understand the "surgical" process of catharsis and can administer "chemotherapy" when needed.

The following two waypoints further explore the liberation and transcendence stages of catharsis, as they relate to life's third and fourth stages. This portion of the journey brings our ultimate goal—the holy grail—into vivid focus.

Enjoyment

Are You Enjoying Your Self, Others, and the World?

The way of *The Quest* is often messy. We've explored the descent into the dark, inner wounds and conflicts, unhealthy Affect, and shipwrecks. However, in the final two waypoints, we get to the fun part of our journey, the climax and the afterglow. But, first, what does it mean to enjoy life?

True happiness comes from enjoying one's self, companions, community, and world. Moreover, a way to savor them best is the aspects of the enjoyment quaternity: integrating pleasure, strengths and essentials, healthy emotion, and gratification.

Maximizing these four aspects of life in ourselves, others, and the world is a simple but profound path to enjoyment. On average, what percentage of time do you feel pleasure, utilize your strengths, express healthy emotion, and experience gratification? To increase that percentage, we need to understand more about this quaternity, these four ways to enjoy life.

Pleasure

Religions denounce it, governments tax it, prudes deny it, education censors it, parents forbid it, and priests repress it. So if you manage people's pleasure, you'll control them.

Invariably, surrounding primary aspects of pleasure, there are institutional procedures about its enjoyment. Myriad rules and laws govern its existence and its cost. Moreover, authorities know pleasure spawns independence. And freedom is why the questions of who gets pleasure and who controls pleasure are always crucial.

The impulse to control pleasure is pervasive and carefully regulated even in the afterlife. The Islamic heaven permits sexual pleasure, while the Christian heaven does not. The existence of sensuality and the role of the body in the afterlife remain contentious issues of debate in various theologies.

However, there is little argument that one of the most significant purposes of life is to activate our reward systems. For example, nature has equipped virtually all healthy human beings with taste buds that respond positively to sweetness. Pleasure is universal. Yet, the myriad ways we experience it are unique. Believe it or not, some people say they do not like dessert.

Pleasures are as individual as we are. Jane likes chocolate, Dick savors cheese, and Harry drinks late harvest wine. Yet, pleasures are also universal, the satisfaction of biological needs. Consider the color, cloth, cut, and cost of one's clothing. So let's briefly consider a quaternity of pleasures.

Simple Pleasures—Me: Song of an indigo blue bunting, lavender, a minor third, a thunderstorm.

You:_____

Sensual Pleasures—Me: Hot stone massage, orgasm, snuggling, a long hot shower.

You:_____

Guilty Pleasures—Me: Erotic poems, masturbation, room service, an afternoon nap.

You:_____

Savory Pleasures—Me: Perfect pairings including merlot and chocolate, Royal Tokaji and blue cheese, cabernet sauvignon and filet mignon, milk and cookies.

You:_____

As you consider and write down *your* pleasures, what percentage of time do you feel pleasure in yourself, give pleasure to others, and find satisfaction in the world? How can you increase the amounts a little every day?

Exploring pleasure is so enjoyable. After all, it is the subtitle of our book. So let's examine six more ways to experience pleasure.

Variety

Over three hundred years ago, William Cowper first used the phrase "variety is the spice of life" in *The Task*. The aphorism has endured for a good reason. Doing different things and interacting with all sorts of people is a way to make life more enjoyable.

Experiencing new things, tasting fresh foods, meeting new people, and traveling to new lands heightens our pleasure. Nature wired our brain to notice and respond to recent events and disregard old ones. As a result, people who enjoy variety are fascinating to be around.

Surprising ourselves and others elicits pleasure. Dr. Martin Seligman suggests allocating five minutes each day to create a pleasing little surprise for yourself, your spouse, your children, or a friend. He lists doing simple things for others, like playing their favorite music when they arrive home or rubbing their back as they work on the computer.[148]

Savoring

When I hear this word, inevitably, it brings my close friend Melissa Greene to mind. Savoring life is one of her life mantras. And she truly epitomizes each of these aspects of pleasure. So it is no wonder everyone enjoys being around her.

A study tested thousands of college students and identified five strategies promoting savoring. Three should be obvious—sharing with others, memory-building, and self-congratulations.

Next is sharpening perceptions, that is, to focus on specific elements and block out others. For example, when listening to music, close your eyes.

The last technique is absorption; let yourself get immersed, and try not to think; instead, sense. Do not remind yourself of other things you should be doing, or wonder what comes next, or consider how you could improve the event.[149]

Basking

Gracefully receive praise and congratulations. My religious background propagated false humility and deflection to God when people gave me words of praise. It always felt disingenuous. There are few things more pleasant than receiving a sincere and well-deserved compliment. Don't deflect them or self-deprecate them—accept and bask in them.

Thanksgiving

Express gratitude for good fortune. This simple act permeates our being with pleasure. For example, every time I finish a long walk or run, I take a moment to whisper words of gratefulness. I think about the many people with health problems who would give anything to accomplish what I did.

Marveling

Lose the self in the wonder of the moment. Twirling shamelessly on the beach, throwing one's hands up in praise of a beautiful day, or reveling in the magic of a priceless moment.

Luxuriating

Indulge the senses. Enjoy a long, hot bubble bath, hike the forests or beach, sip a perfectly mixed cocktail, or relish a splendid post-coital "glow."

****

Pleasure is hard-wired into our deepest parts. The third stage of life should be characterized not by how well one works but by how well one plays. Pleasure should resonate more strongly in this period of life. Expect it, engage it, experience it, enjoy it.

Strengths and Essentials

In the Essentials waypoint, we identify the main characteristics of each aspect of our being. However, the four essentials do not comprise the total of one's power. *The Quest* is not a personality assessment that attempts to place you in a box of a limited number of traits. Our uniquenesses are many.

One of the first tasks on the enjoyment journey is the identification of personal strengths. For those of us who have never examined them, it is eye-opening. Around two decades ago, a breakthrough occurred in the social sciences. Researchers discovered a common language of twenty-four character strengths that make up personality.

Everyone possesses all the character strengths in different degrees; therefore each person has a unique character strength profile. We are indeed one-of-a-kind. The number of potential character strengths profiles is exponentially more than the number of people living on our planet.

Character strengths fall under six broad virtue categories: wisdom, courage, humanity, justice, temperance, and transcendence.[150] They are universal across cultures and nations and valued by moral philosophers and religious thinkers. Moreover, they are methods of solving essential tasks necessary for the species' survival.

There are practical assessments to help determine additional strengths, including one of my favorites, the VIA Survey of Character Strengths.[151] Once we discover our strengths and essentials, we must cultivate and use them. It stands to reason that when we live them out as frequently as possible, we have the opportunity to experience joy.

Let's choose to live, work, and play in our strengths each day. When we use them often, they grow more robust and flourish. Recall a story from your life when you used one of your strengths for good. Living in your strengths will energize and expand you; your weaknesses will drain and diminish you.

Dr. Seligman posits that the formula for a good life is using your strengths and essentials every day. In the main realms of your life, to bring abundant gratification and authentic happiness.

Some of the nagging questions that grow increasingly pressing as we transition to the second half of life concern the proper usage of our strengths. Does my work, family, religion, or parenting have to be this unsatisfying? What can I do about it? By applying our strengths and essentials, we should be able to reestablish these areas of life so that they are fulfilling and meaningful, and in a word, enjoyable.

It not only makes life more enjoyable, but it rejuvenates it into a calling. The word calling means satisfaction and *gratification* (which we explore later in this waypoint) in our daily journey. We live each day not because we have to, but because we want to—purpose and meaning override money and success.

When we sense an unusually intense period of satisfaction, we must pause for a moment and ask why. Inevitably, it is because we have been operating in a strength or an essential.

Recently I marveled to my wife about the exhilaration and contentment I felt after a day of doing nothing but reading. A weekday spent like this would have been unthinkable in my first half of life. But now, in the second half of life, it brings me hours of sheer joy and gratification—not fleeting moments of pleasure. Nevertheless, I must admit there were moments early on when I felt guilty.

But I discovered when I took the VIA Survey of Character Strengths that this deep satisfaction comes from activating two of my top four signature strengths. They are "the love of learning" and "being curious and interested in the world." It gave me inner assurance to know I was not wasting a day. On the contrary, I am recreating my first life "doing" ethic into a second life "being" ethic. And I am exponentially happier.

Furthermore, we can cultivate our strengths by sharing them with others. And even better, it is reciprocal. Studies show that people with a circle of social relationships live longer and happier. Psychologist David Myers says there are few stronger predictors of happiness than a close, nurturing, equitable, intimate, lifelong companionship with one's best friend.

Friendships and companionships flourish when they are regular vehicles for using our strengths and essentials. This "authentic self" is the image we hold when we realize and activate our highest strengths. When our friends and companions acknowledge this, we feel validated.

The happiest people focus on the positive aspect of relationships, focusing on strengths and not weaknesses. As a result, they are the most successful, most healthy, and least depressed. Optimism helps build better relationships. And when we use our unique strengths in the service of others, we become "one-of-a-kind" friends. Dr. Seligman says a significant part of what makes us invaluable to those we love is the profile of our strengths and the unique ways in which we express them.[152]

Today our world requires help more than at any time in history. I firmly believe that nature is also our reciprocal friend.

She gives much to humanity; now, it is time to utilize our strengths in her service.

Few speak to this subject more eloquently than Wendell Berry. He writes that the earth is what we all have in common. The care of the earth is our most ancient and most worthy, and our most pleasing responsibility after all. Berry concludes that to cherish what remains of it and foster its renewal is our only hope.

We can bring our strengths to conservation, restoration, and education activities. A few practical ways include:

- Driving less.
- Biking more.
- Volunteering.
- Conserving water.
- Helping educate.
- Advocating for sustainable resources.
- Supporting research.
- Donating to non-profit conservation organizations.
- Engaging with elected officials.
- Shopping wisely (i.e., less plastic and using reusable shopping bags).

We all have unique strengths to show love to the earth. So that our children, grandchildren, and future generations can enjoy the bountiful goodness of our beautiful world.

Healthy Emotions

We have talked a lot about emotion (Affect) in this book. Healthy and unhealthy Affect permeate everything we do. So it stands to reason that we can attain enjoyment in life by increasing our healthy emotions and decreasing our unhealthy ones.

For example, we explored the nine biological Affects in the Emotions waypoint. Of those, only two were positive. They are *interest-excitement* and *contentment-joy*. However, when we include the low and high ranges of these positive emotions, we have four possibilities, a quaternity of healthy Affect.

Interest

I love the word pique, but one rarely sees it in print. It means "to arouse an emotion or provoke action." As a verb, we can use it with or without an object. So first, let's use it with an object—*interest*. As in, what piques your *interest*?

The way of *The Quest* has prompted me to pay attention to things that spark my *interest*. In the Emotions waypoint, these are called triggers. A few triggers that pique my interest include mixology, historical fiction, foreign culture, beauty, art, and exotic lands.

It is entertaining to be even more specific. A more definitive list of those triggers would be cocktails with rye whiskey, any book by David McCullough, the Italian way of life, the female body, the artist Botticelli, and Greece. An even more exacting list would be a Sazerac cocktail, McCullough's book *Truman*, the passeggiata (a traditional evening stroll in an Italian plaza), the nude female body, the Botticelli painting *La Primavera*, and the island of Mykonos, Greece.

What about you? What piques your *interest*? Try this exercise. It is enjoyable. Make a list of some things that spark your interest. Then create a more definitive list. Finally, compose an exact list.

The simple act of typing these objects of *interest* triggers physical reactions. I sit up a little straighter, lean forward, and breathe a little faster. In other words, this list symbolizes things that pique my *interest*. So it seems apparent that I need to include more of them in the second half of my life.

Perhaps now, spend a few moments daydreaming and fantasizing about how to add more interesting people, places, and events to your life.

Excitement

When something includes multiple qualities that pique my *interest*, it triggers my *excitement*. For example, an *exciting* trip to Mykonos, Greece, would consist of mixology, foreign culture, beauty, art, and exotic lands. To be more specific, Greek spirits mixed with bitters, savoring a yogurt and olive dish, nude bodies at Paradise Beach, and touring the House of Cleopatra while visiting the nearby island of Delos. Composing this *exciting* list makes me long to travel there at once.

As we transition to the third stage of life, the triggers for *excitement* may change subtly. For example, planning a trip to Mykonos triggers my *excitement* in second life. Much more than the trips I made to Colorado during the first half of life while attempting solo summits of rugged fourteen-thousand-foot mountains. I have changed. And that is okay. Gradually, I am adapting to this new way of life and the different pathways to enjoyment.

Look for the opportunities that trigger multiple areas of *interest*, then wait to feel a tingle of *excitement*. Pay attention when your eyes start tracking. And when you are looking and listening intensely—face flushing. Moreover, your breathing is fast, accompanied by thoughts such as Yayyy! and Yippee!

When this happens, act on the event that caused those reactions. Creating additional times of *excitement* that are unique to you will add enjoyment to life.

Contentment

The synonyms for the word "contented" speak volumes. They include fulfilled, glad, happy, pleased, satisfied, serene, thankful, gratified, and comfortable. But unfortunately, many of these peaceful feelings cannot co-exist with the ongoing demands to succeed at all costs in the first half of life.

A friend, Daniel, once told me a memorable story about his parents. He and his wife have busy careers as successful dentists, they have two young children, are gourmands, and love to travel. They are in the epicenter of the rapid pace of first life.

One evening as we enjoyed a fabulous meal, the conversation turned to his mom and dad. Shaking his head in wonder, he waxed nostalgic, recounting memories of his parents in their first life. Then, they were always busy with their jobs and the endless tasks of life. But now, he continued, they sit on their back porch watching the wildlife.

He told of going home and the conflicting emotions he felt as his dad, an electrician, was able to name the many birds that perched on their feeders. His mom would gladly talk of the new animal sightings all evening. Their new appreciation of serenity, comfort, and happiness, although surprising, was undeniable.

A typical person in first life might think they sit on the back porch birdwatching because they are old now. But perhaps there is something more to this story. If finances and time had allowed, I wonder if they would have begun a closer observation of nature at a far younger age.

Only a short time later, Daniel's father died of illness. I can only imagine the priceless memories that his mom treasures of those happy and serene times together on the back porch. In second life, they had discovered an invaluable truth. An example that we all would do well to remember.

When you are discontent, you always want more, more, more. Your desire can never be satisfied. But when you practice *contentment*, you can say to yourself, "oh yes—I already have everything that I need."

When we are in a calm state of *contentment*, the physical manifestations include a mellow voice, graceful movement, and a relaxed walk and posture. Also, there is the mental manifestation of creativity; ideas will float in and out of mind quickly. *Contentment* is a precursor to the concept of *flow*, which we will explore soon in the gratification section.

Joy

First, it is important to note that this biological emotion, this Affect, is different from the conventional idea of happiness. Nathanson uses a 19th-century proverb found in a medical dictionary to convey the concept of *joy* Affect. "*Omne animalium languo post coitum*—all animals are calmed after intercourse."

This relief, the feeling of 'all is right in the world,' occurs after the orgasmic release. Technically, the *reduction* in stimulus level accompanying the ease of any high-density experience will trigger the smiling face of *joy* Affect.

The tears streaming down my face during the psychedelic trip (described in the Unconscious waypoint) while saying, "it's okay, everything is okay," was *joy* Affect. That is why we have the term 'tears of *joy*.' The immense relief and reduction of the *shame* that surrounded my religious upbringing, *fear* of eternal punishment, and *guilt* from past mistakes triggered a biological response of *joy* like few times in my life.

Joy Affect has an intriguing relationship with another aspect of healthy emotion—*pride*. Unfortunately, those with Christian childhoods may inevitably default to the harmful indoctrination that *pride* precedes a fall. And while some undoubtedly possess an unhealthy amount or type of *pride*, there is nothing wrong with a proud feeling of accomplishment.

A childlike response of *pride* can easily be seen all over a three or four-month-old infant's face when they receive praise for accomplishing a task. Imagine how much more we could salvage the treasures of childlike wonder if we gradually undo our institutional brainwashing and accept heartfelt praise.

Furthermore, we can experience both *pride* and *joy* as we reflect on the accomplishments of our first half of life. For most of us, our children are grown and have a home and family around this time. In addition, we are approaching retirement, and we hopefully have financial stability.

Reflecting on our life achievements should trigger the *contentment-joy* Affect. Like a baby's sheer *joy* and *pride* when taking their first steps into the first half of life, we should joyfully manage the first steps into the second half of life.

Therefore, let's raise our hands and pump our arms in triumph. We have survived the first half of life. We have the T-shirt. Integrating healthy emotions gives us the flexibility to adapt to the changes that will inevitably come with aging.

Technically speaking, we finally have a much-deserved reduction of stimulus levels from the high-density experience of the development and establishment stages. Now, all the unique adventures of the second life await us. Whatever that means for you—birdwatching, traveling, golfing, writing, reading, partying, surfing, mountain climbing, or laying on the beach until you look like a raisin. *Be and do* what triggers your *joy* Affect.

Gratification

Identifying and cultivating pleasure, healthy emotion, strengths, and essentials, and gratifications consistently are sure pathways to enjoyment in life. Yet, at first blush, gratifications are challenging to distinguish from pleasures.

But there is a crucial and life-altering difference. The pleasures are about the senses (body) and the emotions (soul). However, gratifications are about enacting personal strengths (mind) and virtues (spirit). So, for example, there is the physical delight of enjoying ice cream and the emotional bliss of making love. Contrast that to the mental gratification of creating art and the spiritual fulfillment of serving a meal to the homeless.

Let's examine the psychological components of gratification.[153]

- The task is challenging and requires skill
- Concentration
- Clear goals
- Immediate feedback
- Deep, effortless involvement
- A sense of control
- Sense of self vanishes
- Time stops

The last two psychological components in the list are particularly noteworthy. First, recall that the conscious aspects of self are ego and persona. When they dissolve (like during a psychedelics trip), it alters the control of one's trajectory. As a result, an intense state of enjoyment is possible. This type of gratification is also called *flow*. This concept is introduced in the Unconscious waypoint while exploring therapy as a communication vehicle.

Flow suspends consciousness when we are absorbed. Time seems to stop. A high level of gratification occurs when we utilize our strengths and essentials in an activity with a noble purpose more significant than our self.

The purposeful increase of gratification and flow will make our lives, the lives of others, and the life of our world a better place. It can be as simple as choosing the gratification of reading a good book rather than the perceived pleasure of surfing social networks or mindlessly watching a sitcom.

Surveys repeatedly show that habitually consuming social networks and sitcoms lead to depression. Likewise, a lifestyle of choosing easy pleasures over the more challenging gratification tasks may have unhealthy consequences. There are few shortcuts to enjoyment.

Depression has been growing in every affluent country across the globe. As nations become wealthier, they have access to shortcuts to pleasure. Television, addictive drugs, social media, empty sex, and spectator sports are a few examples. But unfortunately, these shortcuts lead to self-absorption.

At the age of twenty-eight, I moved from rural Tennessee to the melting pot of South Florida. Soon after, I met Marvin "Bunny" Jensen, who was fifty years my senior. He was from the south side of Chicago and had a big personality to prove it. Sporting a crewcut, substantial paunch, slurred speech, and limp from a stroke, he was legendary for still being able to shoot his age in golf.

Bunny had retired from the highly successful furniture and moving company he had founded and led for many decades. He bought a modest home at a golf resort upon relocating to sunny Florida. He played golf for over one hundred days straight. But he eventually was bored and depressed. Subsequently, he started a tiny furniture store near a strip mall. The business grew, and he soon added a small moving company.

When I met him, I worked a demanding job, attended college full-time, and managed a family, including two little ones. Someone had suggested his store as the most economical way to furnish my girls' nursery. We immediately hit it off.

Hearing my story, he exclaimed that I was working too much and promptly invited me to a complimentary round of golf. It was a blast. Later we savored lunch at his country club (also his treat). I learned that the furniture and moving business, which had been such a chore in Chicago, was now one of the most enjoyable things of his life.

He took me back to the store and helped me pick out baby furniture. I would never have been able to purchase the pieces he chose. But he insisted on selling them to me for ninety percent off and delivered them for free. Over the years, I watched him provide countless people down on their luck with beautiful furniture, complimentary rounds of golf, and help with moving.

The endless rounds of golf when he first moved to Florida had brought him temporary (and much-needed) pleasure. But it was the ability to help others that brought him gratification and lasting enjoyment. He was one of the most pleasant men I've ever known and a joy to be around.

Using his strengths of kindness, creativity, and honesty in a noble way alleviated his depression and replaced it with meaning and enjoyment. His story is a perfect example of an integrated life of pleasure, healthy emotion, strengths and essentials, and gratification.

****

Integration is crucial for this portion of *The Quest*. The key to becoming whole is dissolving the lines between body, mind, soul, and spirit. Further, integration implies merging the unconscious with the conscious. Finally, wholeness requires the dissolution of ego, persona, shadow, and gender through practices such as mindfulness, life review, and life repair.

However, many institutions of the world, particularly religion, split our being. They say the body and mind are profane; therefore, we should deny them. Furthermore, dogma says that only the soul and spirit are sacred and redeemed. But *The Quest* posits that all four aspects of our being are excellent and essential to wholeness.

When life institutions fragment us, we become less than who we are. That brokenness results in our deepest longings and desires being repressed, suppressed, denied, and projected. But a key to enjoyment in life is integrating all the aspects of who we are.

The subjects we've explored in this waypoint are proven pathways to enjoyment. And now, as we contemplate utilizing them in service to something greater than ourselves, let's travel to our ultimate destination.

To prepare, let's consider the following questions.

- Is it possible to enjoy aging?
- Can our life still have a noble purpose?
- Can our lives have meaning that transcends our past?
- What is enlightenment?
- Am I prepared for the afterlife?

The way of *The Quest* now comes into sharper focus. We've explored symbols, essentials, transitions, stages of life, emotion, consciousness, the unconscious, catharsis, and enjoyment. Finally, at the next waypoint, we arrive at the ultimate goal of our journey, the holy grail of enlightenment.

Enlightenment

Have You Done Shadow and Mortality Work?

There are many definitions for the word enlightenment. For example, Buddhists believe it is a final blessed state marked by the absence of desire or suffering. Another explanation is to free our self from ignorance and misinformation. Furthermore, to add to the confusion surrounding the word, it was a philosophical movement of the 18th century that rejected traditional social, religious, and political ideas and emphasized rationalism.[154] However, for *The Quest*, our definition encompasses the state of cultivating the knowledge and understanding of being.

Most of us approach life's final stage as an afterthought instead of exploring its potential to be the most enjoyable time of our life. Elderhood is the fourth act, and what it will look like is up to us. In *The Quest*, this waypoint is the ultimate destination. The holy grail of enlightenment is not becoming good or perfect but becoming whole. Ideally, elderhood is that period of life when a person is clear about who they are and what they value. As a result, they possess a quality of innocence reconciled to experience.

Let's talk about life after age seventy-five. The second-class citizenship of older adults is entrenched and systematic in our culture. Most Americans view old age as an unsavory time and fail to acknowledge its great pleasures adequately.

"Aging," writes the Pulitzer Prize-winning geriatrician Robert Butler, "is the neglected stepchild of the human life cycle." However, barring an early death, the elderhood stage is every person's ultimate destination.

Westerners do not understand how well this stage can (and often does) go. It offers decades with new opportunities for contentment, learning, and contributing. Perhaps it is because the effects of age are visible in even the healthiest older adults that we try to ignore it. Despite clear evidence of its myriad joys and endless variety, we reduce the final stage of life to a single, dreaded state.

Dr. Louise Aronson is a practicing geriatrician and Harvard Medical School graduate. She distills many enlightened thoughts in her Pulitzer Prize-nominated book *Elderhood: Redefining Aging, Transforming Medicine, Reimagining Life.* I consider it one of the most insightful books of my second life.

It is ironic that although almost one in six of us is old, aging remains the subject of cultural jokes and fears. For example, in one passage, she lists a few common insults for old people: biddy, blue-hair, codger, crone, geezer, goat (older man with a sexual interest in women), has-been, old bag, old fart, old fogey, old-timer, and over-the-hill.[155]

These words ridicule and reduce human beings who possess vast quantities of wisdom and experience. Moreover, they widen the gulf of interdependence between age groups. It is ironic that although almost *one in six of us is old*, aging remains the subject of cultural jokes and fears.

Aronson writes that we fail to properly consider the positives of advanced age that accompany most years of this stage of life: the decreases in stress and hurry and the increases in contentment and wisdom. Unprecedented numbers of us in old age will be doing many of the same things younger people do, though sometimes in different ways. In addition, there will be many opportunities that weren't possible during our more demanding life stages.

Studies show that older adults surpass younger adults on all positive measures by the later sixties or early seventies. They exhibit less stress, depression, worry, and anger and more enjoyment, happiness, and satisfaction.

In these and similar studies, people between sixty-five and seventy-nine years old report the highest average levels of personal well-being, followed by those over eighty, and then those who are eighteen to twenty-one years old.[156]

Ironically, it's those who are in the second and third stages, generally thought to have the most power and influence in culture, who are the unhappiest and the least satisfied among us. It may not be a coincidence, then, that this is the group most responsible for the nearly ubiquitous false messages about old age.

Therefore, as in the transition between first and second adulthood (mid-life), our identity can once again feel challenged. But if we are lucky, many of these years will resemble the best parts of midlife. We will experience a more solid sense of who we are and have more say about how we spend our time.

The complex reality reveals that elderhood will probably be one of the most extended and most exciting periods of our lives. This stage now lasts longer and includes many more healthy years than our forefathers. As a result, there are more elders alive today than at any time in human history.

The number of centenarians (over one hundred years old) and supercentenarians (aged 110 or more) grows steadily worldwide. If we are lucky enough to join that club one day, we'll need a robust retirement fund, a plan, and a purpose.

I recently (at age sixty-three) took the Living To 100 longevity assessment[157] and was stunned to find it estimates I will live to be 101. That means thirty-eight more years of life. So that is *four additional decades of life*.

As I struggled for perspective, I quickly did the math. Thirty-eight years ago, I was a young man of twenty-five, entering the transition to first adulthood. It took a moment to place my life's various themes in context and realize I could have so much life remaining.

If that calculator is correct, I want to live fully the essentials and strengths of who I am. But moreover, I want to use that additional time for generosity and encouragement of others and to experience wholeness and thus a profound sense of life satisfaction. That is why in the way of *The Quest*, we call this the enlightenment stage.

The goal of the previous nine waypoints now comes into focus. We understand that our symbols are communication tools. They help us identify and live out our essentials. We need to recognize which stage of life we are in. Next, we must navigate the universal journeys of transitions, regulate our emotions, and move the contents from the depths of our unconscious to the freedom and clarity of our conscious. Finally, we must experience catharsis to embrace enjoyment fully.

This integration of our being (body, mind, soul, and spirit) is a way to the holy grail of enlightenment, in a word, wholeness. It transcends the disappointments, challenges, victories, and suffering of first life into the contentment and joy of fully being who we are.

Our previous seventy or more years of experience and the themes of our life become sources of meaning and reflection that have the power to render us ageless. We should know what matters when we successfully reach the waypoint and stage of enlightenment.

The ultimate aim of *The Quest* is to discover a way to accept, integrate, and cultivate the diverse experiences of a lifetime. We don't have to be like the ninety-one-year-old woman when asked about her life story. She responded, "I'd enjoy talking with you but between the things I've forgotten, the things I've repressed, and the things I will not discuss, there's not much left."[158]

What, then, is a healthy approach to old age? There are many positive aspects of our fourth stage beyond not being dead. Enjoyment. Contentment. Clarity of self. Less need for external validation. Newfound freedoms. And a clearer sense of meaning.

Life satisfaction studies in wealthy English-speaking countries show marked increases in enjoyment during old age despite rampant ageism. Imagine the added satisfaction of aging in a community that doesn't ignore or demean older people.

The quaternity of enlightenment is physiological (body), philosophical (mind), psychological (soul), and cosmological (spirit). To attain the holy grail of *The Quest,* we seek to integrate the four aspects of our being into a cohesive oneness —in short, wholeness. Let's explore this waypoint further.

Physiological (A Resilient Body)

At this stage of life, the body increasingly calls the shots. Objectively, it is what most people respond to, and subjectively, it limits what the self can do. A resilient elder overcomes the tendency to look at old age and only see a bodily decline. They understand that inside the body is a fellow human being.

Aging has now become a marathon. Therefore, it behooves us to take care of our bodies in the best way possible. Dr. Aronson believes that a person should have a specialist for each of the four major life stages: first a pediatrician, the next two an internist, and then a geriatrician.

You may not be familiar with the last term. Only a few thousand geriatricians are practicing in the United States. The best ones know that it's not only about the person or their diseases. It's also about their care and what other factors (besides the usual medicine and doctors) might promote their health and well-being. Keeping people healthy and out of the hospital is among their primary goals.

Consider these staggering statistics from her book *Elderhood*. Over forty-million Americans are sixty-five years old or older. A group accustomed to active, engaged lives with considerable financial power. Eleven million Americans—the fastest-growing population segment—are over age eighty.[159]

Dr. Aronson writes that a person's attitude about oldness doesn't simply affect how they feel about growing or being old. It affects their health, how they spend their time, and how long they live. Preventive health measures improve health at all ages, yet older adults are the age group least likely to engage in them.

Beliefs about aging are self-fulfilling prophecies. Our health and well-being in old age often become what we imagine they will be, whether what we imagine is good or bad. Biology matters, but it's only one part of a far more complex equation that includes attitude, behaviors, relationships, and culture.

She continues, that's a terrifying thought in a culture where ageism is more common than sexism or racism. Most people of all ages see old age through a window rendered dark and dirty by negative stereotypes.

Putting philosophical explorations of rampant ageism aside, we must proactively and creatively grow and seek the proper support to meet the physical challenges of the fourth stage of life. Some of us are doing this. Most are not. Could it be that much of the lack of enjoyment and enlightenment in old age is caused by little forethought or strategy about physical health and medical care?

Our culture rarely considers what older people need or want. To better enjoy this stage of life, we must make careful considerations. For example, each would have one or more kind and competent human caregivers in an enlightened and perfect world. They would help support our physical, mental, emotional, and spiritual needs as we age.

Aging has changed quickly in recent years, yet our language and institutions that "support" the years of life after age fifty haven't caught up. Our senators and representatives deprive constituents of health care coverage while continuing their own extra-special congressional health benefits. Many doctors and healthcare professionals display systemic ageism and behave as if they believe that older people get what they deserve.

Dr. Aronson says, follow the money and hype in medicine, and unfortunately, you will find that in the United States, we prefer treatment to prevention. Bones matter more to us than children or older people. And the patient's benefit is not a prerequisite for treatments or procedures. Unfortunately, the American healthcare system believes that drugs work better than exercise, that doctors treat computers, not people, that death is avoidable with the proper care, and that hospitals are the best place to be sick.

We must thoughtfully choose what essential aspects make the whole of our physical being and promote resilience—our health, activity, and engagement. They should not be determined by our doctors, children, or friends. Instead, we must ask ourselves these vital questions and allocate the time to decide and make damn sure we (and those who care for us) know the answers.

Ageless elders experience and exemplify resilience in themselves, their companions, their community, and the world. They realize that the body is but one aspect of wholeness.

Philosophical (A Serene Mind)

As elders on *The Quest*, we must cultivate the mind, in other words, expand our consciousness. One way to grow is by coming to terms with our shadow. By confronting our shadow, we learn to dissolve the ego further and ultimately discover the serenity of knowing our place in the world.

Self-confrontation and self-reformation are crucial if we desire to become elders and grow wise with age, and not become stuck and bitter. Furthermore, by learning to integrate and cultivate the shadow, we can forgive ourselves for human imperfections.

As we began our exploration of the unconscious, I mentioned that we have almost no training for exploring our depths. Fortunately, Dr. Connie Zweig has invested her life developing what she calls *shadow-work*.[160]

She says the shadow is that part of us that lies beneath or behind the light of awareness. It contains our rejected and unacceptable traits and feelings. However, it also includes hidden gifts and talents that have remained unexpressed or unlived. As Jung put it, the essence of the shadow is pure gold.

A vital question Zweig poses is this. "What is it like internally to make a shift from an unconscious senior, living in denial, to a conscious elder, living with deep awareness and sharing one's gifts?"

She raises a profound and enlightening question. The answer provides an emerging sense of becoming who one was always meant to be, and profound gratitude for how one's life unfolded. It also creates a quieter mind, which gives us space from negative emotions about aging and death.

Zweig provides contemplative exercises in her remarkable book, *The Inner Work of Age*. She calls them shadow-work practices that move one's attention into unfamiliar, and at times, uncomfortable territory. Yet she gently asks us to heed the poet Ranier Maria Rilke's instruction to "live our questions now."[161]

We learn how our mind operates with these practices. And how to observe our shadow characters (such as the inner critic, doer, victim, provider, inner ageist) instead of obeying them. With more profound practice, she says, we can let go of our past roles and beliefs about ourselves, expand our identity to something more significant, and move into a new stage of awareness.

Shadow-work helps us drop our conditioned personas, chronic fears, and automatic reactions. It allows us to choose to be fully real, transparent, and free, perhaps for the first time in our life.

We must begin to examine the unconscious issues beneath our feelings. They block our ability to let go of the ego's self-image and release the establishment stage values of success and productivity. Shadow-work is a vehicle for slowing down, reorienting to the inner world, watching the breath, being fully present, and learning to witness the internal obstacles as they arise.

Dr. Zweig has a natural gift of teaching. She combines techniques such as meditation, journaling, and dream analysis with reflective questions that address the issues of retirement, ageism, awareness, illness, changing roles, and life completion. The book also includes an invaluable shadow-work handbook that outlines her step-by-step process.

I have made these practices a vital part of my *Quest*. They have provided additional communication vehicles to confront the dark and light sides of myself. The uncomfortable work with the dark places has resulted in serenity gained by acknowledging and releasing them. It cultivates the discovery of lost treasure in my shadow that ego had relegated to the depths of my unconscious. Shadow-work has proven priceless as I continue my journey to elderhood.

Cultivating the mind by incorporating reflective practices such as shadow-work, meditation, journaling, and connecting with dreams comes naturally to those who are introspective. Yet, I believe extroverts can also learn these techniques to salvage the treasures within and expand consciousness. And in the fast, furious, and loud times we live, who of us does not want to cultivate a quieter mind?

Mindful elders experience and exemplify serenity in themselves, their companions, their community, and the world. The body and mind comprise our material substance. Now we move to integrate further by cultivating the emotional and spiritual aspects.

Psychological (An Equanimous Soul)

If you think equanimous looks like it has something to do with equal, you've guessed correctly. The word comes from the Latin phrase *aequo animo*, which means "with even mind." The word quickly evolved to suggest keeping a level head under any pressure. Eventually, it described an extended sense of general balance and harmony.[162]

The original meaning has enormous implications for the last stage of *The Quest*. I heard ministers expound on the crucial importance of balance all my life. But once I moved to a wilderness retreat and lived for several months in a leaning recreational vehicle teetering on blocks, it forever impressed upon me the foundational importance of being level.

Learning this principle the hard way inspired me to take meticulous care to ensure my mountain cabin's floor was perfectly level. One can be perfectly balanced, but it is hard to stay upright if no level surface exists. I was vindicated about my distaste for the word balance when reading these words by David Whyte, one of my favorite poets and thinkers. He said, "poets have never used the word balance, for good reason. First of all, it is too obvious and therefore untrustworthy; it is also a deadly boring concept and seems to speak as much to being stuck and immovable, as much as to harmony."[163]

Buddhism teaches that one approach to developing equanimity is cultivating the practices of the mind that support it. Thus, it comes together in mindfulness and meditation practice. Almost all of our spiritual traditions advocate times of seclusion or withdrawal as a first step.

Furthermore, equanimity is an inner strength that keeps our soul, the seat of emotions, level in the middle of all that is unbalanced. It gives us the power to be equal to difficulties and large enough for the drama of life.

Script Work

Another approach to developing equanimity is practicing what I call *script work*. In the Emotions waypoint, we explored the four aspects of Affect—trigger, emotion, script, and mood. It is tough to change our triggers. And we know our emotions (Affect) are innate and universal. However, we can all do the work of rewriting our unique scripts.

For example, I have gradually lost my hearing over the years. There are times during my walks when a cyclist (usually an inexperienced tourist) will whiz uncomfortably close by me without warning. Because tourists don't know the proper etiquette of the trail, they do not announce they are coming up on my left. Because I cannot hear their approach until they are within a hair-breadth away, it triggers my *surprise-startle* Affect.

My first-life script sounds something like a loud "fuck!" or worse, "fuck you!" One could not characterize this response as levelheaded. At times, it has led to mutual hostility and ill-will.

Happily, during my years-long research writing this book, I discovered it is possible to rewrite our scripts to promote equanimity. So while the ill-mannered cyclist still triggers my *surprise-startle* Affect, my revised script sounds more like "oh wow!"

It is fascinating how a simple script edit drastically changes the resulting mood. Instead of subsequent triggers of *anger* and *anxiety*, the new script leads to an air of exasperation that dissipates quickly and is far more healthy and conducive to the continuance of an enjoyable walk.

As we discover which emotions are healthy and unhealthy for us, it becomes obvious which scripts need work. Often, it is a simple edit, while knowing it may take some time to make it routine. Intentional script work promotes equanimity. And who doesn't want to spend time with a person who is "abundant, exalted, immeasurable, without hostility and ill-will." That sure sounds like qualities of an enlightened elder to me.

Cosmological (A Transcendent Spirit)

Let's first look at the meaning of these two rarely used words—cosmological and transcendent. Most religions and cultures include some kind of cosmology to explain the nature of the universe. In modern astronomy, the leading cosmology is still the Big Bang theory, which claims that the universe began with a massive explosion that sent matter and energy spreading out in all directions. One reason fans watch *Star Trek* is for the various cosmologies depicted in the show, including different conceptions of space, time, and the meaning of life.[164]

The word transcendent derives from the Latin verb "to climb" or "move beyond." Transcendence has the basic meaning of climbing so high that one crosses some boundary. A transcendent experience takes us out of ourselves and convinces us of a more meaningful life or existence. In this sense, it means something close to "spiritual."

The American writers and thinkers known as the Transcendentalists, including Ralph Waldo Emerson and Henry David Thoreau, believed in the unity of all creation, the essential goodness of humankind, and the superiority of spiritual vision over mere logic. When we speak of the transcendent importance of an issue such as climate change, we may mean that everything else on earth depends on it.[165]

Both words, cosmological and transcendent, are often erroneously thought to have only religious connotations. However, the life-altering book, *From Age-Ing to Sage-Ing: A Revolutionary Approach to Growing Older* by Zalman Shalomi and Ronald S. Miller, provides invaluable guidance for cultivating a cosmological (spiritual) vision of elderhood—with or without religion. The authors posit humanity's crucial need for transcendent elders—enlightened ones they call sages.

Sage Work

Let's take the first steps into the largely unexplored region of enlightened eldering. It is the culminating stage of *The Quest* and a way to a more fulfilling old age. Aging does not need to mean diminishment or exile from the living ranks. On the contrary, we have now reached the pinnacle of our journey, which provides a panoramic view of life. We have explored ways to cultivate resilience, serenity, and equanimity. Now, ultimately, we cultivate transcendence.

We finally have time to contemplate our life review and identify the motifs (significant objects of interest or concern) that have given our life more profound meaning. As each life is unique, so are our themes. We formulate themes by interpreting our journey's events, experiences, conditions, and priorities. A thoughtful life review helps us make connections and draw conclusions. In this way, we come to know ourselves and explain who we are to others.

Therefore, life themes are the building blocks of spiritual identity in this context. Contextualizing the significance of experience and events and our current understanding of meaningful symbols is foundational to cultivating enlightened elderhood, that is, becoming a sage.

Shalomi and Miller beautifully describe the traits of a sage. They are wisdom-keepers who have an ongoing responsibility for maintaining culture's well-being and safeguarding the health of our ailing planet earth.

They are pioneers in consciousness who practice contemplative arts from our spiritual traditions to open up greater intelligence for their late-life vocations. They use tools for inner growth, such as meditation, journal writing, life review, life repair, and mortality work. As a result, elders come to terms with their mortality, harvest the wisdom of their years, and transmit a legacy to future generations.

Serving as mentors, they pass on the distilled essence of their life experience to others. The joy of passing on wisdom to younger people not only seeds the future but crowns an elder's life with worth and nobility. Sage-ing is a process that enables older people to become physically vital, mentally curious, emotionally stable, and spiritually radiant elders.[166]

Transcendence of Aging Paradigm

For many Westerners, the traditional view of the fourth stage of life is negative. It looks at old age as an unpleasant and unrelenting decline of all that is joyous and full in life. However, Dr. Barry Barkan, a gerontologist, looks at aging differently.

He describes an enlightened elder, a sage, as a person who is still growing, still a learner, still with potential, and whose life continues to have promise for and connection to the future. Elders are still pursuing happiness, joy, and pleasure and have the same rights as young people.

Moreover, an elder is a person who deserves respect and honor and whose work is to synthesize wisdom from life-long experience and formulate this into a legacy for future generations. Therefore, sages refuse to follow the well-trodden path marked "aging."[167]

Instead, they are pioneers and heralds blazing new and unmarked paths that lead to new frontiers and the promise of an exciting and fulfilling late life. In the words of philosopher Jean Houston, "they are lured by the prospect of becoming harbingers of the possible human."[168] These elders refute the notion that older people are close-minded, set in their ways, slow, and often senile. They are no longer "old dogs who can't learn new tricks."

However, a word of clarification is necessary here. This elderhood concept differs from the "successful aging" paradigm that stresses extending middle-age values and preoccupations into late life. This approach prioritizes activity in later life, a process that Connie Goldman, a specialist in aging issues and author of *The Ageless Spirit*, playfully calls "aerobic grandparenting." [169]

Instead of feeling rested and whole in old age, she says aerobic grandparents feel compelled to be as busy, active, and involved as they were in middle age. Conversely, those elders who prefer to sit quietly, plant a garden, meditate, or walk on the beach can quickly feel like failures if they aren't exhausted in a frenzy of activity.

Instead of lamenting the passing of the third stage of life, why not accept and explore where we are. And resist the temptation to take heroic measures to conform to earlier images of optimal functioning. The more we reject old age, the less opportunity we have to mine its physical, intellectual, emotional, and spiritual issues.

A better and emerging term seems to be "conscious aging." All of humanity stands to benefit from the elders who accept the mantle of sage—who transcend and go beyond the archaic Western paradigm of aging.

Transcendence of Wisdom

Sages look upon aging as a developmental process whose goal is cultivation—an ever-widening expansion—of consciousness and a growing sense of the unity of life. They use growth tools such as meditation, relaxation techniques, and breathing exercises to transcend the world's wisdom.[170]

They also draw from the techniques developed by neurologists, such as integration of both sides of the brain, journal writing, and memory enhancement—resources that grow our mental essentials. Enlightened elders exhibit the quaternity of consciousness. They are awake, aware, attentive, and growing.

After age seventy-five, there is less becoming and more being. There is no longer a need for socially required identities or acquiring positions of social status. Despite current medical literature, many researchers have found that meaning in late life does not come from continuing earlier roles. Nor does it come from creating new roles in later life.

There is no longer a need to be perceived as wise. An enlightened elder *is* wise. The self draws meaning from past themes. It interprets and recreates over seventy-five years of experience as a resource for being in the present. The enlightened elder serves as an interpreter of experience.

Sharon Kaufman writes that one's unique symbols reveal an elder's identity.[171] These usually appear in images, fantasies, dreams, and times of altered consciousness. Enlightened elders do not allow identity to become frozen in a static moment of the past; symbols change as growth occurs.

They formulate and reformulate personal and cultural symbols to create a meaningful, coherent sense of self. And by living consciously, the wise sage emerges.

Connie Zweig sums it up beautifully. The sage experiences newfound freedom from the constraints of past roles and identities, an emerging sense of becoming who you were always meant to be, and profound gratitude for the way that life unfolded. As we make this internal shift in awareness, she continues that natural generosity arises within us. We seek to share our gifts of wisdom as a lasting legacy. [172]

Transcendence of Legacy

To begin the transcendence of legacy, Shalomi and Miller recommend a practice they call harvesting your life.[173] It involves bringing one's earthly journey to successful completion, enjoying the contributions one has made, and passing on a legacy to the future. To begin the process, ask yourself:

- If I had to die now, what would I most regret not having done?
- What remains incomplete in my life?
- What are the things for which I'm most grateful?
- What are my values?
- What matters most to me?

Then contemplate the answers utilizing journal writing, meditation, and relaxation techniques. As we review and "harvest" our lives, we express gratefulness for all we lived through. We recall the triumphs and the tragedies, the realized dreams and the bitter disappointments, the acts of love and the shock of betrayal. This remembrance frees us to convert this rich experience into wisdom.

Suppose our lives indeed are a drama, as Shakespeare tells us. In that case, elderhood is when the play's meaning becomes clear. First, we complete our life review and repair (see Catharsis waypoint). Then we do script work, shadow work, and life harvesting. As a result, we experience a beautiful and fulfilling time of enlightenment.

Finally, now is the time to gift our boon, the treasure that is our uniqueness, to the world. One of the crowning achievements in life is to leave a legacy that only we can provide. We do this by being fully who we are.

There are many types of elders. For those who have lived a life of serving others, the enlightened path may be a contemplative life of meditation, writing, and art. Conversely, for those who lived the first life secluded in the home raising a family, the enlightened path may be one of activism.

The paths of enlightenment are as varied as our uniqueness. No one way is better than the other. We transcend legacy by bringing forward our unique combination of strengths and gifts. Traits include self-awareness, a sense of social justice, deep empathy, love of nature, consensus-building skills, creativity, and spiritual thirst.

The types of elders who transcend legacy are endless. For example, activist, spiritual, psychedelic, "kirtan" chanter, mythologist, storyteller, shaman, doula, mentor, artist, and philosopher, to name a few.

As we discover the deepest longings of our soul that have persisted throughout our journey despite the obstacles, they reveal our legacy. In the words of James Hillman, "Tell me what you yearn for, and I shall tell you who you are."[174] As we identify, accept, integrate, and cultivate these desires, they fill this ultimate stage of life with inner beauty and wholeness. And it is this enlightenment that we can share with the world—to make it a better place because we lived.

Transcendence of Mortality

Neurologists tell us our brains are hardwired to prevent us from imagining the totality of death. Nearly every religion has the concept of an afterlife. Because it is almost impossible for us to imagine our deaths, our brains are built on the faulty premise that there will always be that next moment to predict. We cannot help but imagine that our consciousness endures.[175]

However, the transition and preparation for dying are as necessary as the first life preparation for a career or family. When we confront and transcend (climb above) our mortality, a shift occurs in our attention that makes us more aware of how precious life is.

As enlightened elders, we can face death with a sense of humor. The author and psychedelic elder Ram Dass playfully reminds us, "Death is absolutely safe. Nobody ever fails at it."[176]

Yet we live in a culture that denies death. Psychologist Stanley Keleman urges elders to discover a new path, to formulate a new myth and vision for maturity and longevity. This challenge helped me construct the Elder's Journey, a new version of the universal journey we discover in the Transitions waypoint.

Keleman says our bodies know how to die. We are born knowing about dying. However, the concept of death is yet another way our ego and institutions (in this case, culture) have caused us to deny and suppress the truth. In first life, we form deeply ingrained habits to deny the presence of death.[177]

Utilizing the powerful symbolism of art, comedian Ricky Gervais addresses our complex emotions about death in his television series *Afterlife*. The show centers around Tony, a man whose life is turned upside down after his wife dies from breast cancer.

In a *60 Minutes* interview, Gervais addresses the question, why are we here? He answers, "Well, we just are. The chance of us being born, that sperm hitting the egg, is 400 trillion to 1. We're not special, we're just lucky."

When asked about death, his response makes much sense. Gervais says, "We're gonna die. Everyone we know is gonna die. We're all going to be dead. That's it. Parties don't last forever. Nor should they. People would hate to live forever, they'd hate it."[178]

Our superstitions cause us to believe that contemplating death will hasten its arrival mistakenly—it will somehow "jinx" us. Like many other treasures, we sink the ship of our mortality deep in the sea of our unconscious. But to transcend mortality, we must salvage the riches in that sunken vessel, raise it to the surface, and courageously confront and acknowledge our inevitable demise.

In her thought-provoking book *Deathing*, Anya Foos-Graber writes practically about the transition to the afterlife, a process she calls conscious dying. She points out that doctors formerly anesthetized women in a surgical room apart from family during birth. But over the past few decades, women began practicing conscious birthing techniques such as the Lamaze method.

Foos-Graber suggests taking a similar approach to the dying process. She provides a methodology to transform death from a terrifying experience to an occasion for spiritual awakening. Drawing from yoga and Tibetan Buddhism, her methods include relaxation, breathing techniques, meditation, and mental-focusing exercises. A trusted guide should be available to coach the dying person—whether awake or in a coma— through the various phases of the death process.

There are many similarities to a purposeful psychedelic trip. The importance of setting and intention are also stressed. Foos-Graber writes in *Deathing*, "By allowing yourself to think about the unthinkable, you can make it less forbidding." She also emphasized that it is the most selfless and giving thing you can do for your loved ones.

Instead of insulating ourselves from death by banishing the dying to a hospital and entrusting one's well-being to strangers and technology, we should encounter mortality together with dignity, physical presence, and a sense of equanimity.[179]

A qualified support person such as a death doula can help the dying person and their family remain calm and regulate their fears. Their guidance brings comfort and advocacy to the dying. The companion's knowledge and support allow families to focus on grieving, take breaks, let go, and spend quality time to love and honor their loved one.

Please note that death doulas are non-medical and holistic practitioners and do not facilitate death. Nor do they produce or assist individuals in having a "good death," or help people realize they are dying. They do not place judgment or define what a good (or bad) death is. Their primary function is to support and be alongside individuals in their final transition and release from their physical bodies.[180]

We can transcend mortality no matter our religious belief or unbelief. Simply come to terms with death in whatever way is best for you. Shalomi suggests that those who don't accept theological notions about the continuity of life might consider surrendering themselves at death into the greater life of Gaia—viewing the earth as a vast self-regulating organism.[181]

The enlightened elder will begin preparations for transcending the death experience now. By courageously confronting our last known transition, we better learn the art of living.

The Holy Grail

The mid-life and late-life crises are periods of upheaval and disorientation that accompany life's transitions. They can be times of extreme turmoil. As a result, our life's journey rarely progresses smoothly.

However, suppose we successfully navigate these waypoints. In that case, the universal journeys can show us how to cast off the constricting and outdated life pathways. Old symbols and ways of life may be reviewed and repaired, and new, more life-affirming routes adopted.

We are designed to grow into wholeness. The great teachers of our time describe this growth. Carl Rogers calls it an "actualizing tendency," Carl Jung "individuation," and Sam Harris "non-duality." Stan Grof describes it as "holotropism," Jean Piaget "equilibration," Ken Wilbur "eros," and Martin Seligman "well-being."

We discover the holy grail through the ongoing struggle between growth and stagnation. And between the pull of transcendence and the seduction of the familiar. The psychologist Abraham Maslow said, "If you deliberately plan to be less than you are capable of being, then I warn you that you will be deeply unhappy for the rest of your life."[182]

If you have persisted through this book and life, you realize that becoming whole can be messy. It is a journey marked by periods of disorientation, questioning, and for some of us, trauma and despair. Dr. Roger Walsh poignantly tells us that the twin lions that guard the gates of the Eastern temples are said to symbolize confusion and paradox, and anyone seeking wisdom must be willing to pass through both.[183]

However, our explorations show that those courageous ones who choose growth become enlightened ones. They cultivate resilience, serenity, equanimity, and transcendence.

Here is a summary of *The Quest*—a journey of questions. The adventure usually begins with a crisis, when heroic dreams collapse.

- What four symbols have you chosen to understand and communicate with your inner self?
- What four essentials have you identified to symbolize your body, mind, soul, and spirit?
- How have the previous stages of life formed you, and what stage are you in now?
- What universal journey are you on now?
- What transitions have you survived?
- Are you prepared for the transitions that await?
- Which of the nine Affects are healthy and which are unhealthy for you?
- Have you started your script work?
- How awake, aware, attentive, and growing are you?

- What are your spiritual practices?
- Are you emptying your unconscious and integrating your self (ego, persona, gender, and shadow) by utilizing your preferred communication vehicles?
- Have you entered catharsis? If so, which stage are you in?
- Do you genuinely enjoy yourself, your companions, your community, and your world?
- Have you begun life review, life repair, shadow work, and mortality work?
- Are you becoming enlightened by cultivating qualities such as resilience, serenity, equanimity, and transcendence?
- Do you have the holy grail of wholeness, not goodness or perfection, but *wholeness* as the ultimate goal of your *Quest?*

The answers to these universal questions form the unique waypoints of *your* journey. They comprise your GPS, your treasure map to the holy grail. The whole point of *The Quest* lies in the questioning.

In the subtitle of this book, I utilize the term "discover a way to enjoy the second half of life." And yes, the word "enjoy" posits a beautiful ideal. However, we sum up the holy grail of *The Quest* in one word—wholeness. A whole person enjoys life. It is both simple and complex, unique yet universal.

If we discover the holy grail of *The Quest*, we will know who we are and what matters to us. We *can* discover an enjoyable life even when our first identities are fragmented and even when we are disillusioned in work or devastated by love. And perhaps, at the epicenter of all this deep emotion and the final stages of the journey, we may discover a life worth living. One we can call, despite all the difficulties and imperfections, our very own.

Acknowledgments

This book exists only because of the endless patience of my wife and muse Gina over the past decade. She has endured me slipping out of bed in the wee hours of the morning, listened to me read countless iterations, discussed ideas and improved them, and lovingly endured all the quirks of this highly sensitive artist. For that, and so much more, I am grateful beyond measure.

Also, a special thanks to *TSG Creative Studio* for the cover creation consultation. And to all the incredible team at cre:ate 2.0 publishing. Also to the thoughtful folks who were willing to take time out of their busy schedules to "beta" read and greatly improve this book: Vanessa Cordes, Melissa Greene, John Chancellor, Charlie Flatley, and Jimbo Gulley. Finally, my heartfelt appreciation goes out to all the many people who have experienced *The Quest* live experience over the years. You have enriched my life and added priceless layers to this book.

The Quest

For all things *Quest* related (live experiences, online experiences, cruises, resources, and more) go to: randyelrod.com/quest

Also By Randy Elrod

Sex, Lies & Religion
Beauty Is Calling
Letters From A Devastated Artist
A Renaissance Redneck In A Mega-Church Pulpit
Ruminations
God, I Have A Question...or Two
My Confession
The Loss of Belonging

Mandalas

On the following pages are mandalas I created as mnemonic devices and visual representations of the waypoints, sub-waypoints, and selected ideas of *The Quest*. They are basic mandalas that can be used to create your own. Many of the sub-waypoints are unique to me, however, I feel the waypoints are universal. I look forward to seeing countless unique mandalas, from crude sketches to ornate works of art, as fellow *Questors* create personal mandalas.

Quest Mandala (Your Symbols)

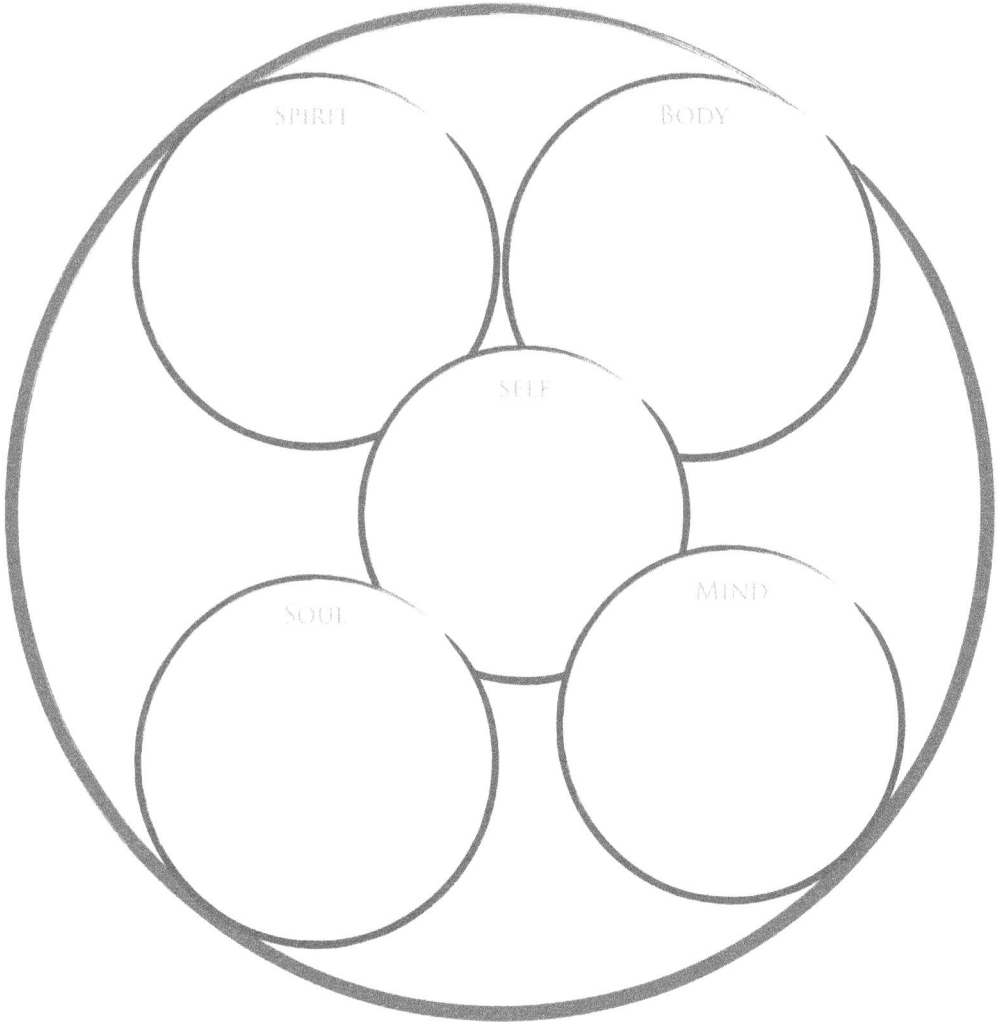

QUEST MANDALA
(YOUR ESSENTIALS)

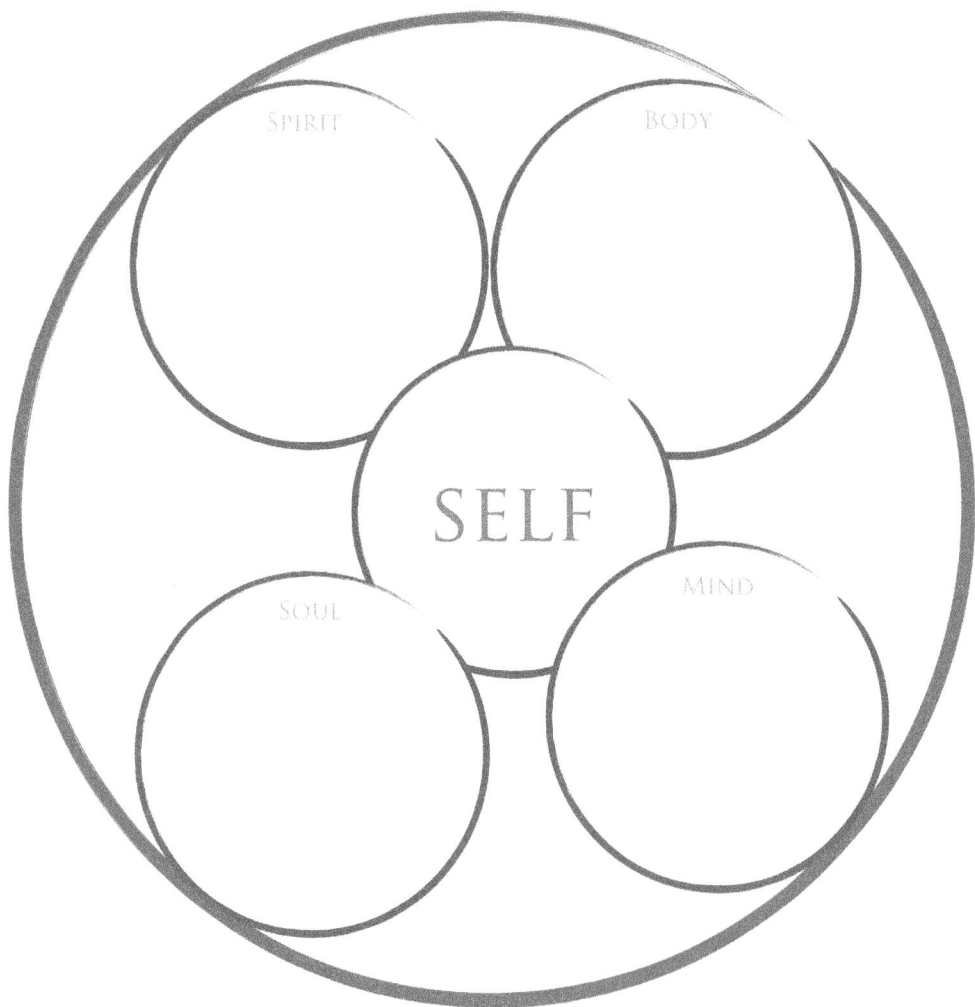

SPIRIT

BODY

SELF

SOUL

MIND

SYMBOLS QUATERNITY

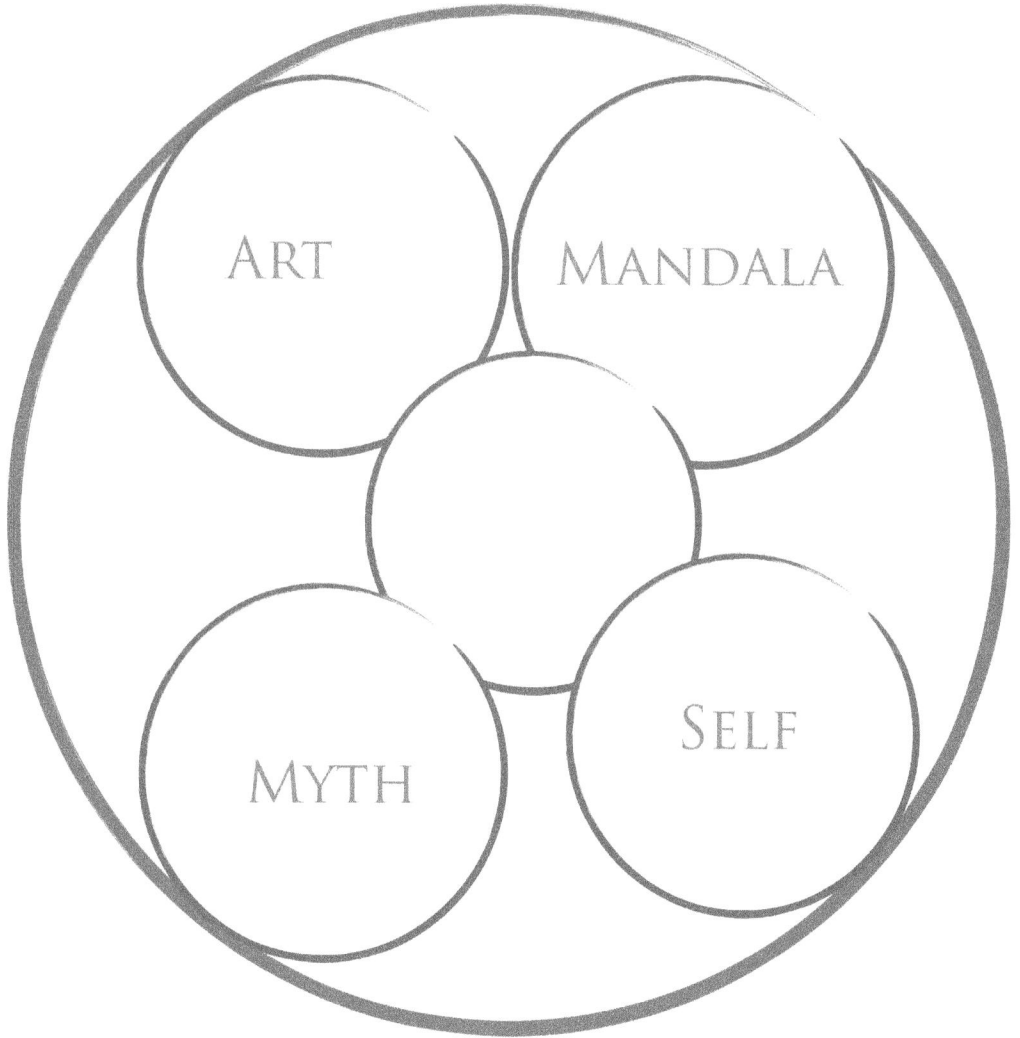

ART

MANDALA

MYTH

SELF

SYMBOLS SUB-WAYPOINTS MANDALA

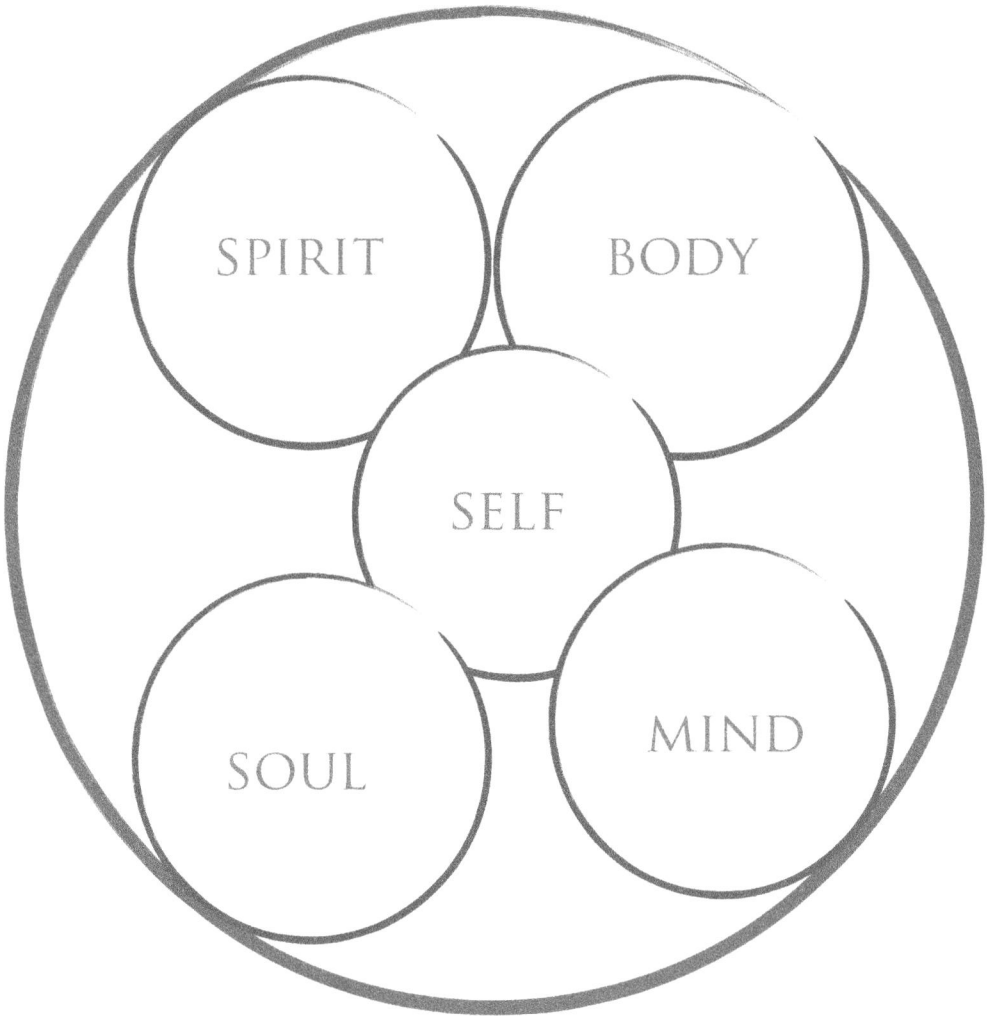

SPIRIT

BODY

SELF

SOUL

MIND

SYMBOLS SUB-WAYPOINTS
SELF

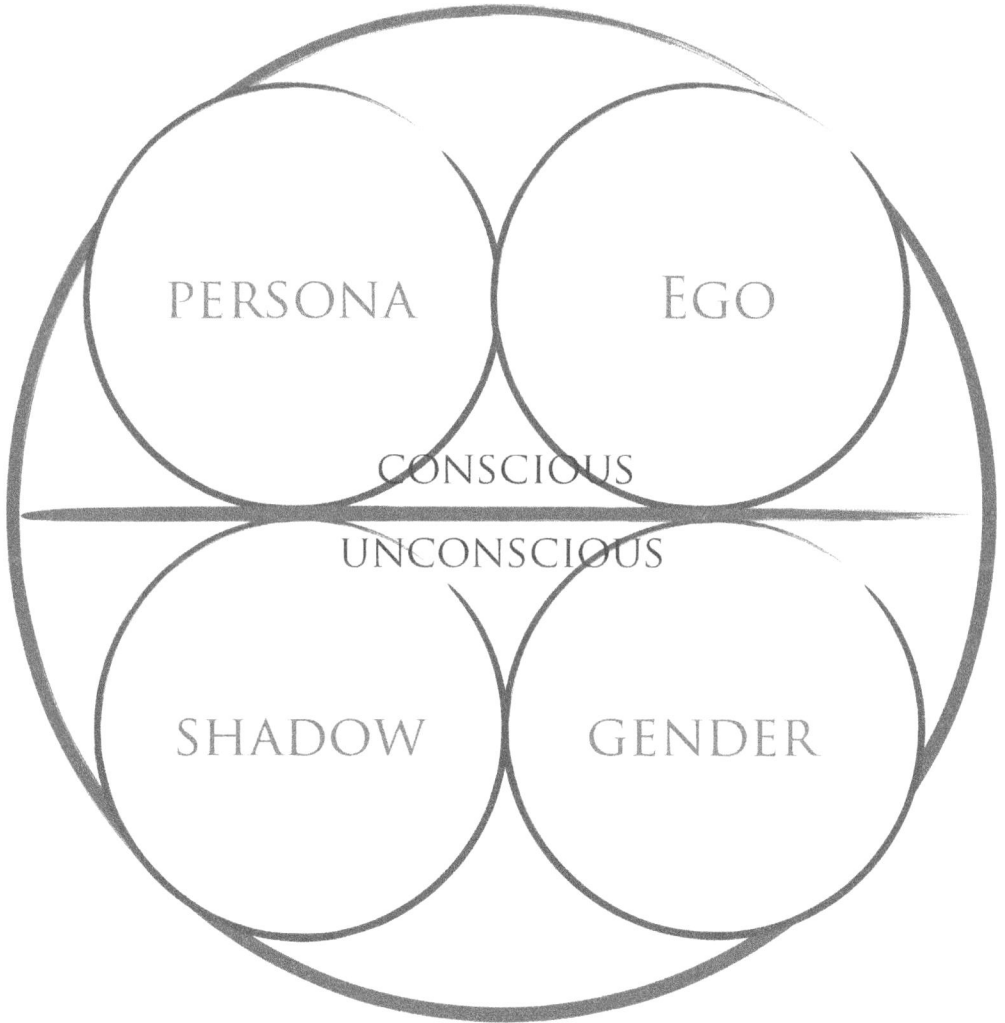

PERSONA

EGO

CONSCIOUS

UNCONSCIOUS

SHADOW

GENDER

SYMBOLS SUB-WAYPOINTS
MYTHS

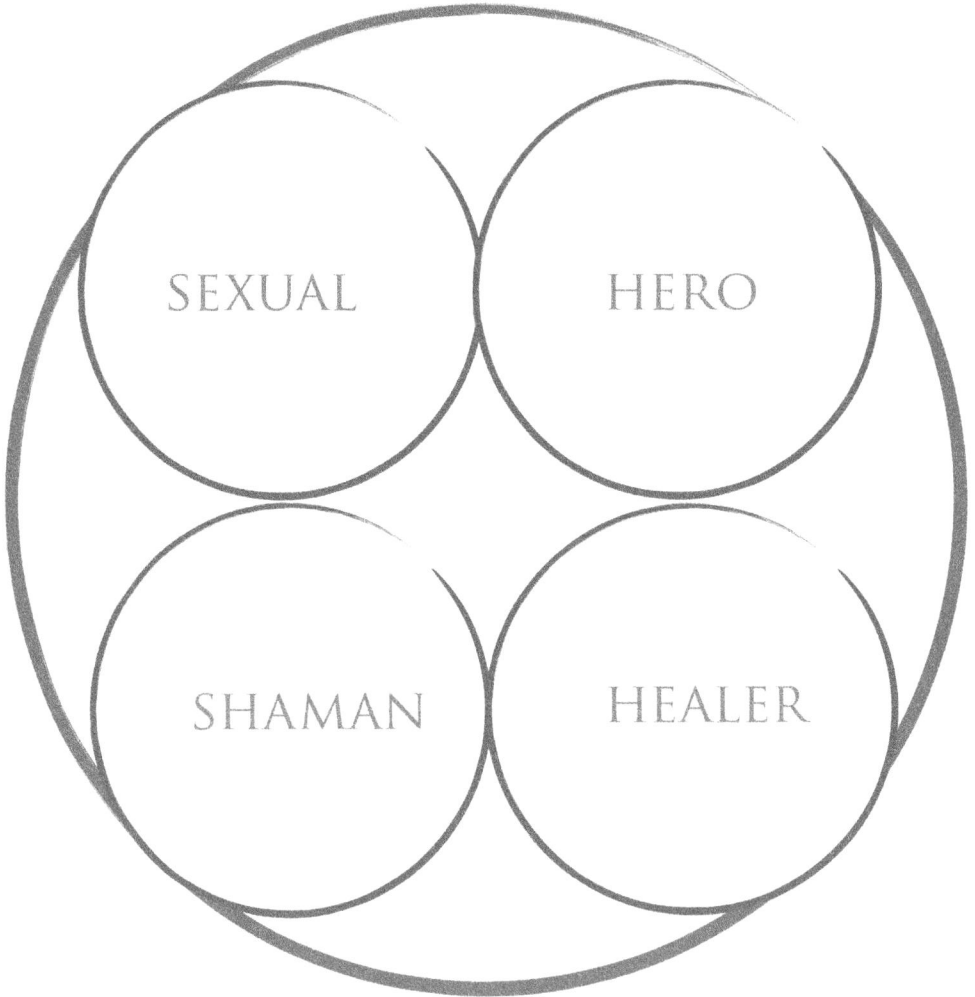

SEXUAL

HERO

SHAMAN

HEALER

SYMBOLS SUB-WAYPOINTS ART

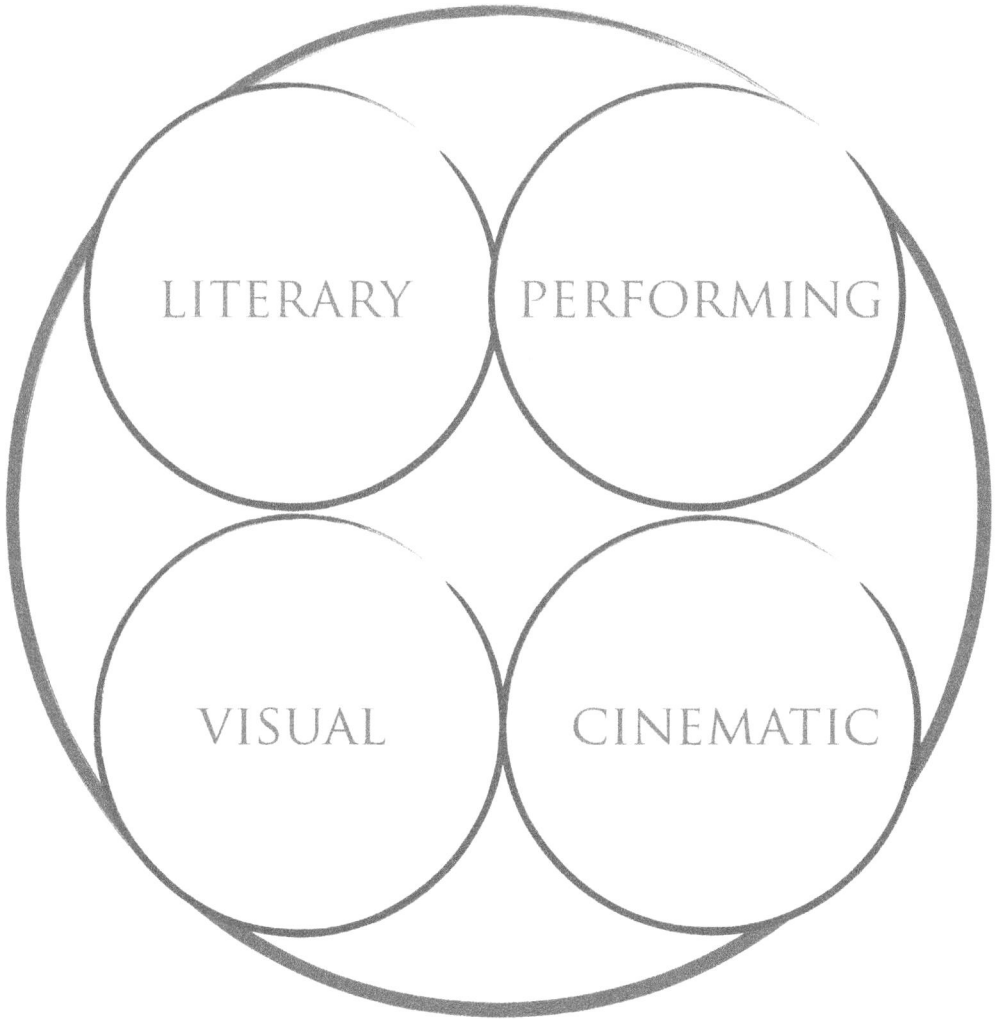

LITERARY

PERFORMING

VISUAL

CINEMATIC

ESSENTIALS QUATERNITY

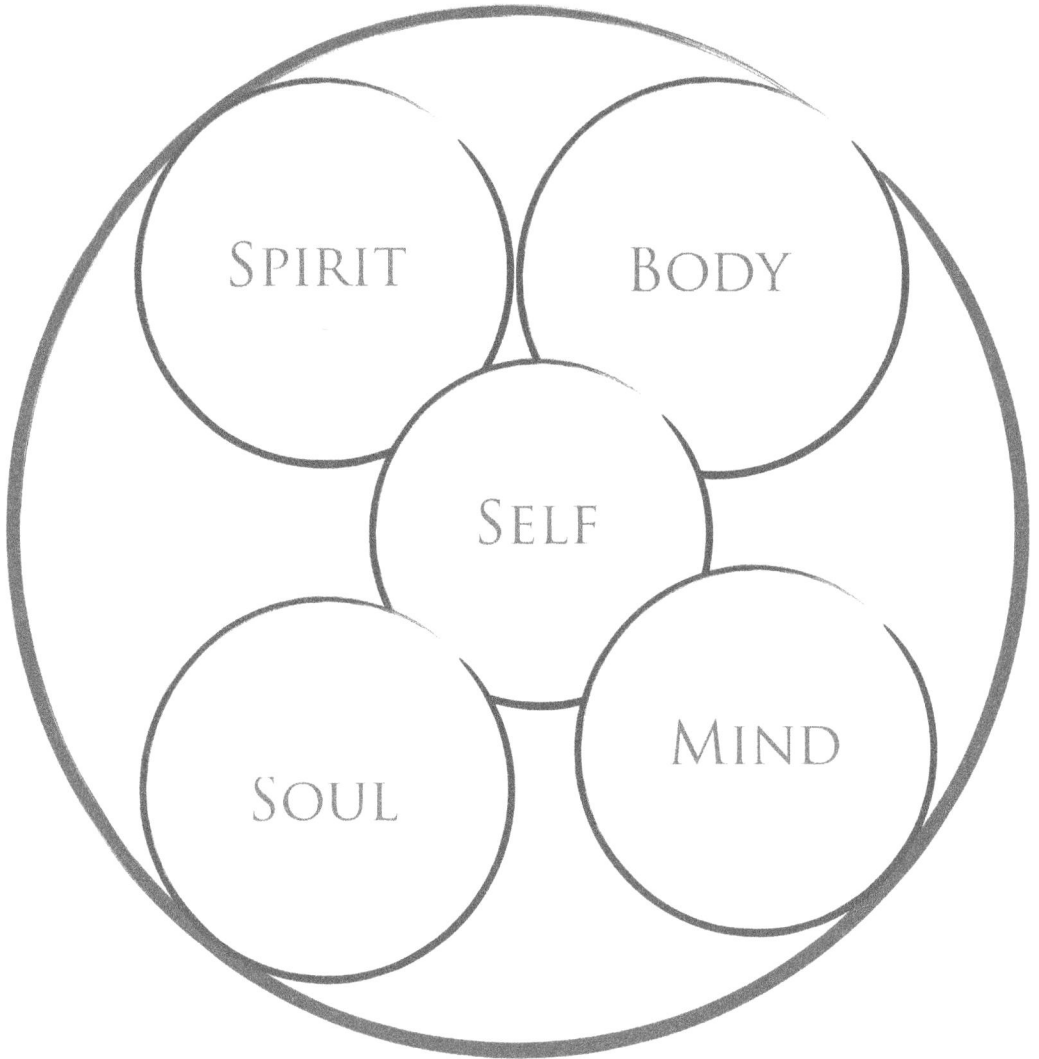

SPIRIT

BODY

SELF

SOUL

MIND

ESSENTIALS SUB WAYPOINTS
(BODY/PHYSICAL)

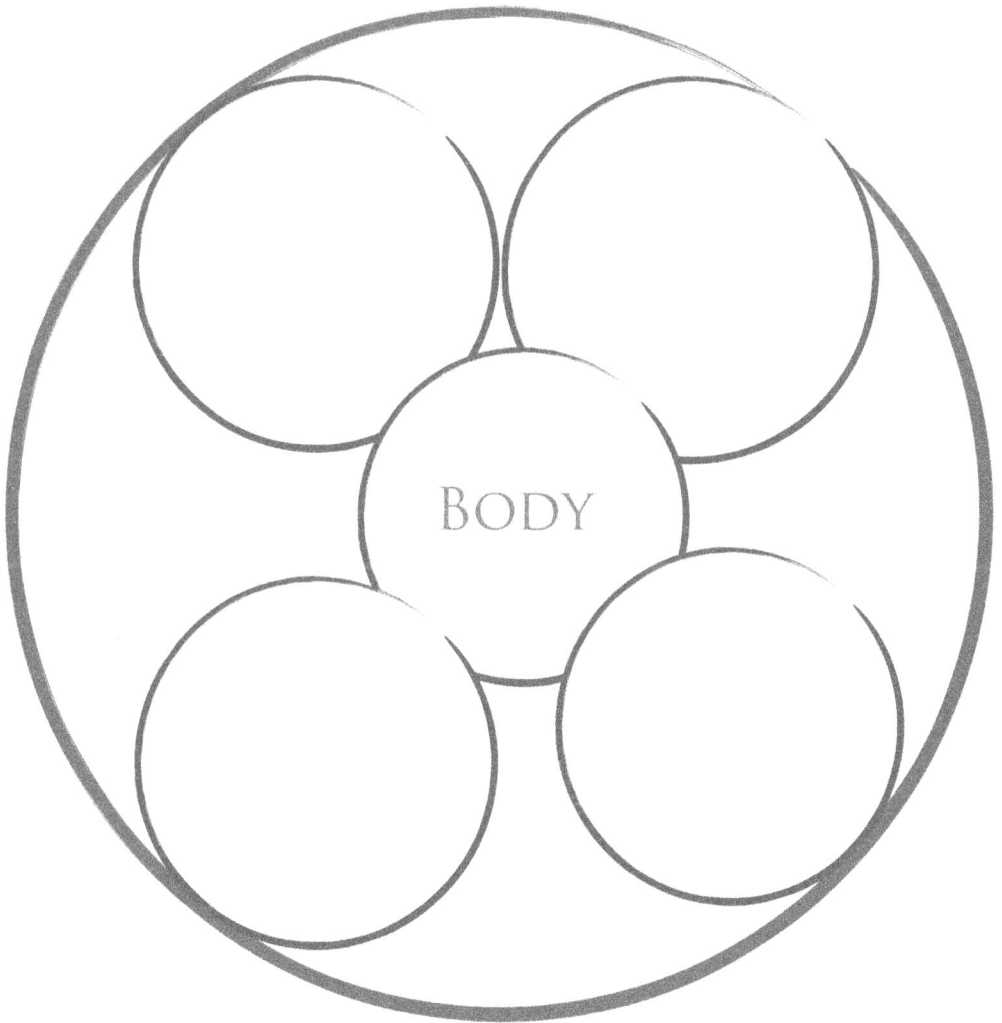

BODY

ESSENTIALS SUB WAYPOINTS (MIND/MENTAL)

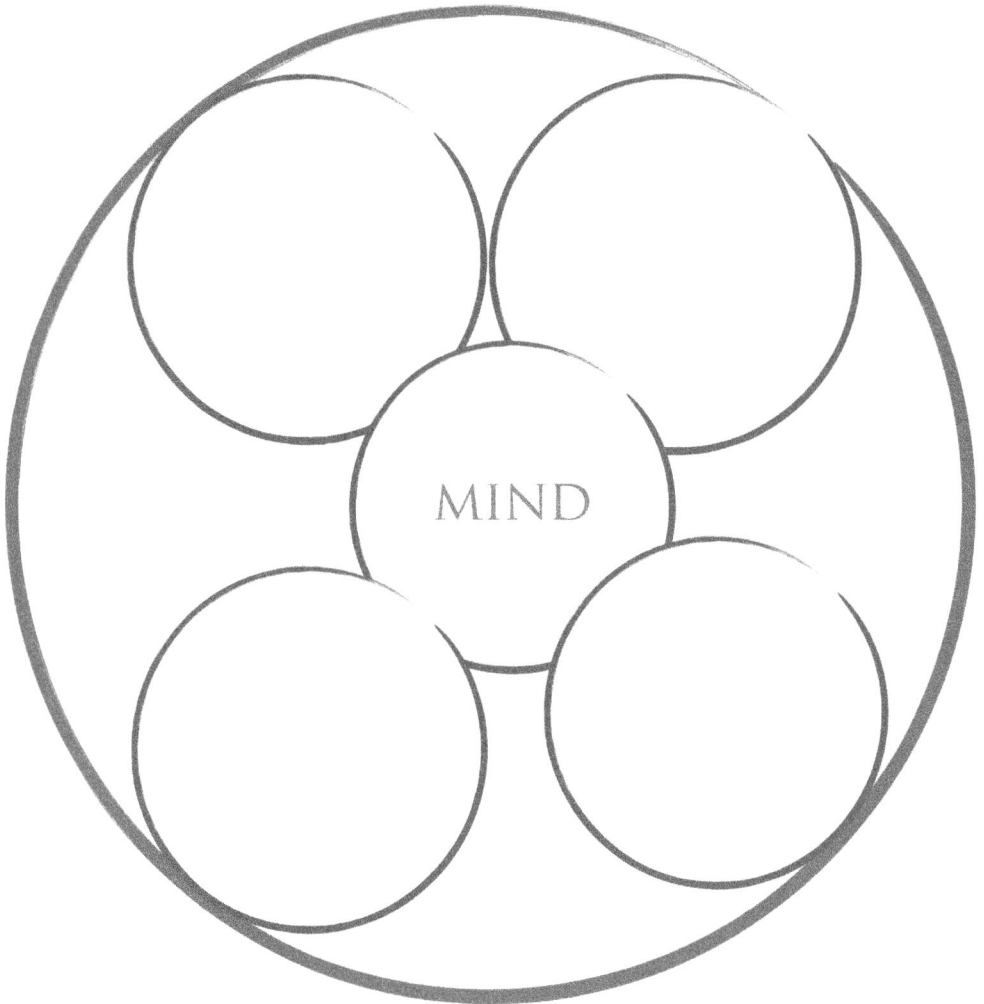

MIND

ESSENTIALS SUB WAYPOINTS
(SOUL/EMOTIONAL)

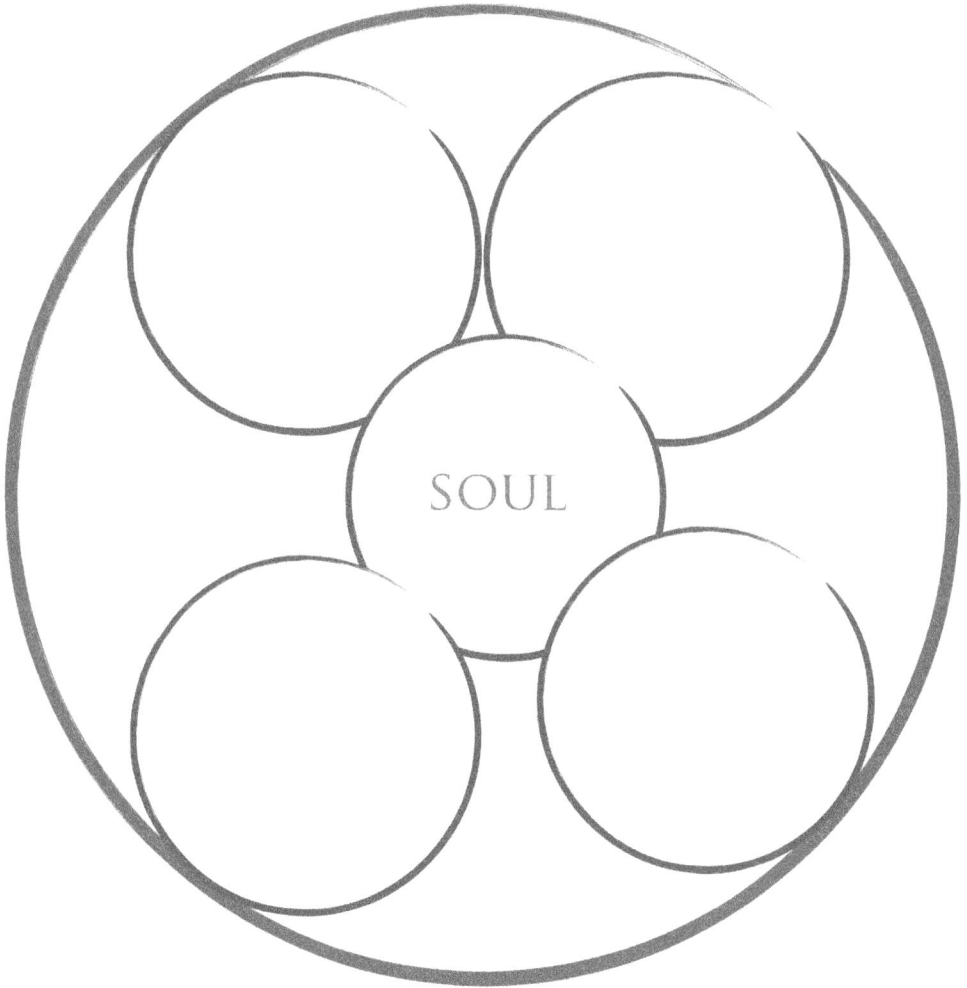

SOUL

ESSENTIALS SUB WAYPOINTS (SPIRIT/SPIRITUAL)

SPIRIT

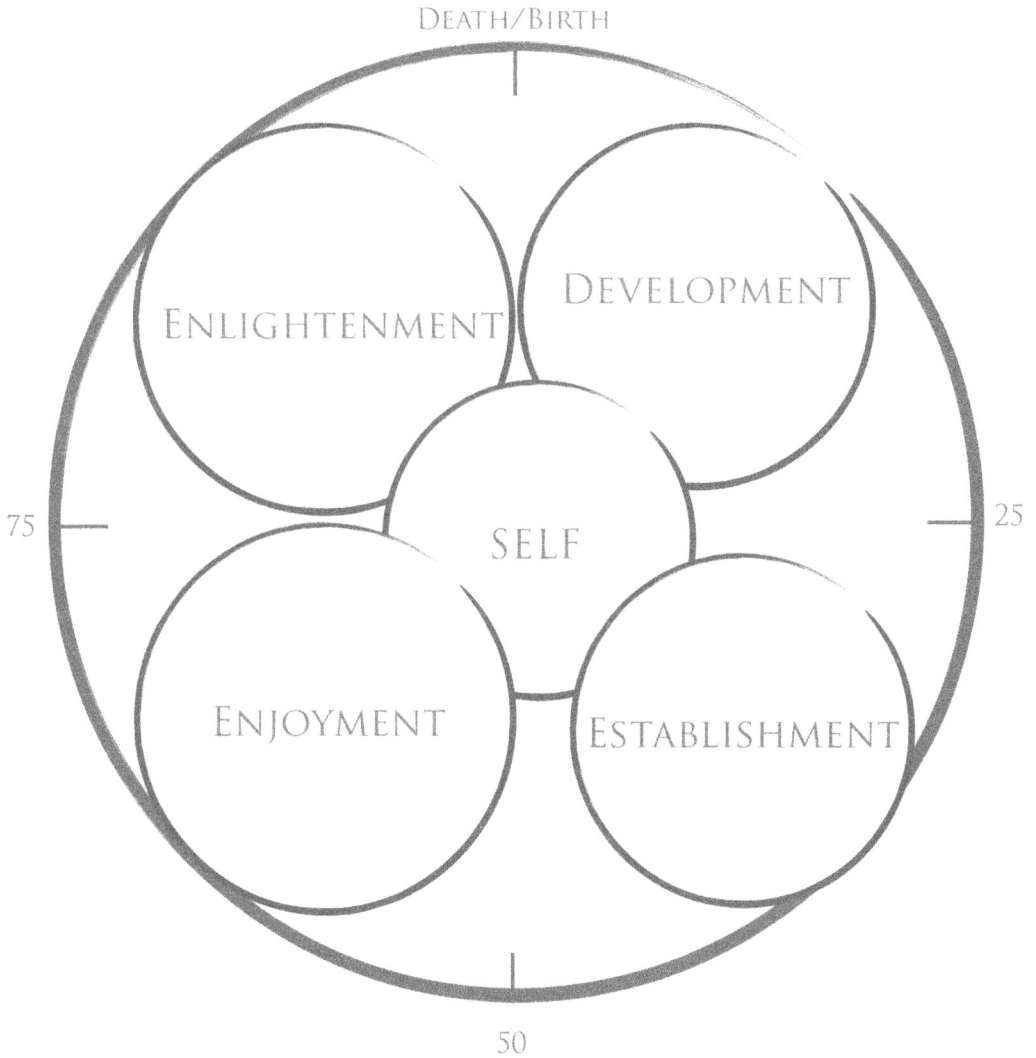

STAGES QUATERNITY

DEATH/BIRTH

75

25

50

ENLIGHTENMENT

DEVELOPMENT

SELF

ENJOYMENT

ESTABLISHMENT

STAGES SUB-WAYPOINTS DEVELOPMENT

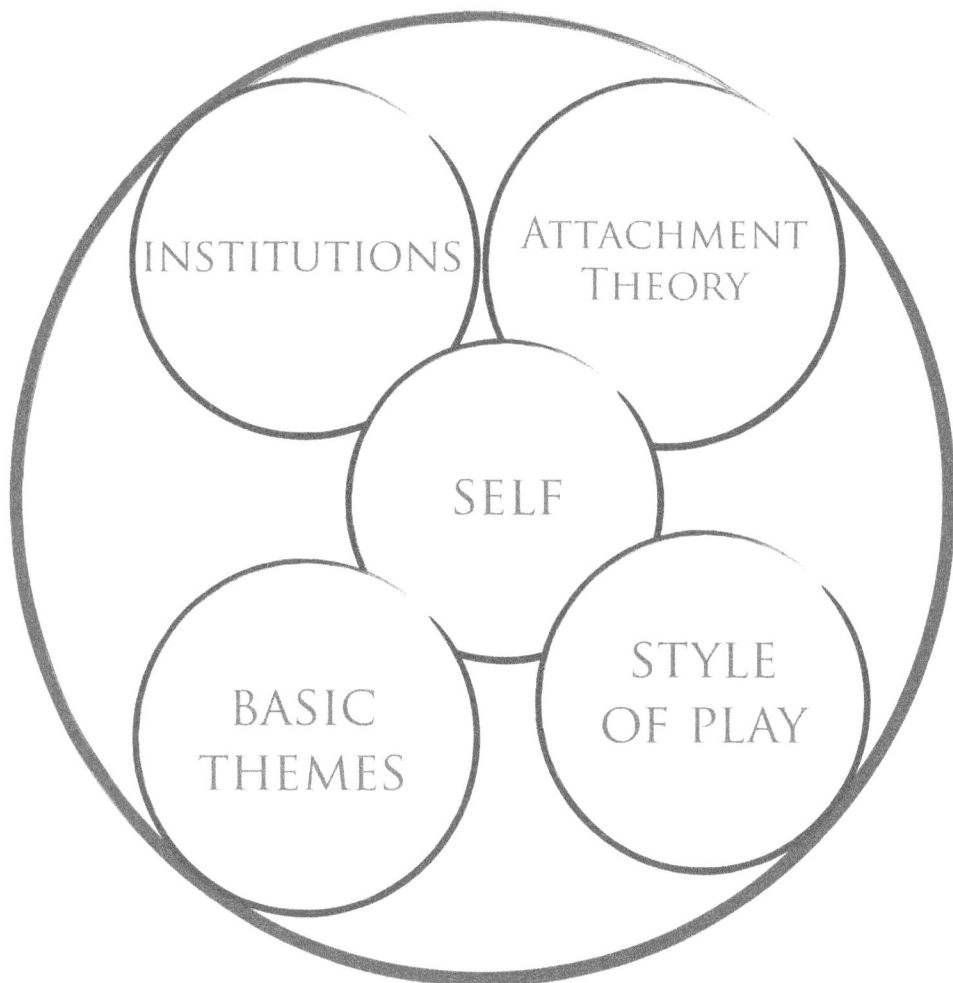

INSTITUTIONS

ATTACHMENT THEORY

SELF

BASIC THEMES

STYLE OF PLAY

STAGES SUB-WAYPOINTS
DEVELOPMENT/ATTACHMENT

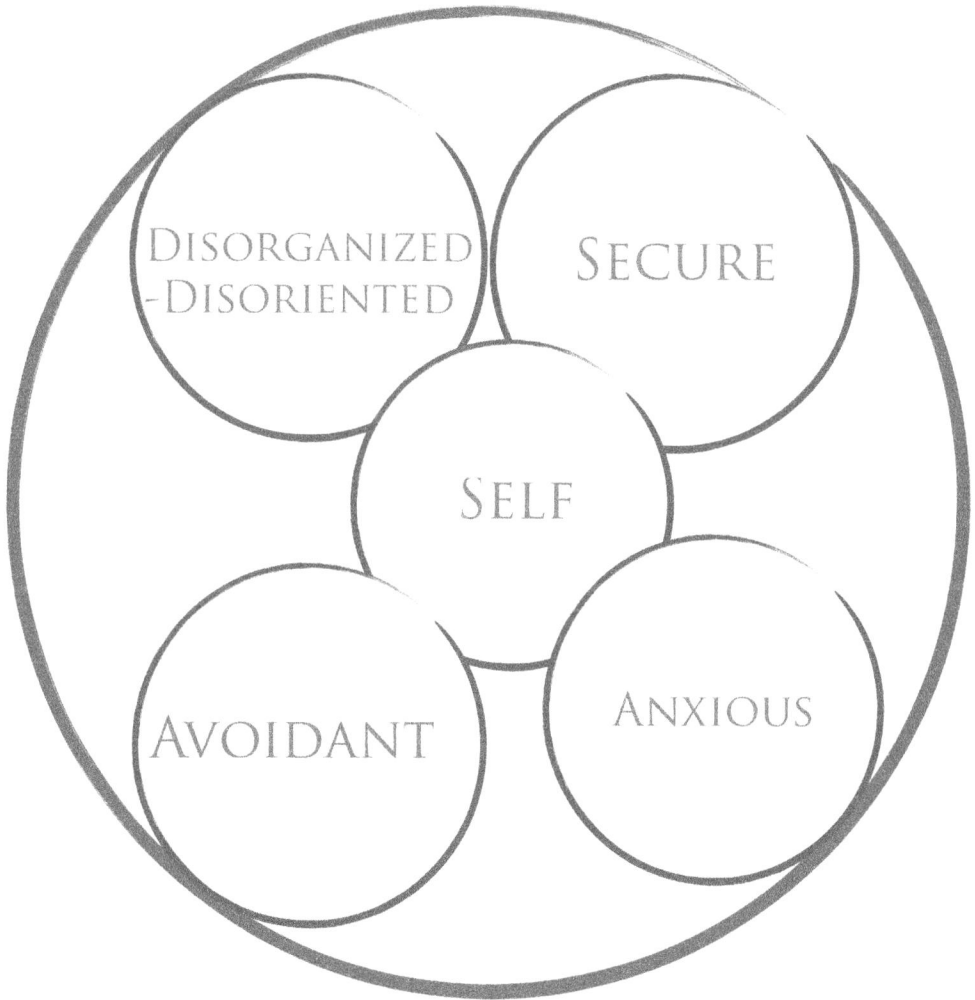

DISORGANIZED -DISORIENTED

SECURE

SELF

AVOIDANT

ANXIOUS

STAGES SUB-WAYPOINTS
DEVELOPMENT/STYLES OF PLAY

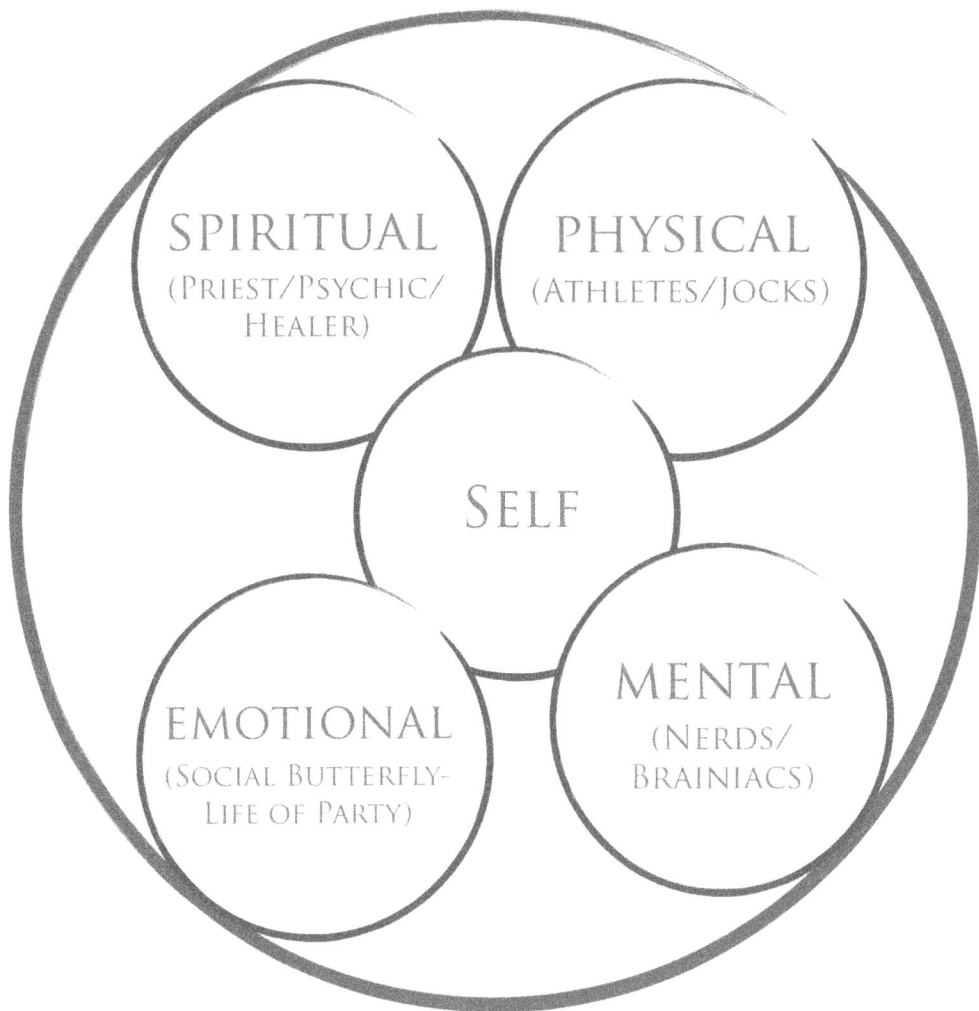

SPIRITUAL
(PRIEST/PSYCHIC/
HEALER)

PHYSICAL
(ATHLETES/JOCKS)

SELF

EMOTIONAL
(SOCIAL BUTTERFLY-
LIFE OF PARTY)

MENTAL
(NERDS/
BRAINIACS)

STAGES SUB-WAYPOINTS DEVELOPMENT/BASIC THEMES

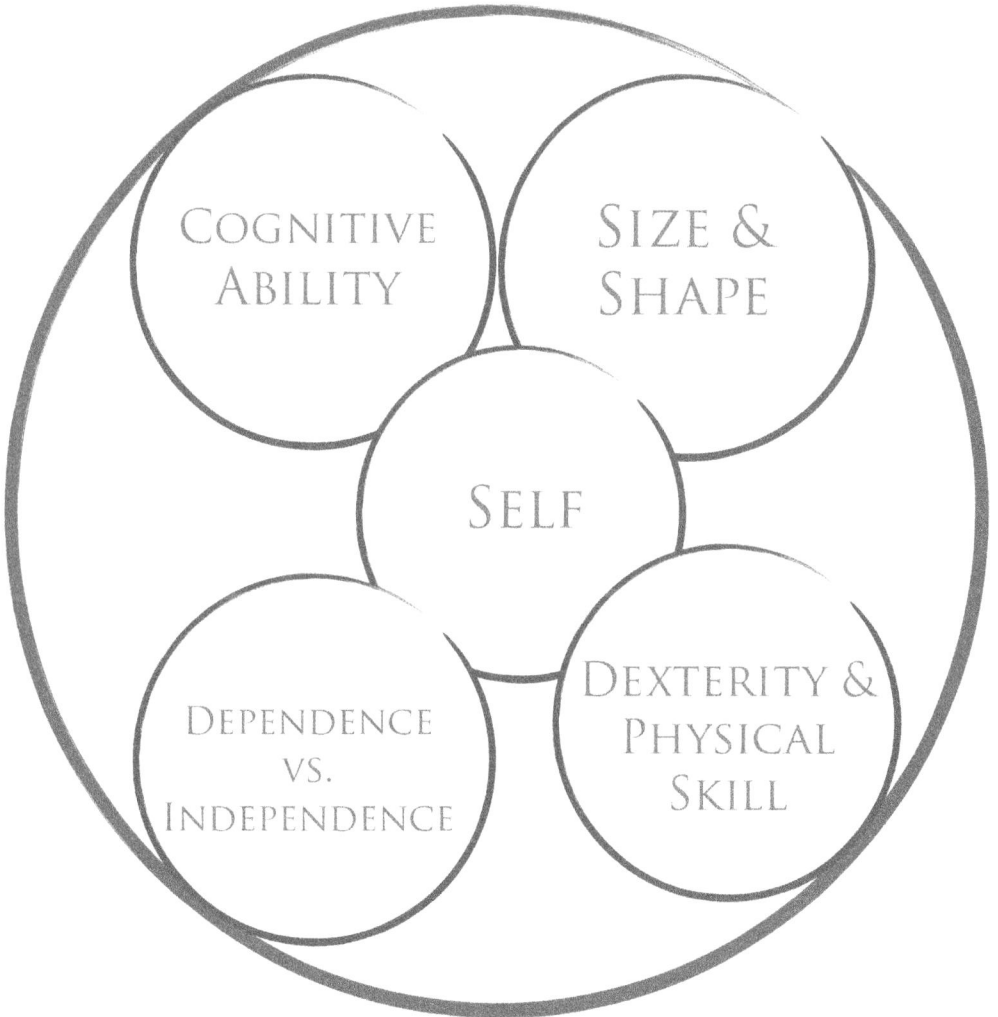

COGNITIVE ABILITY

SIZE & SHAPE

SELF

DEPENDENCE VS. INDEPENDENCE

DEXTERITY & PHYSICAL SKILL

STAGES SUB-WAYPOINTS
DEVELOPMENT/INSTITUTIONS

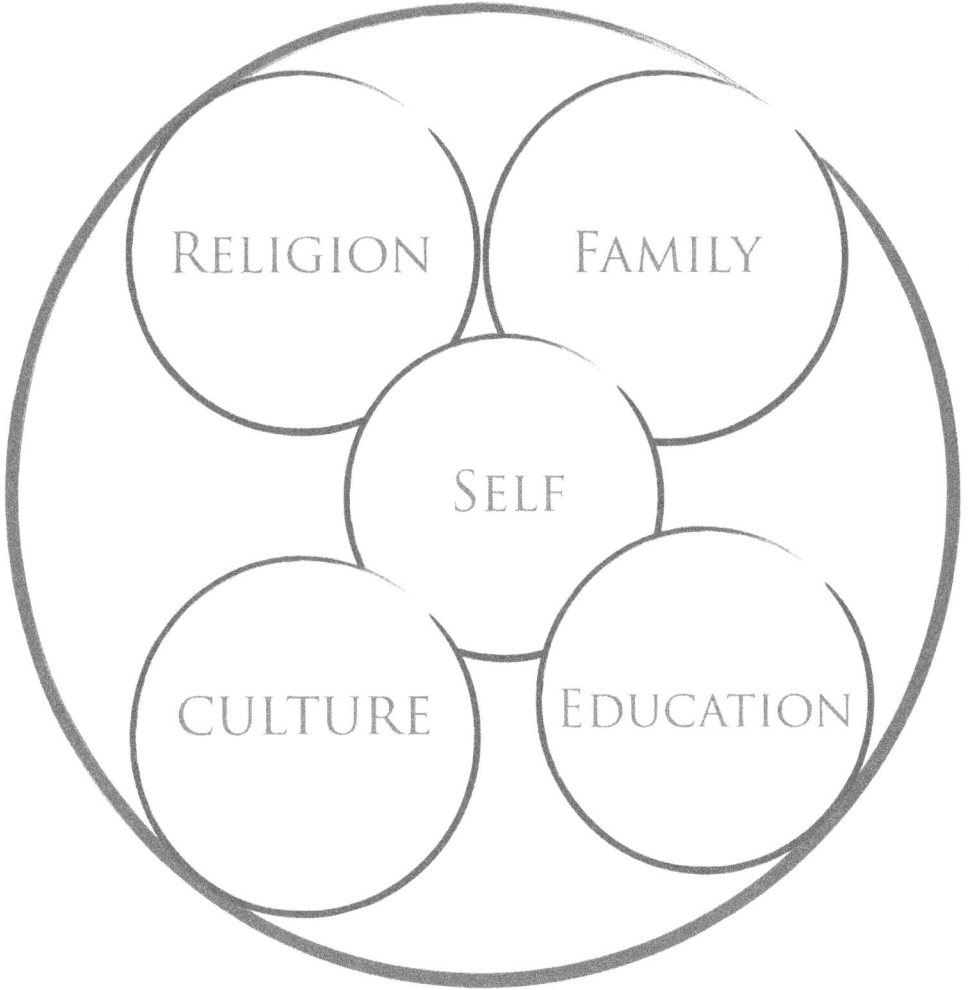

RELIGION

FAMILY

SELF

CULTURE

EDUCATION

STAGES SUB-WAYPOINTS
ESTABLISHMENT

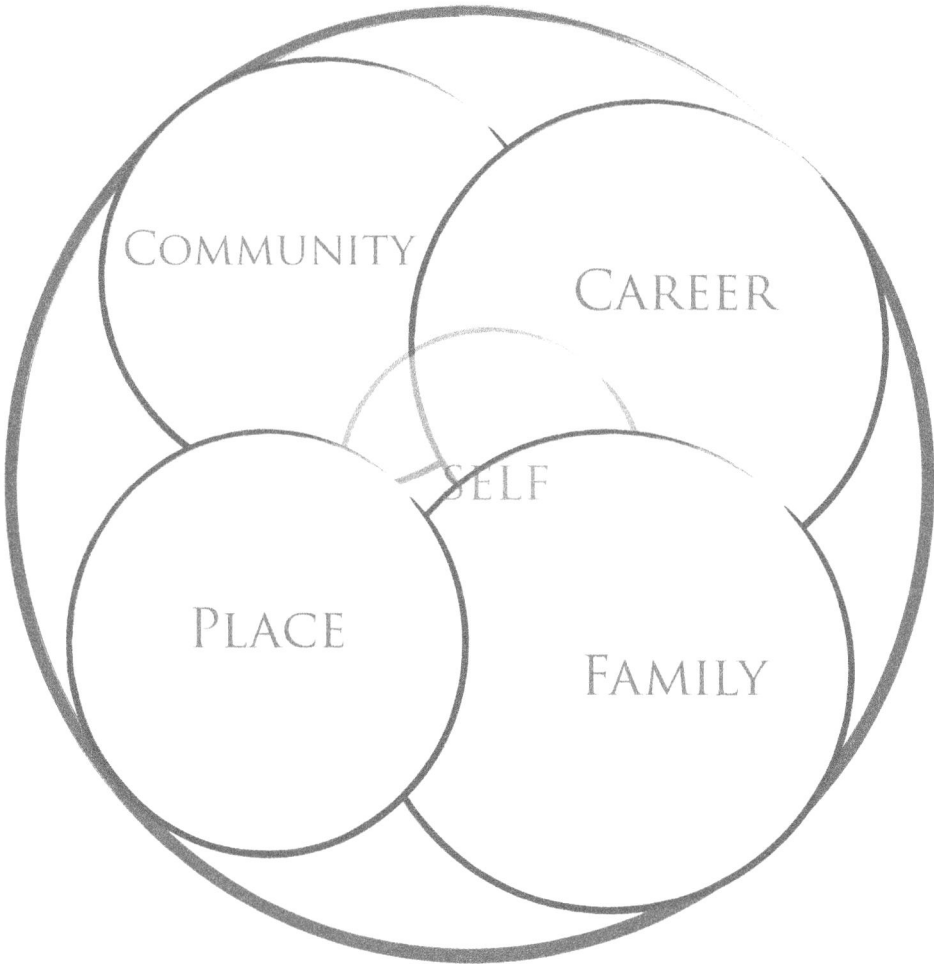

COMMUNITY

CAREER

SELF

PLACE

FAMILY

STAGES SUB-WAYPOINTS
Establishment/Career

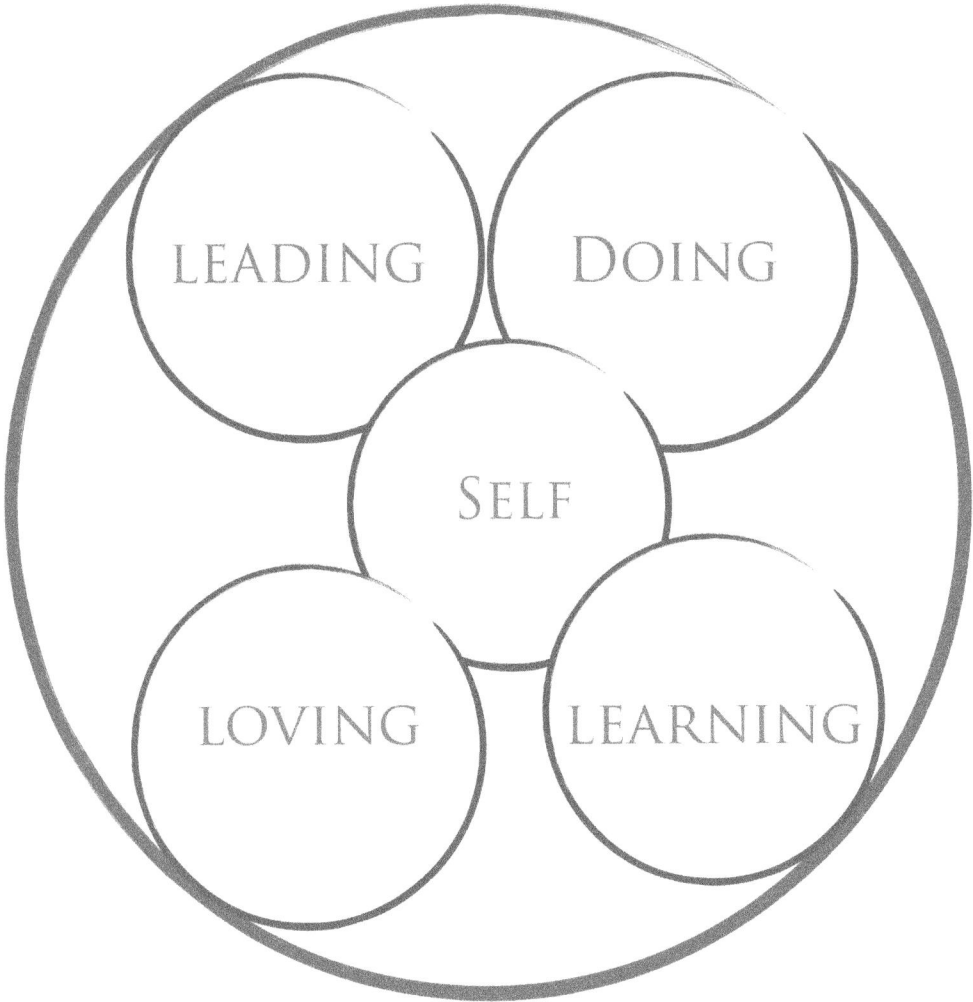

LEADING

DOING

SELF

LOVING

LEARNING

STAGES SUB-WAYPOINTS
ESTABLISHMENT/PLACE

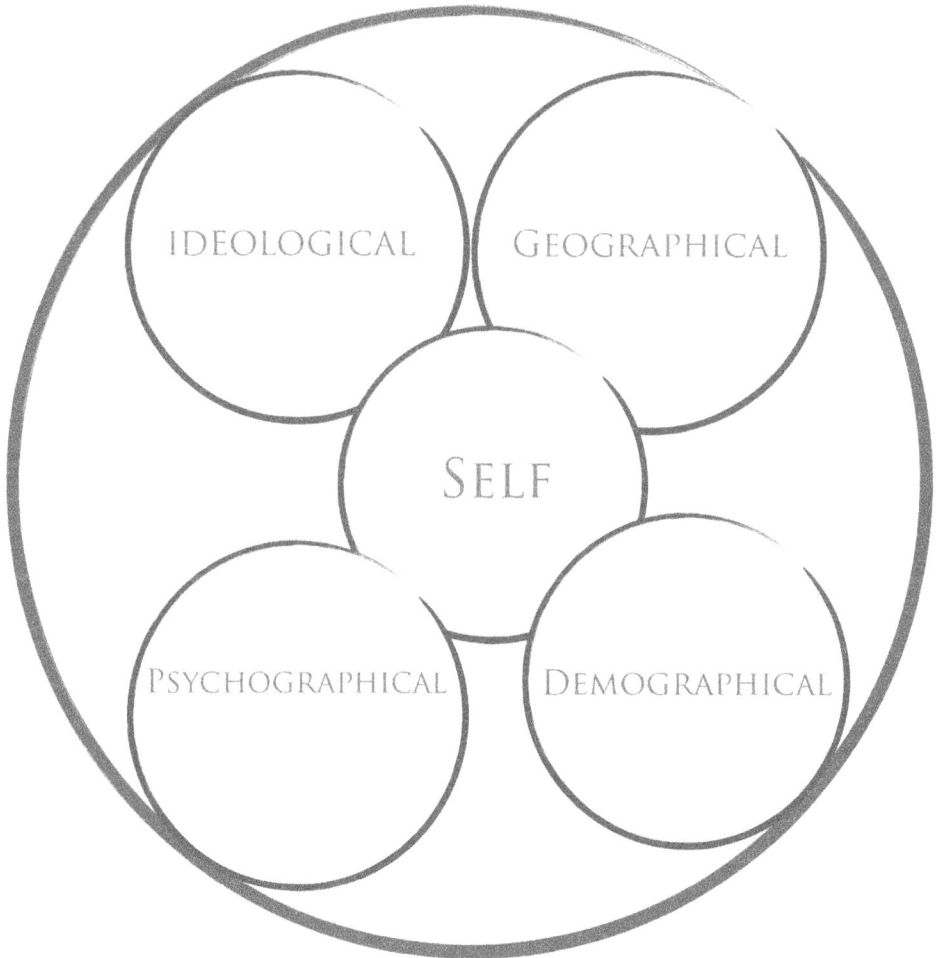

IDEOLOGICAL

GEOGRAPHICAL

SELF

PSYCHOGRAPHICAL

DEMOGRAPHICAL

STAGES SUB-WAYPOINTS
ESTABLISHMENT/TRIBE

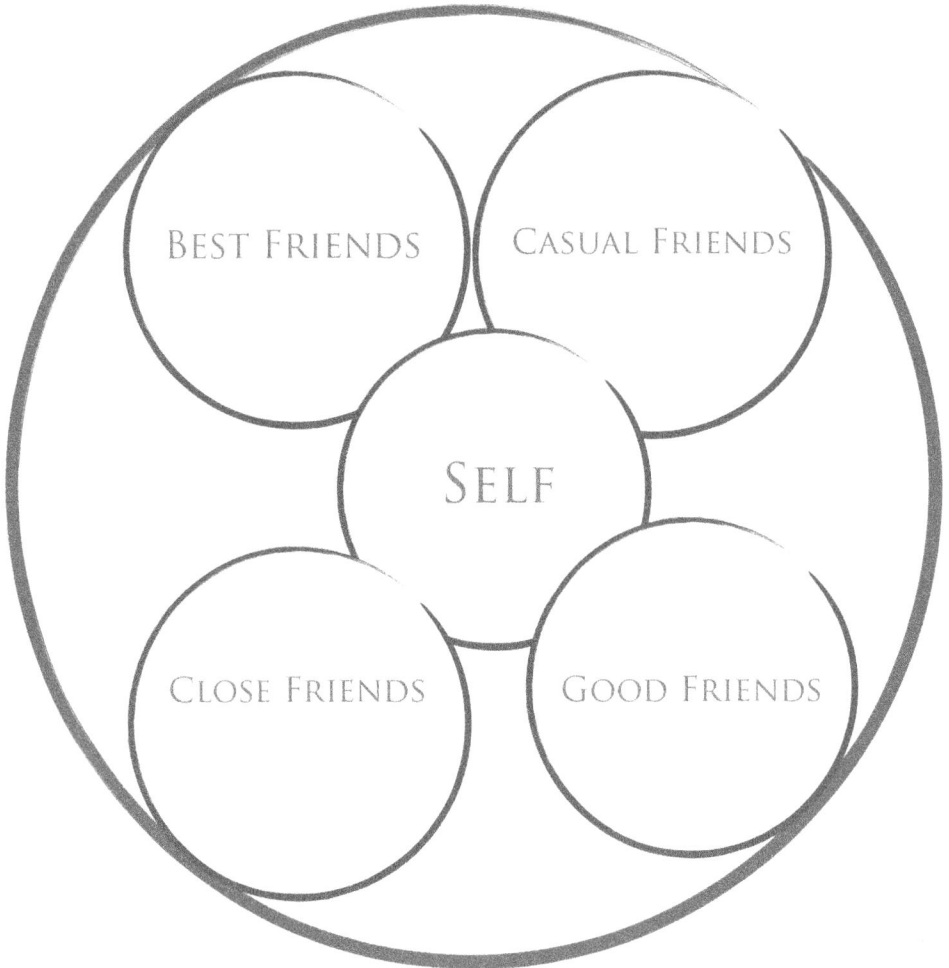

BEST FRIENDS

CASUAL FRIENDS

SELF

CLOSE FRIENDS

GOOD FRIENDS

Your Archetype For Each Stage of Life

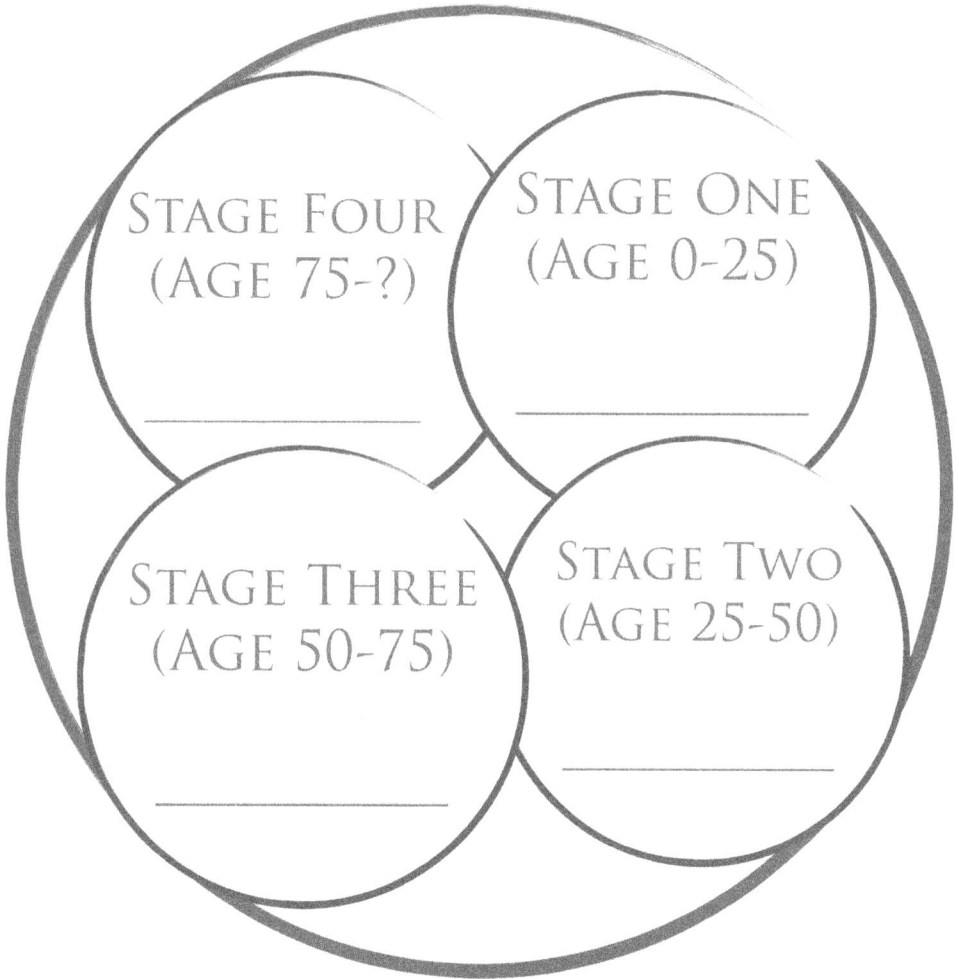

Stage Four (Age 75-?)

Stage One (Age 0-25)

Stage Three (Age 50-75)

Stage Two (Age 25-50)

EXAMPLE: AUTHOR ARCHETYPE FOR EACH STAGE OF LIFE

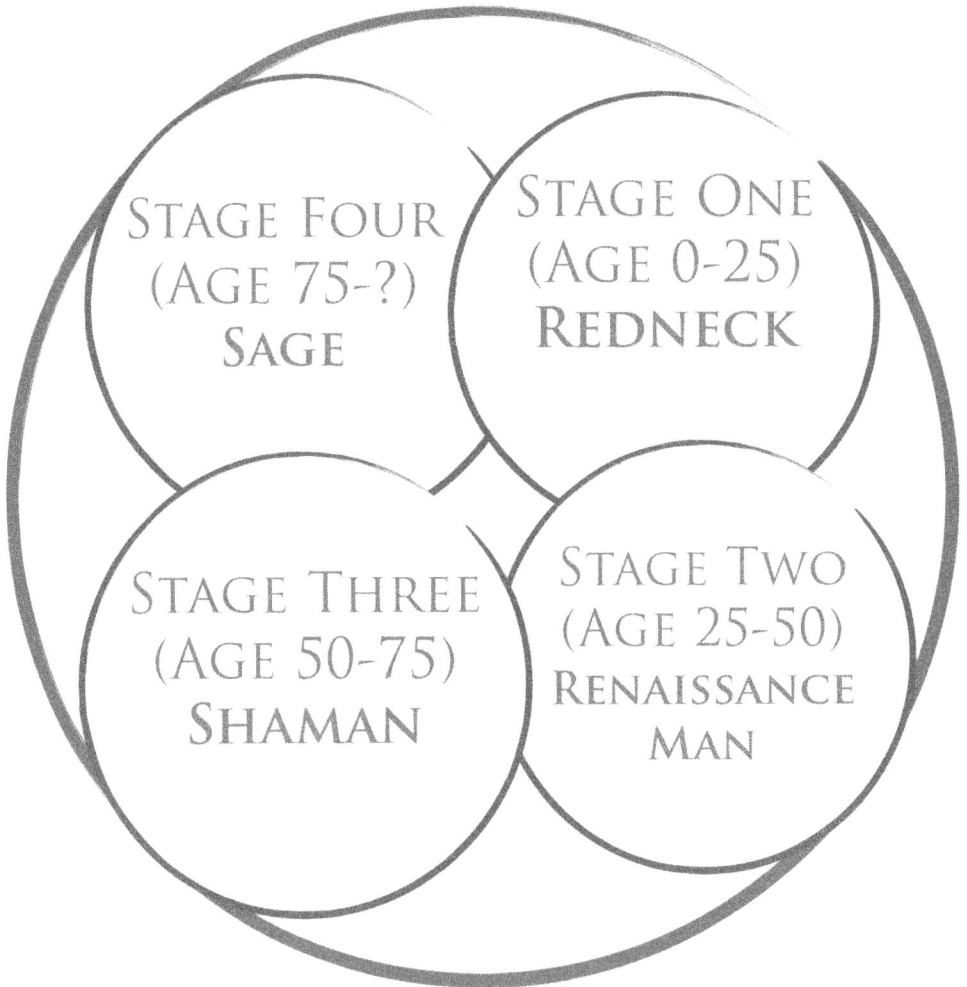

STAGE FOUR
(AGE 75-?)
SAGE

STAGE ONE
(AGE 0-25)
REDNECK

STAGE THREE
(AGE 50-75)
SHAMAN

STAGE TWO
(AGE 25-50)
RENAISSANCE
MAN

TRANSITIONS QUATERNITY

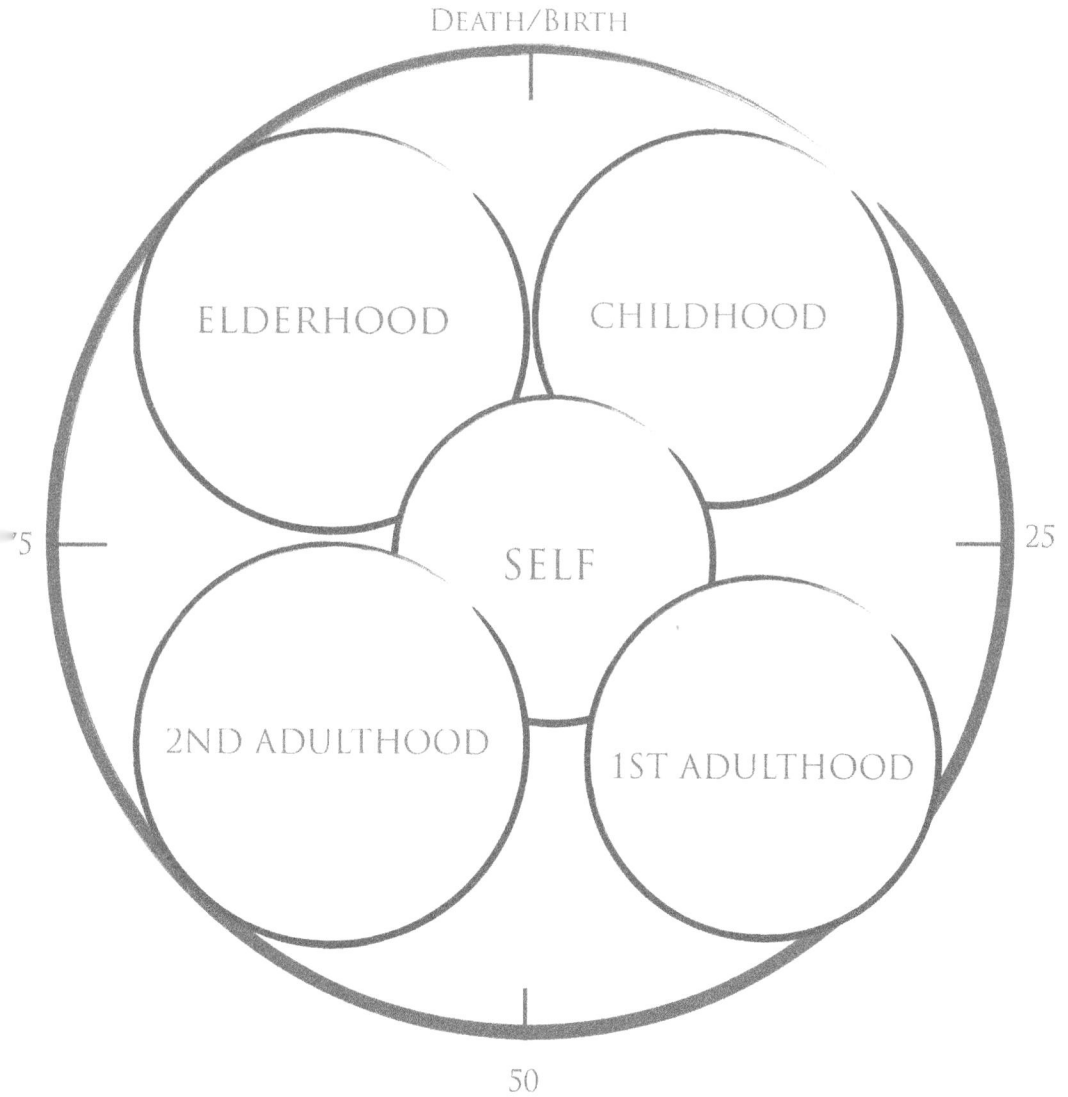

DEATH/BIRTH

ELDERHOOD

CHILDHOOD

SELF

2ND ADULTHOOD

1ST ADULTHOOD

75

25

50

TYPES OF CRISIS QUATERNITY
(ENANTIODROMIA)

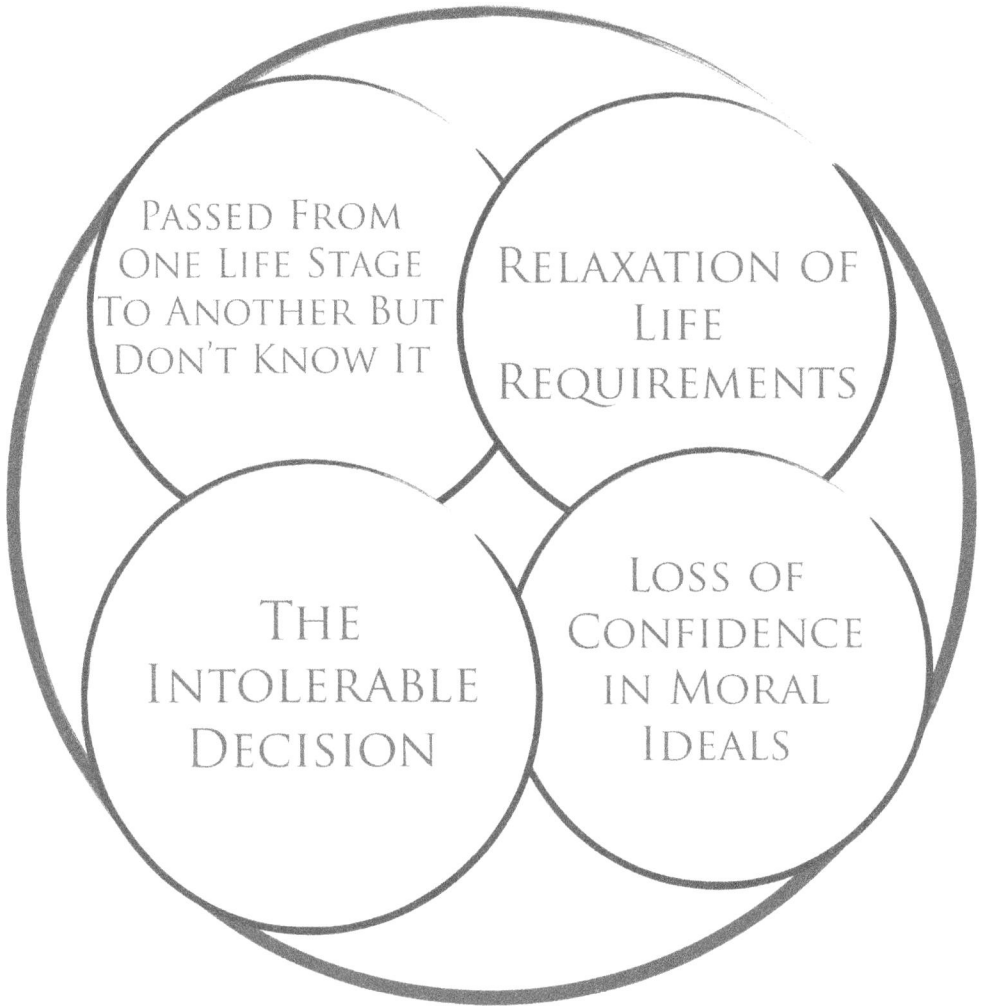

PASSED FROM ONE LIFE STAGE TO ANOTHER BUT DON'T KNOW IT

RELAXATION OF LIFE REQUIREMENTS

THE INTOLERABLE DECISION

LOSS OF CONFIDENCE IN MORAL IDEALS

Universal Journey

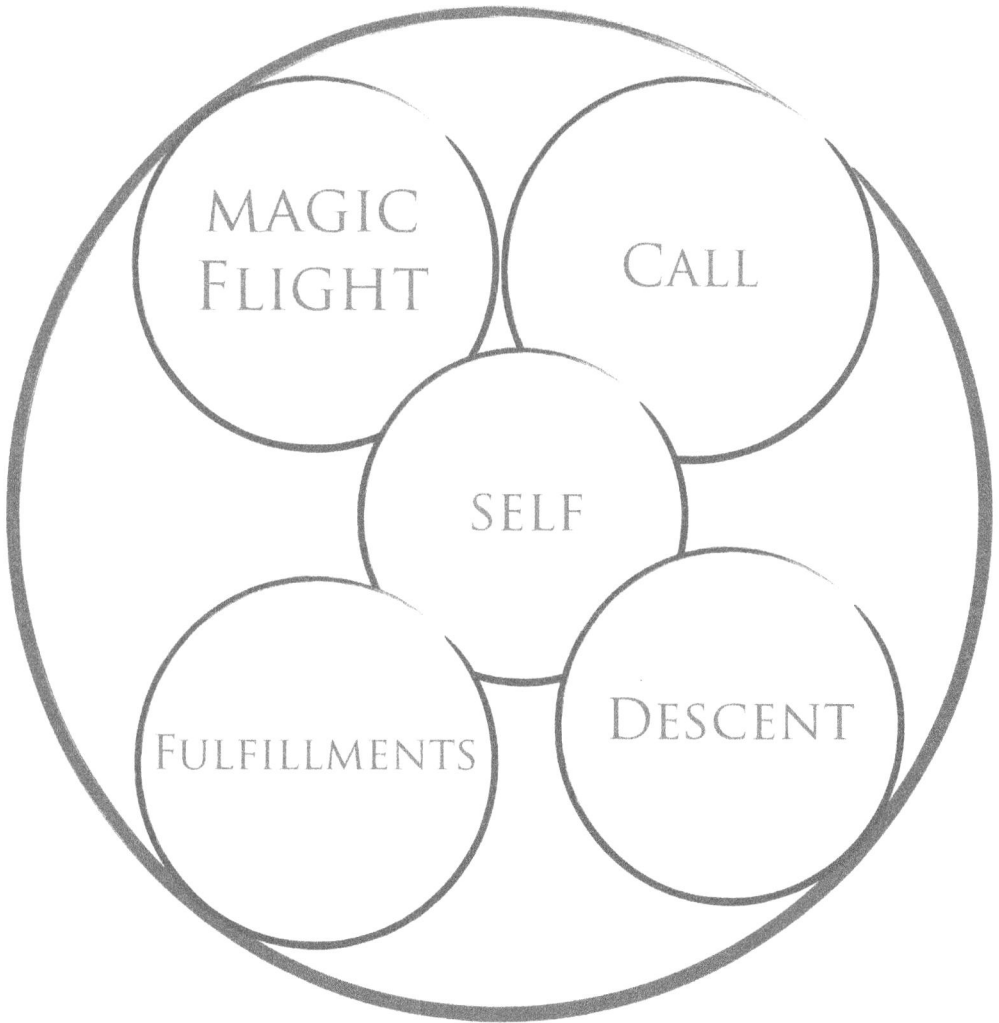

MAGIC FLIGHT

CALL

SELF

FULFILLMENTS

DESCENT

TRANSITIONS SUB-WAYPOINTS
UNIVERSAL JOURNEYS

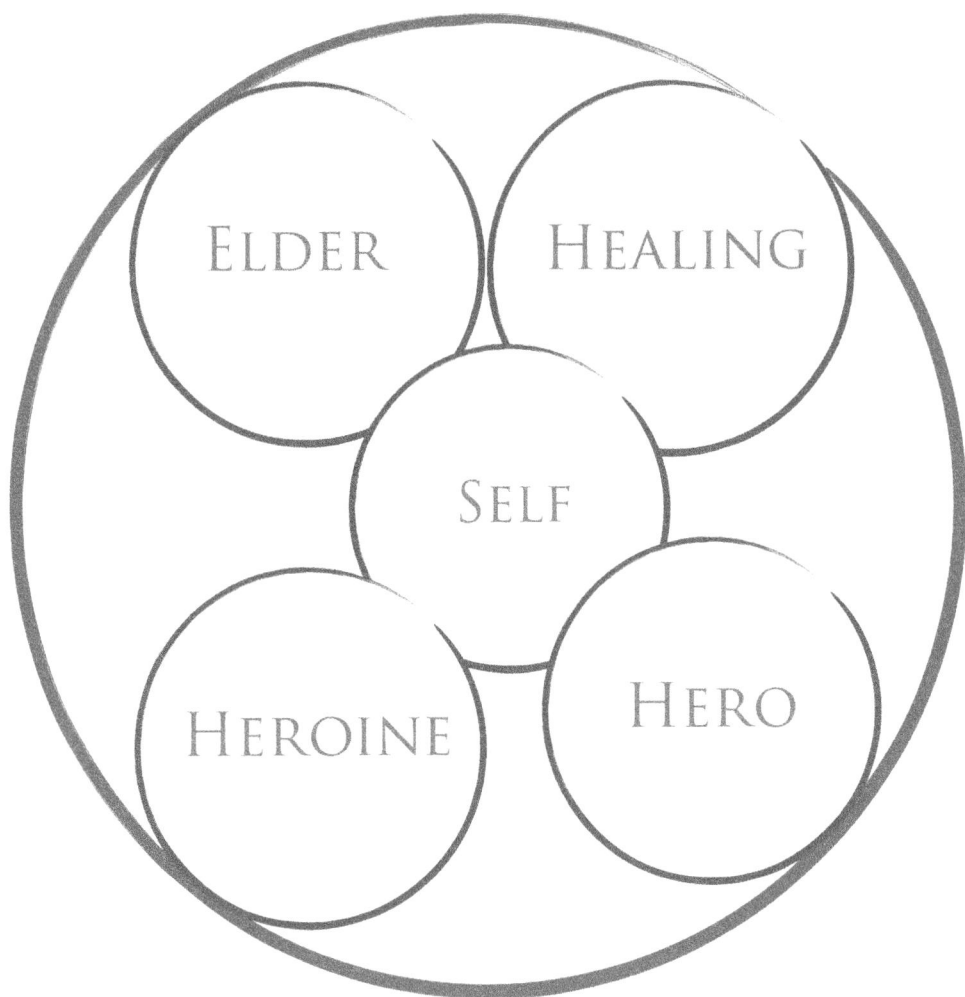

ELDER

HEALING

SELF

HEROINE

HERO

AFFECT QUATERNITY

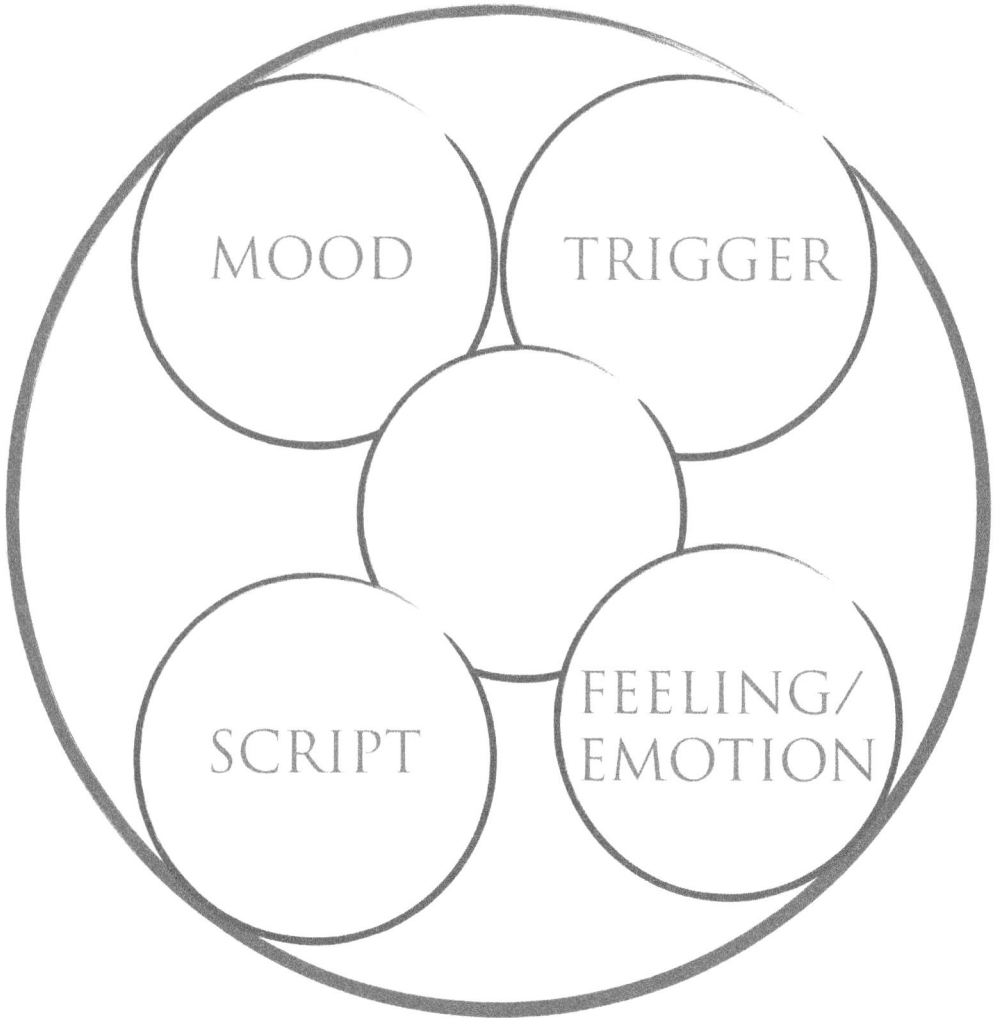

MOOD

TRIGGER

SCRIPT

FEELING/
EMOTION

IDEAL PRIMARY AFFECT (EMOTION) FOR EACH STAGE OF LIFE

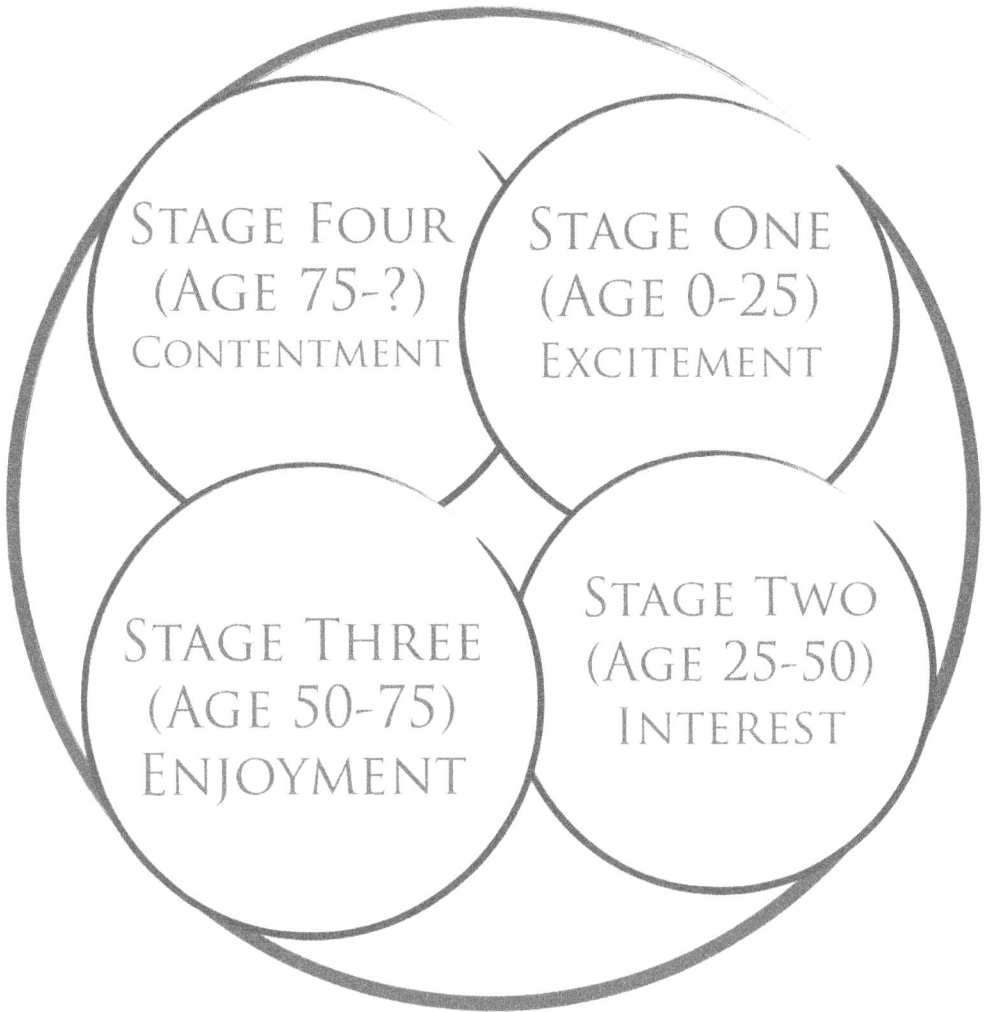

STAGE FOUR
(AGE 75-?)
CONTENTMENT

STAGE ONE
(AGE 0-25)
EXCITEMENT

STAGE THREE
(AGE 50-75)
ENJOYMENT

STAGE TWO
(AGE 25-50)
INTEREST

CONSCIOUS QUATERNITY

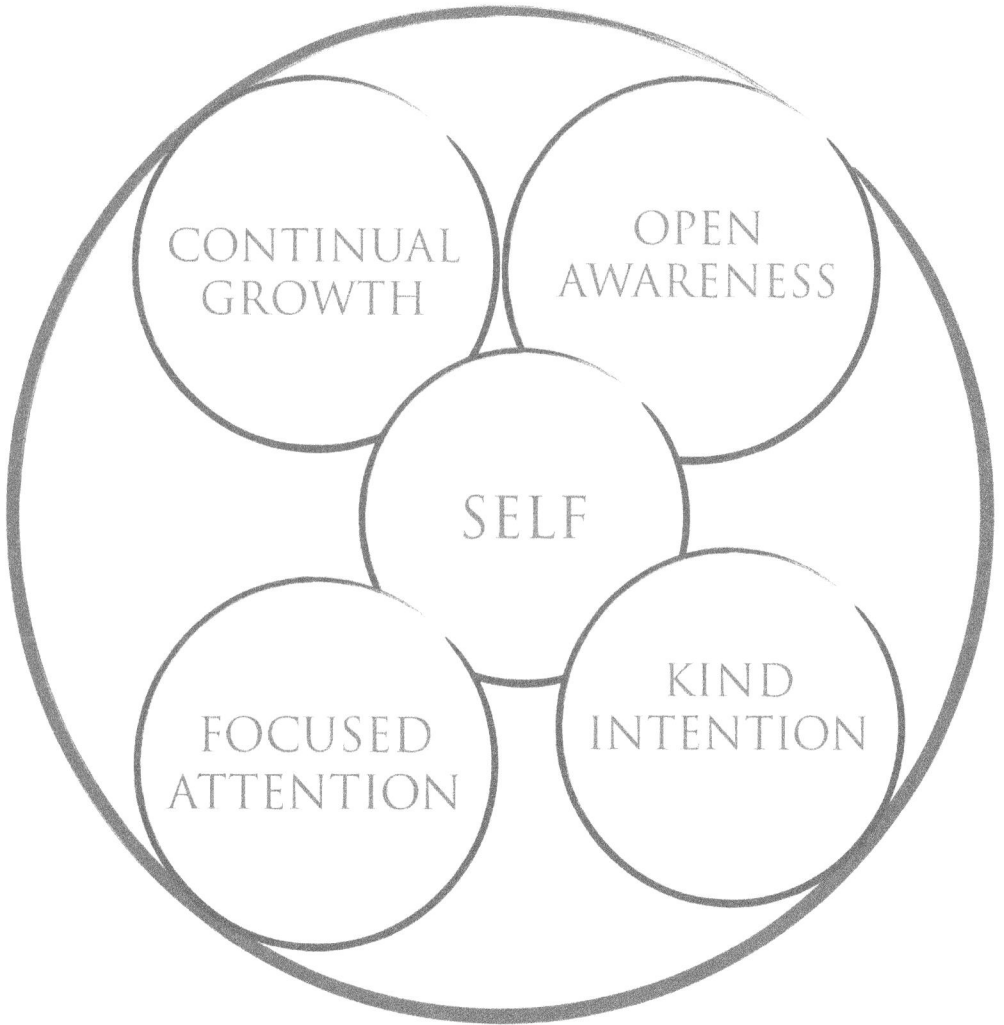

CONTINUAL GROWTH

OPEN AWARENESS

SELF

FOCUSED ATTENTION

KIND INTENTION

CONSCIOUS SUB WAYPOINTS (OPEN AWARENESS)

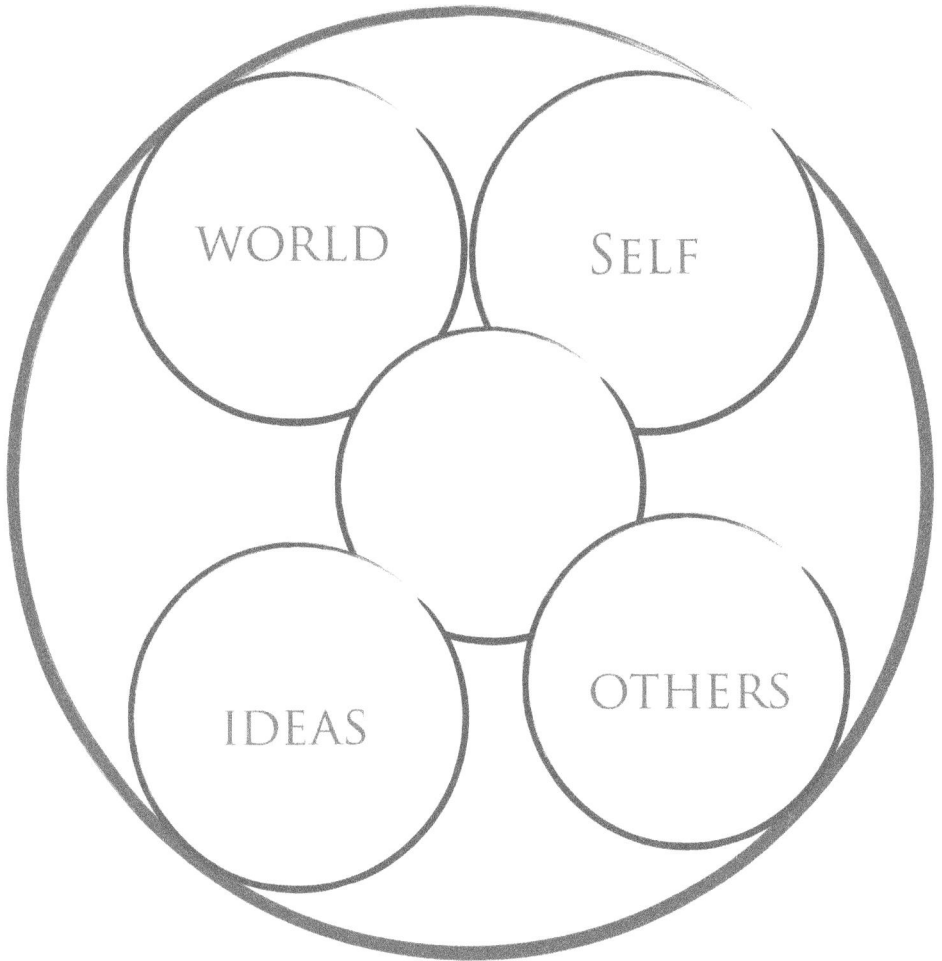

WORLD

SELF

IDEAS

OTHERS

CONSCIOUS SUB WAYPOINTS
(KIND INTENTION)

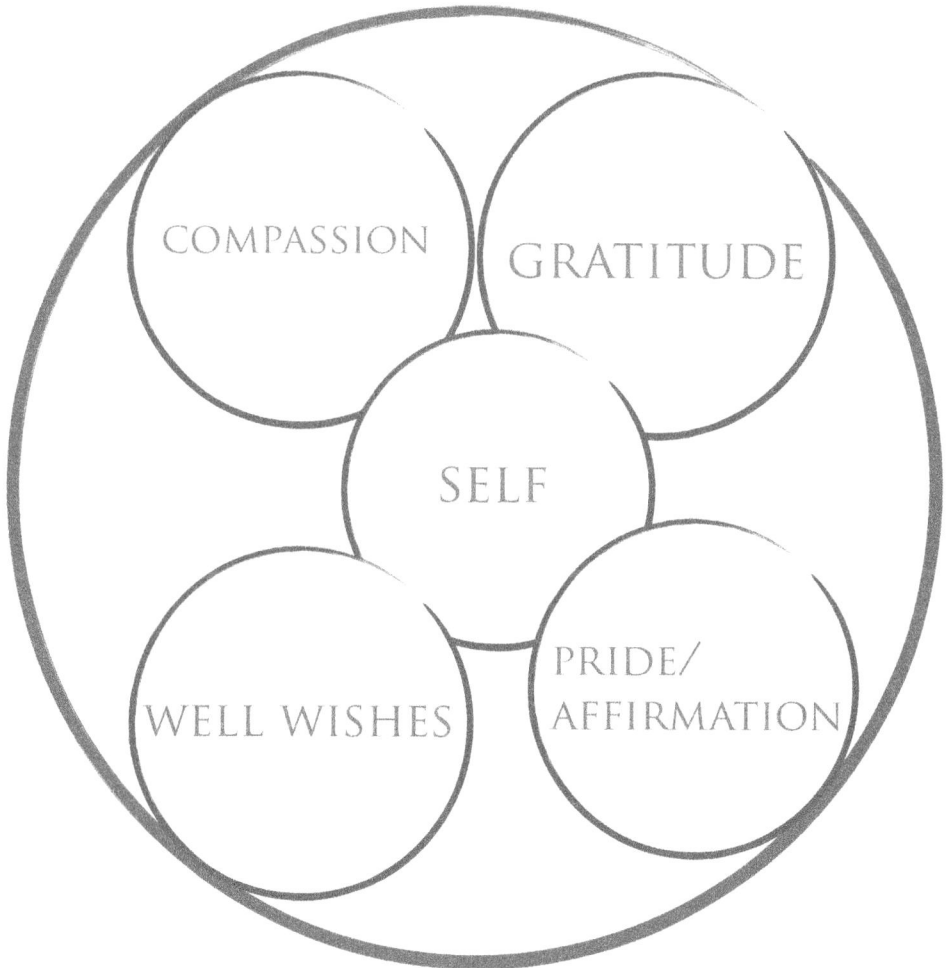

COMPASSION

GRATITUDE

SELF

WELL WISHES

PRIDE/
AFFIRMATION

CONSCIOUS SUB WAYPOINTS (FOCUSED ATTENTION)

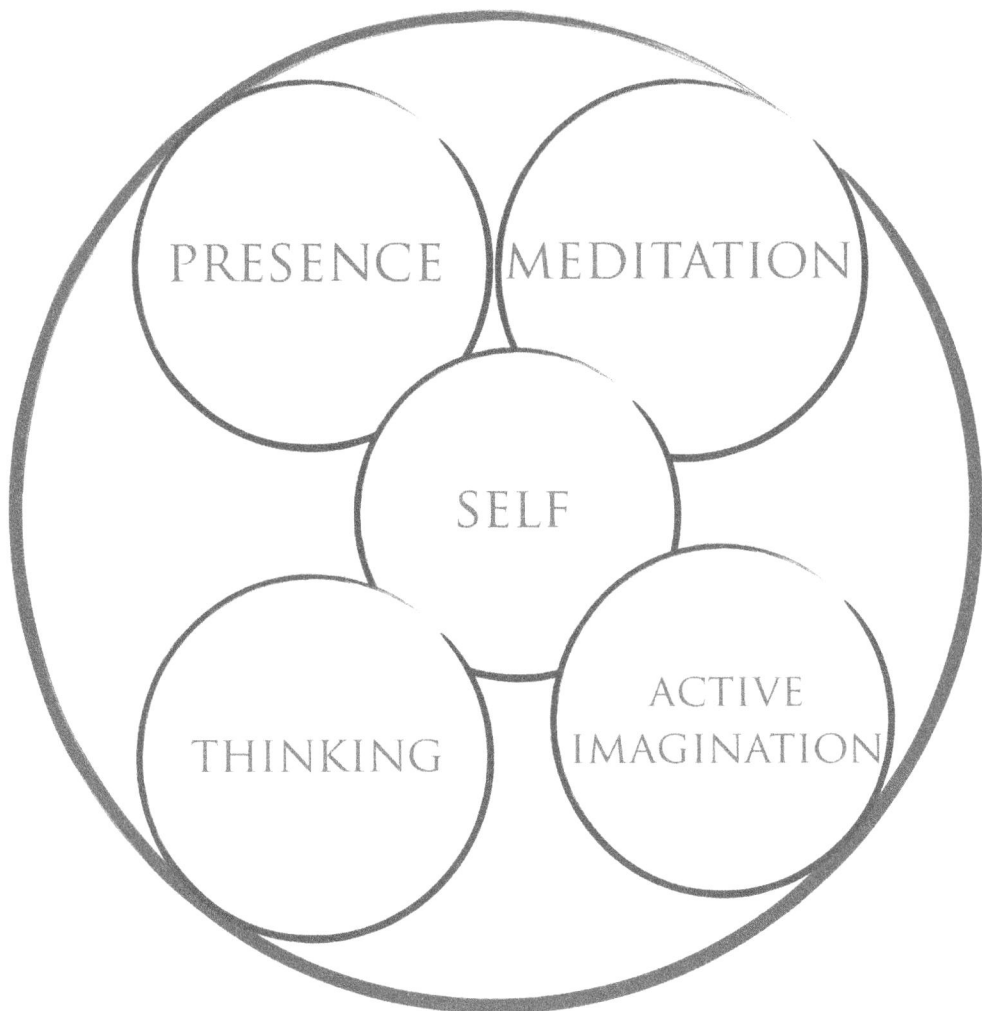

PRESENCE

MEDITATION

SELF

THINKING

ACTIVE IMAGINATION

Conscious/Presence Quaternity

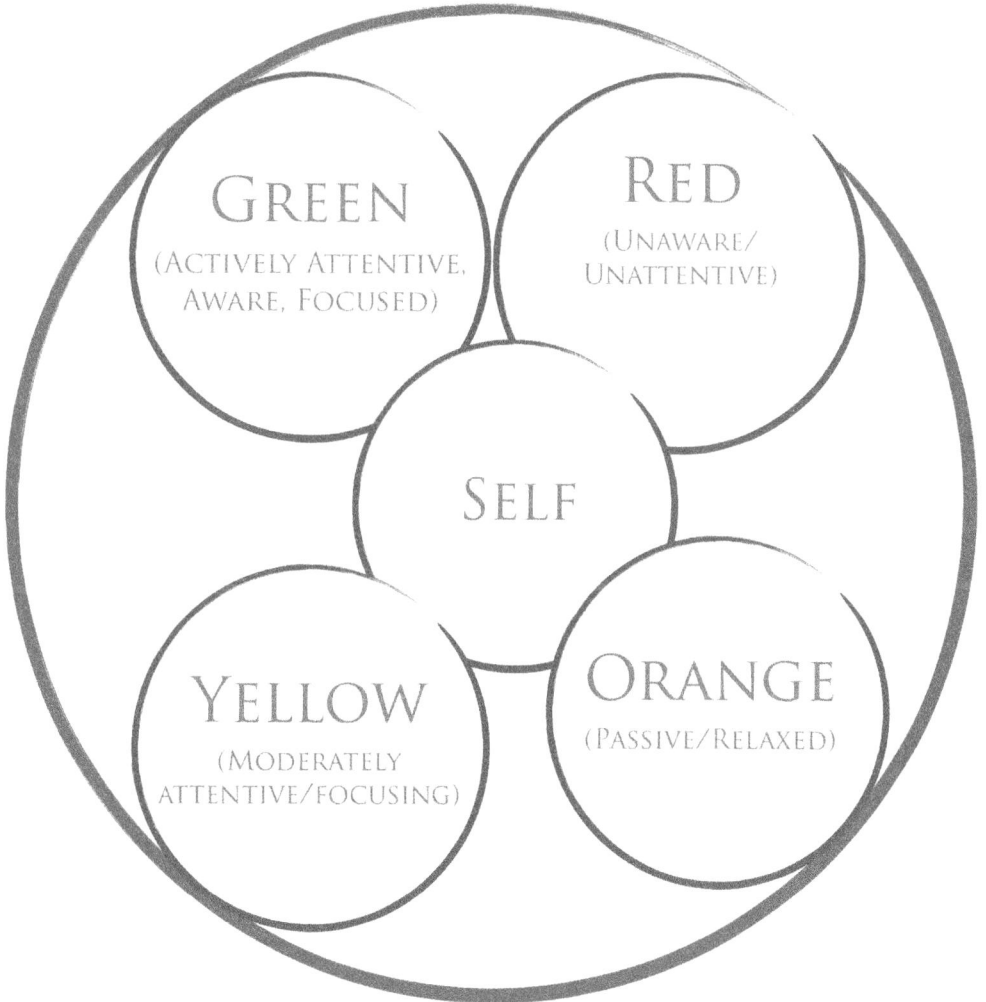

GREEN
(ACTIVELY ATTENTIVE, AWARE, FOCUSED)

RED
(UNAWARE/ UNATTENTIVE)

SELF

YELLOW
(MODERATELY ATTENTIVE/FOCUSING)

ORANGE
(PASSIVE/RELAXED)

CONSCIOUS SUB WAYPOINTS (CONTINUAL GROWTH)

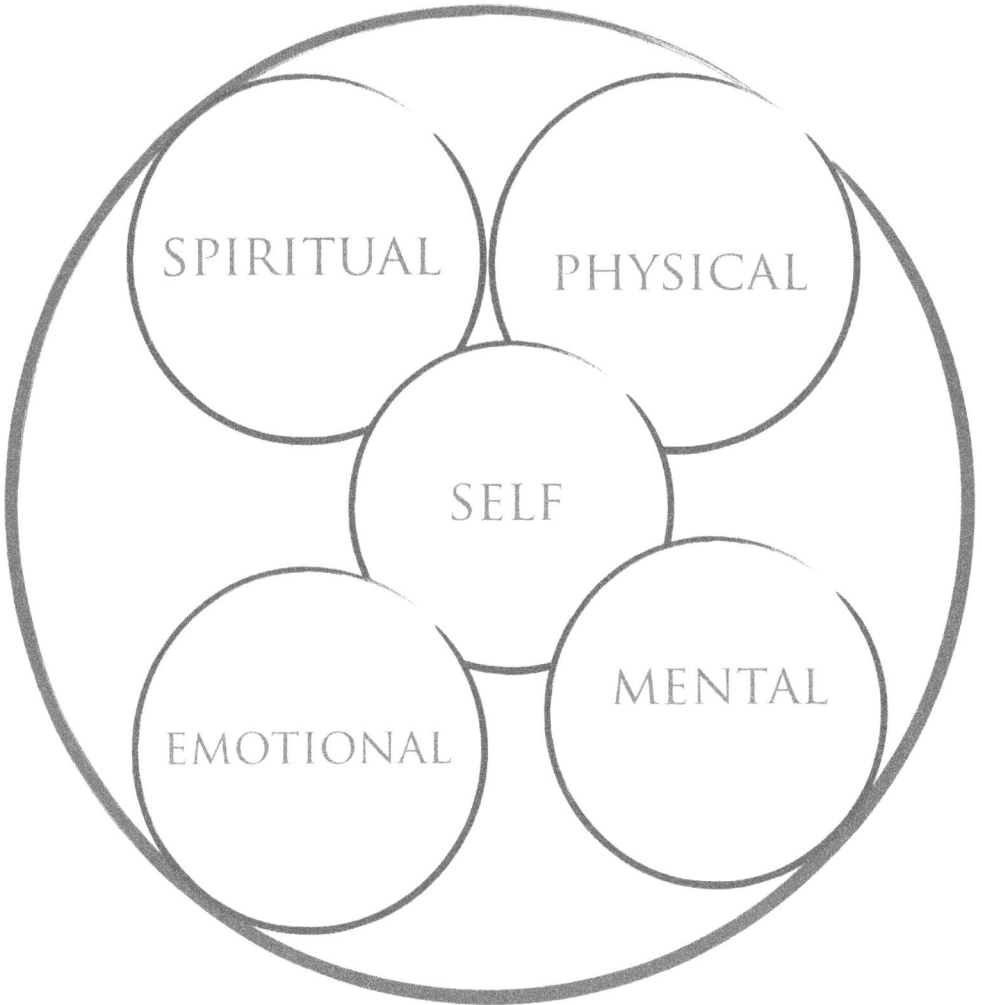

SPIRITUAL

PHYSICAL

SELF

EMOTIONAL

MENTAL

UNCONSCIOUS QUATERNITY

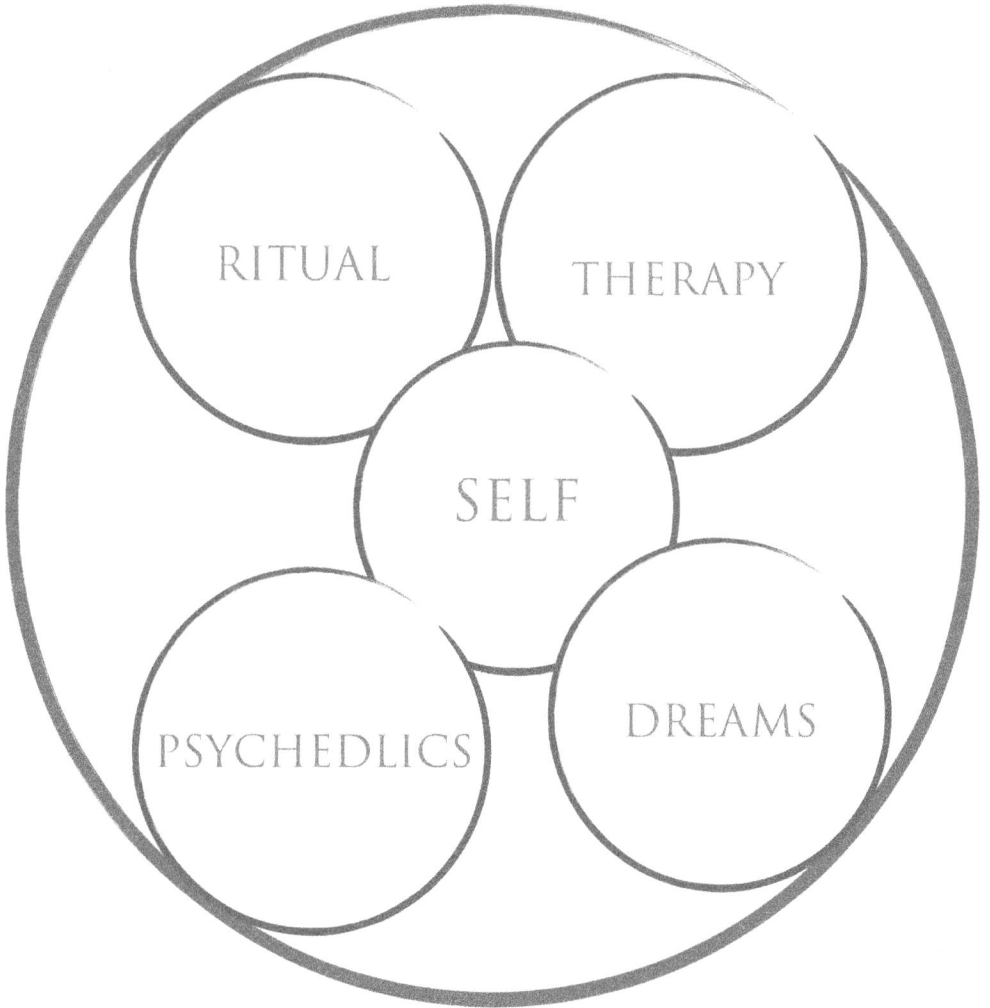

RITUAL

THERAPY

SELF

PSYCHEDLICS

DREAMS

Unconscious sub waypoints Therapy

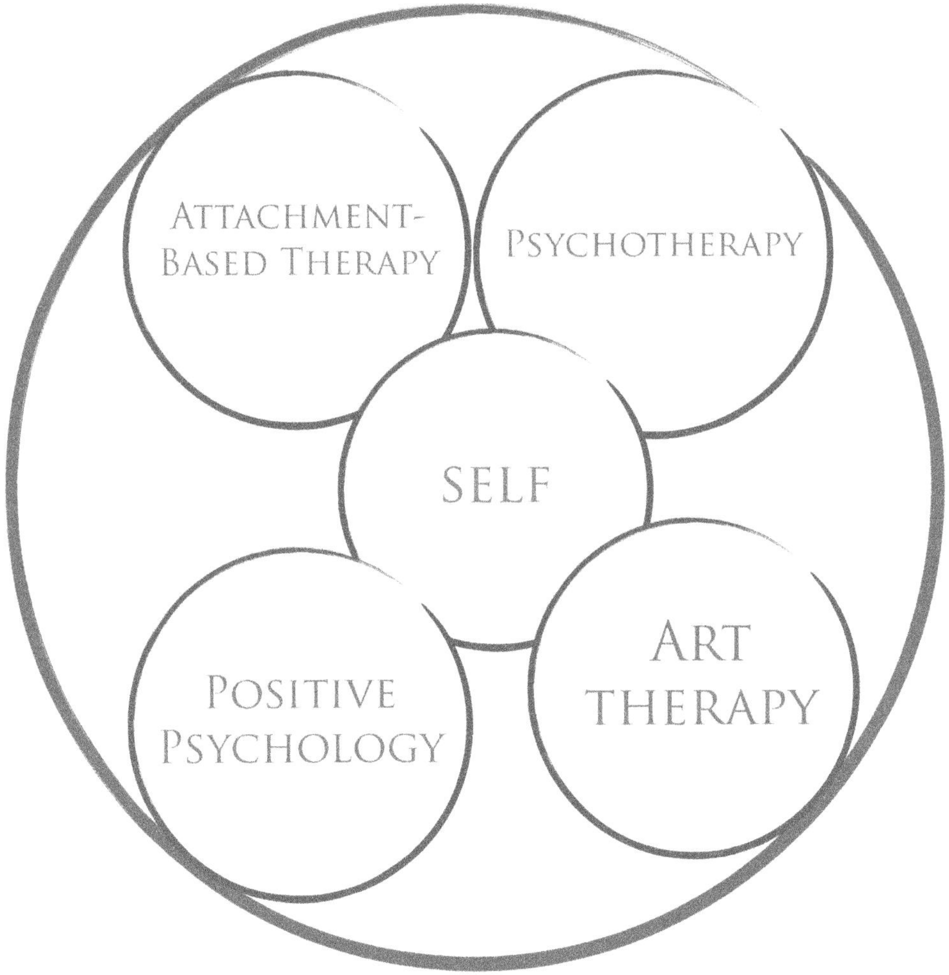
Attachment-Based Therapy
Psychotherapy
SELF
Positive Psychology
Art Therapy

Unconscious sub waypoints
Dreams

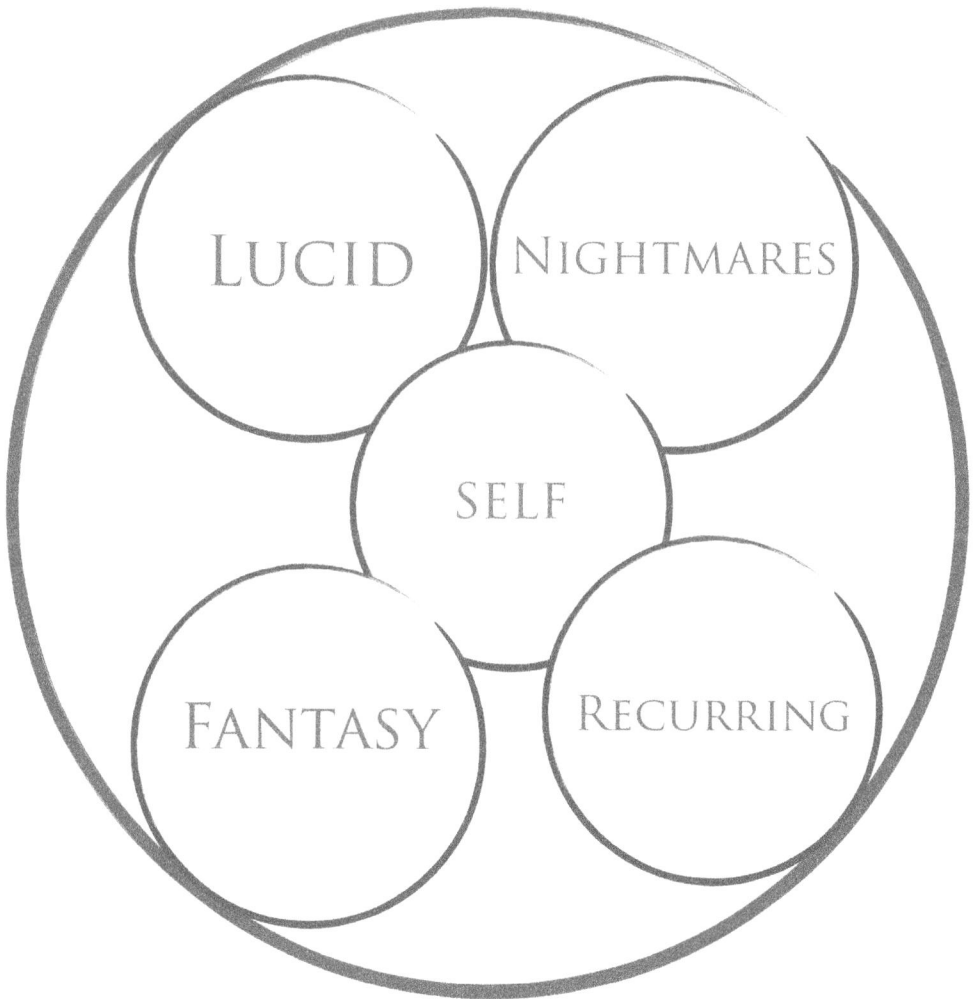

- Lucid
- Nightmares
- Self
- Fantasy
- Recurring

Unconscious sub waypoints
Psychedelics

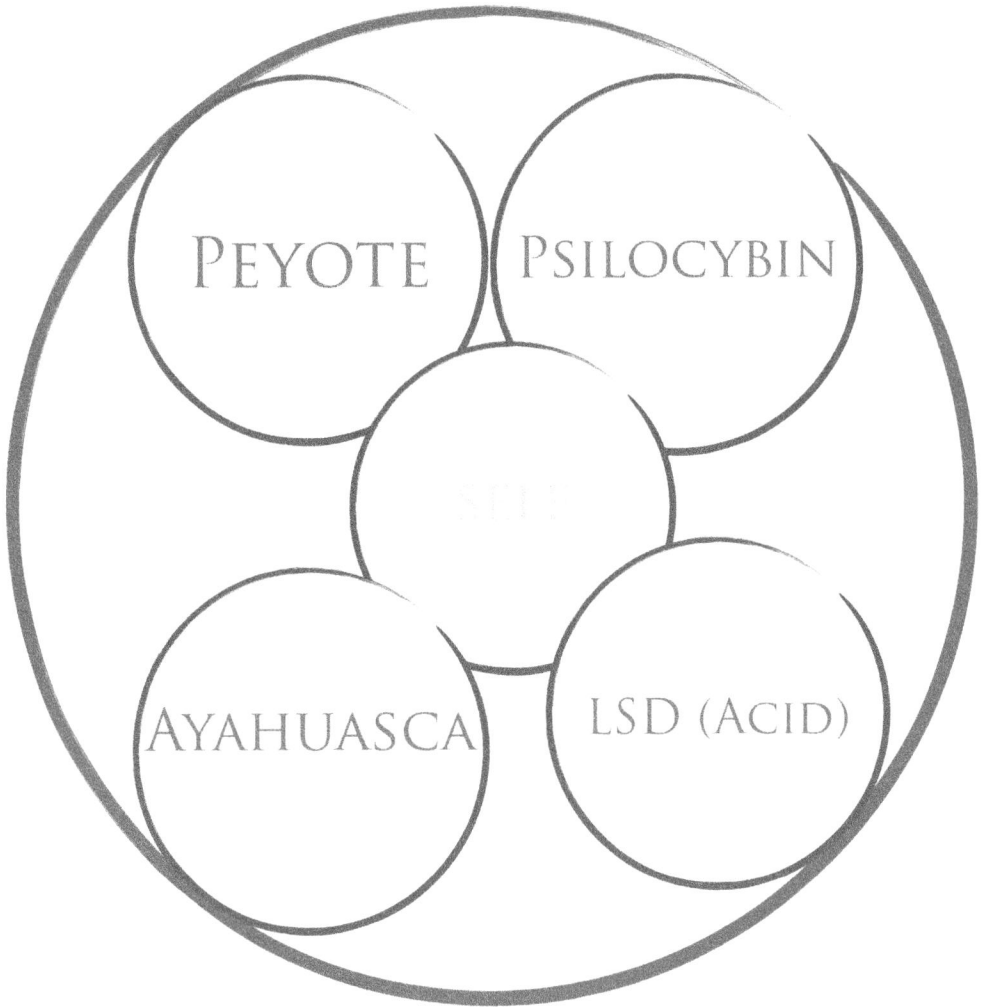

PEYOTE   PSILOCYBIN

STEP

AYAHUASCA   LSD (ACID)

Unconscious sub waypoints
Ritual

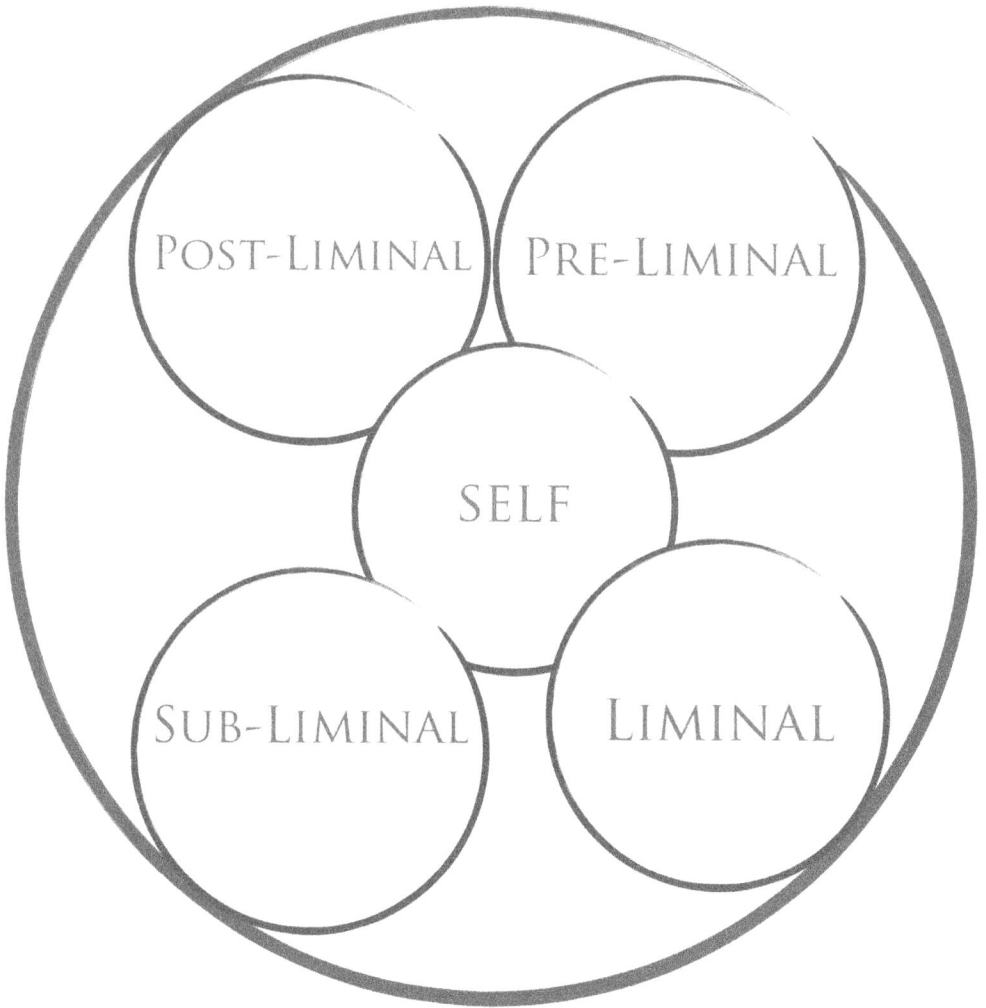

POST-LIMINAL

PRE-LIMINAL

SELF

SUB-LIMINAL

LIMINAL

CATHARSIS QUATERNITY

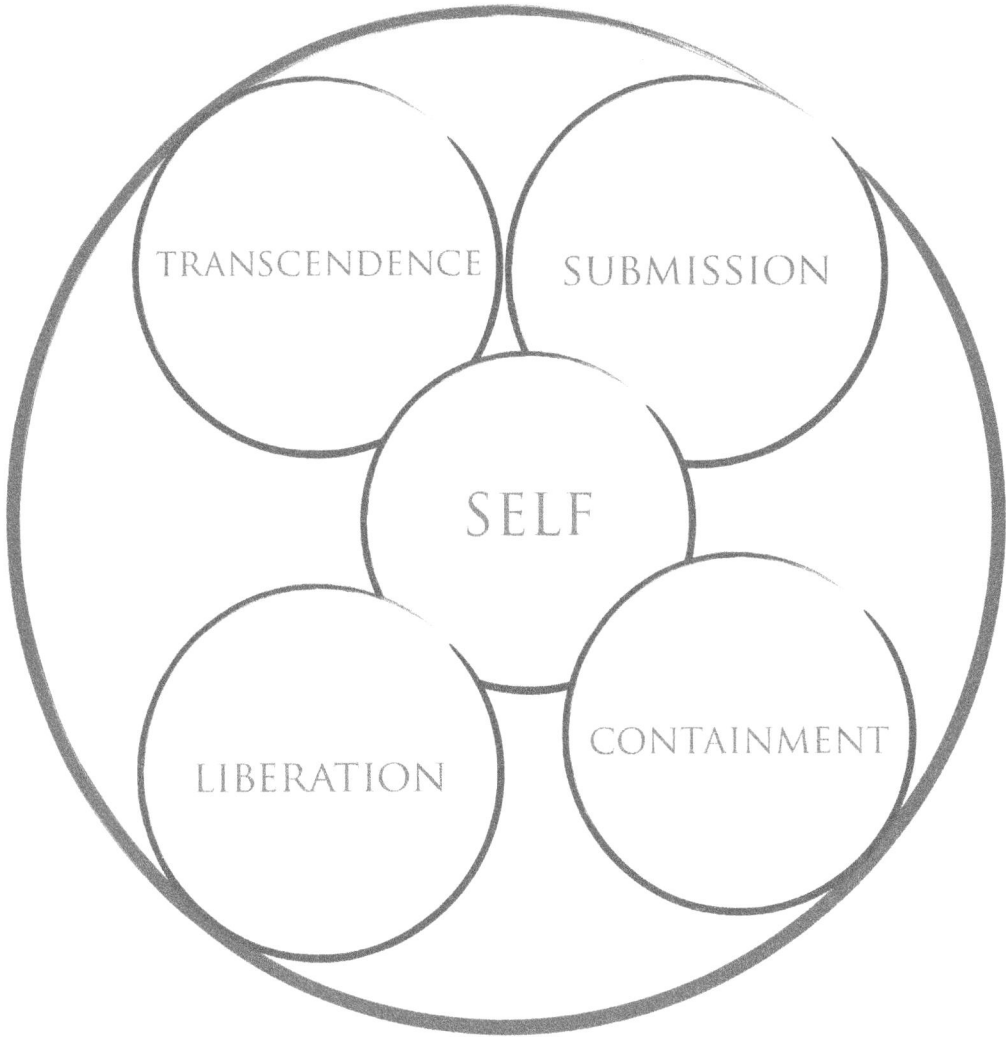

TRANSCENDENCE

SUBMISSION

SELF

LIBERATION

CONTAINMENT

ENJOYMENT QUATERNITY

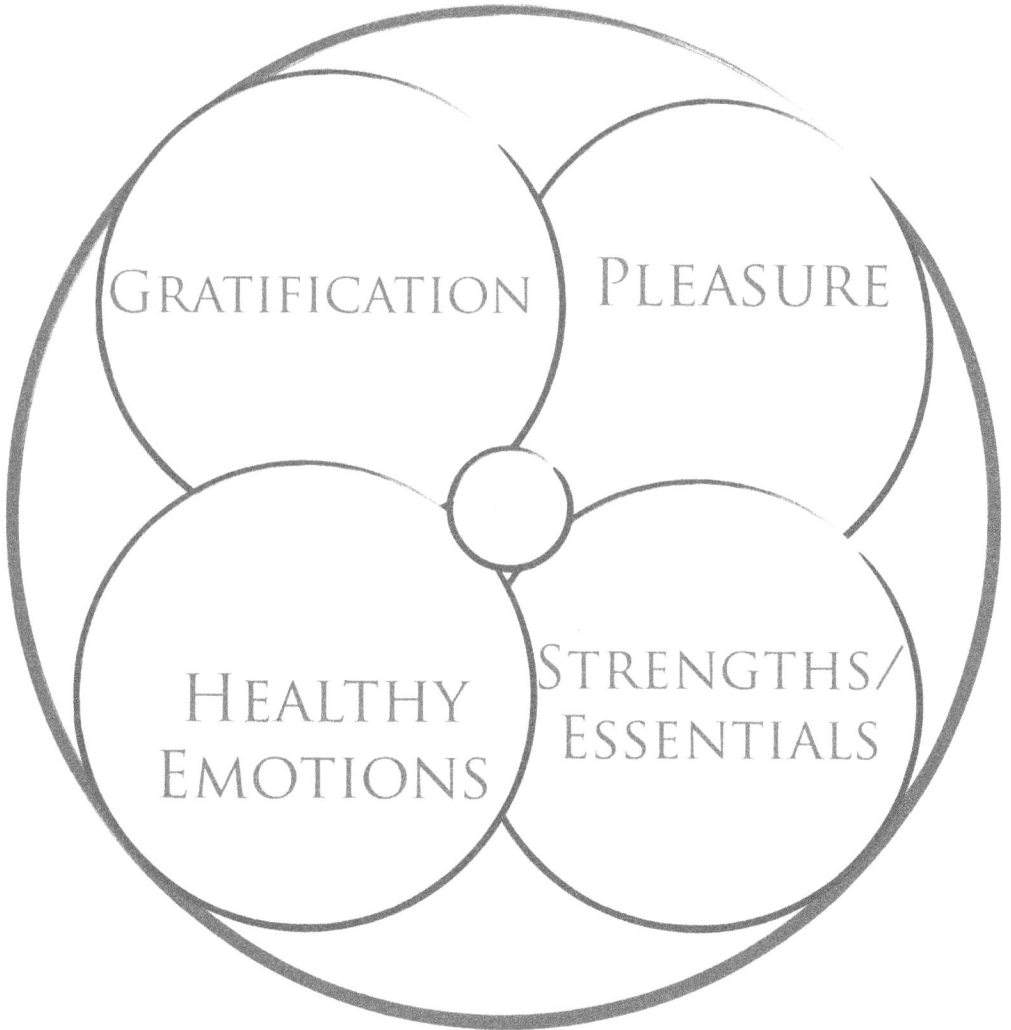

GRATIFICATION

PLEASURE

HEALTHY EMOTIONS

STRENGTHS/ ESSENTIALS

Enjoyment sub waypoints
Pleasure

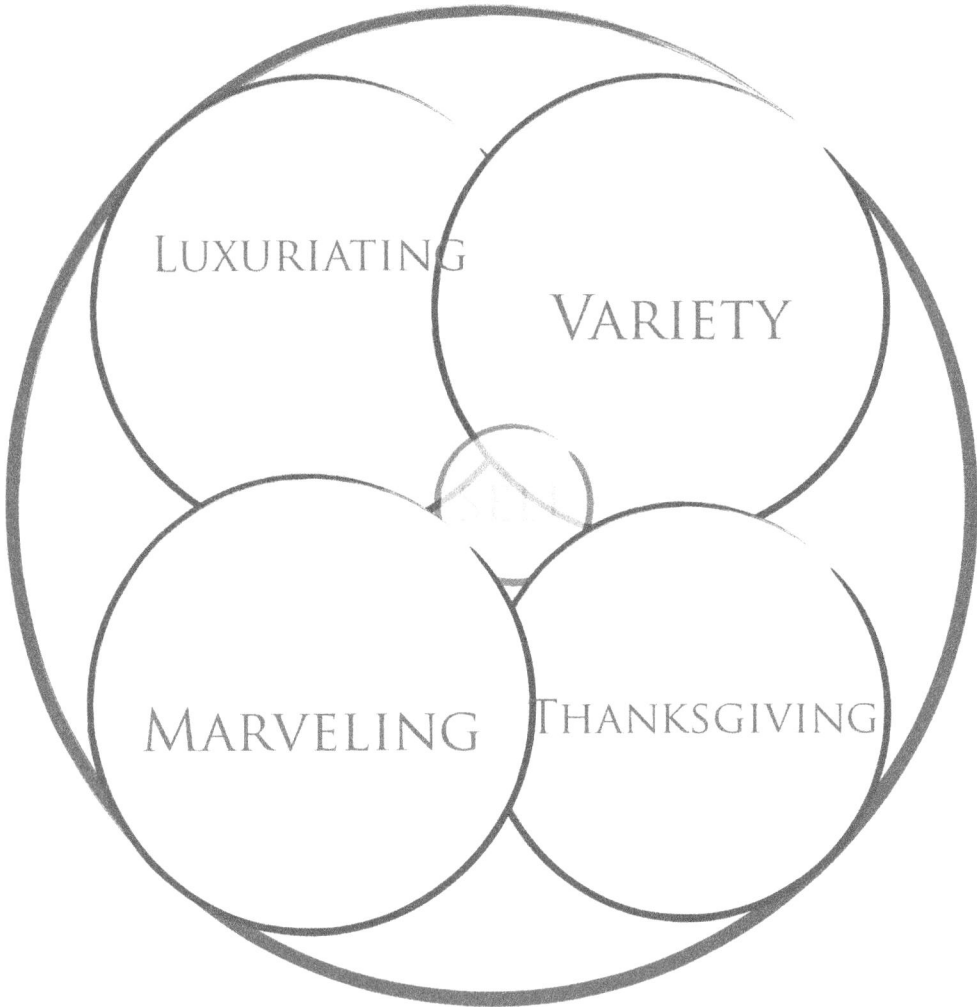

Luxuriating

Variety

Marveling

Thanksgiving

Enjoyment sub waypoints
Healthy Emotions

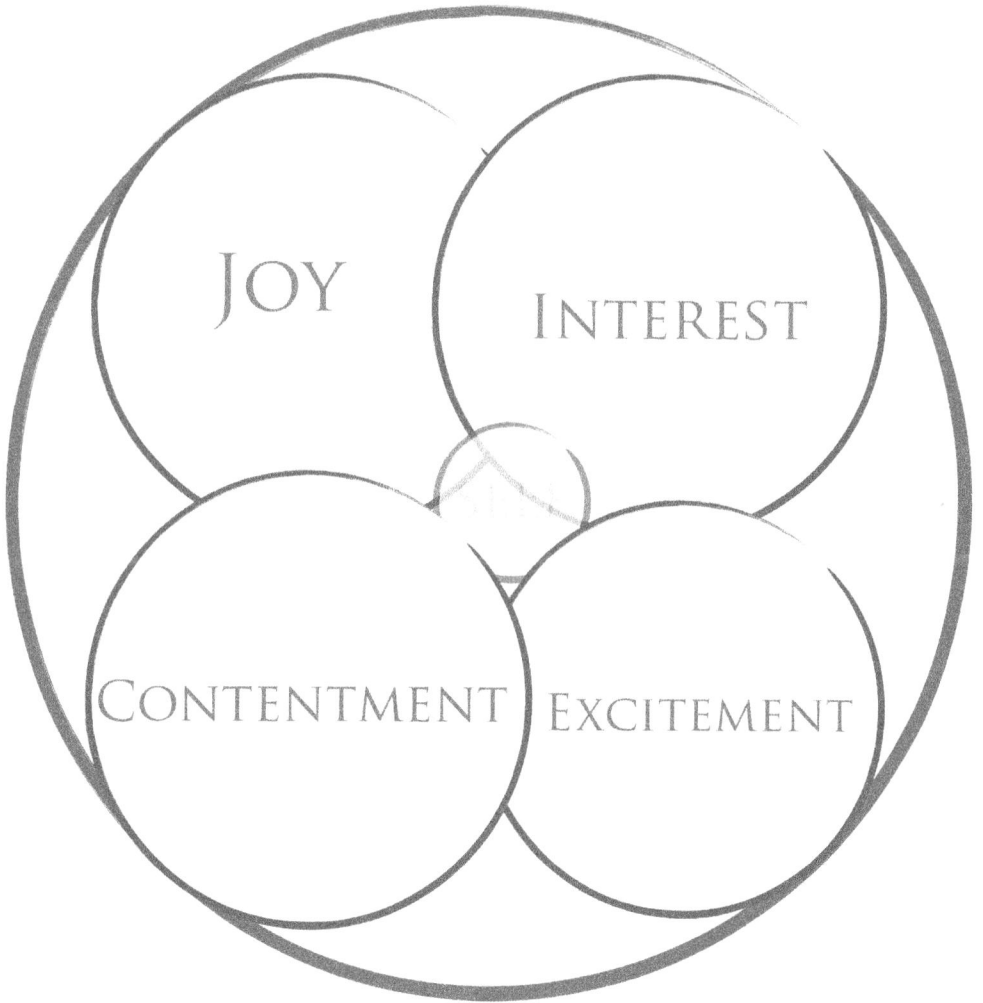

Joy

Interest

Contentment

Excitement

ENLIGHTENMENT QUATERNITY
TRAITS

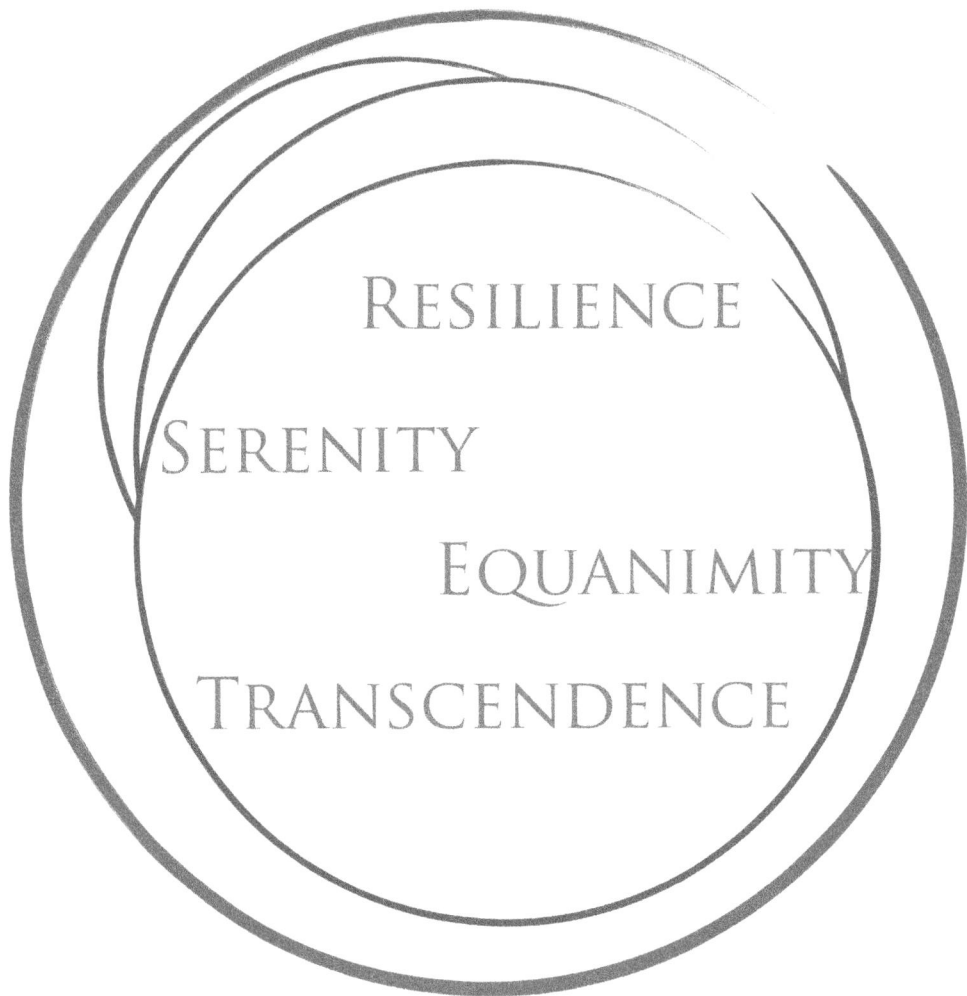

RESILIENCE

SERENITY

EQUANIMITY

TRANSCENDENCE

ENLIGHTENMENT/COSMOLOGICAL/ TRANSCENDENCE/ SAGE WORK SUB-WAYPOINTS

TRANSCEND AGING PARADIGM

TRANSCEND WISDOM

TRANSCEND LEGACY

TRANSCEND MORTALITY

PROJECTIONS OF ANXIETY QUATERNITY

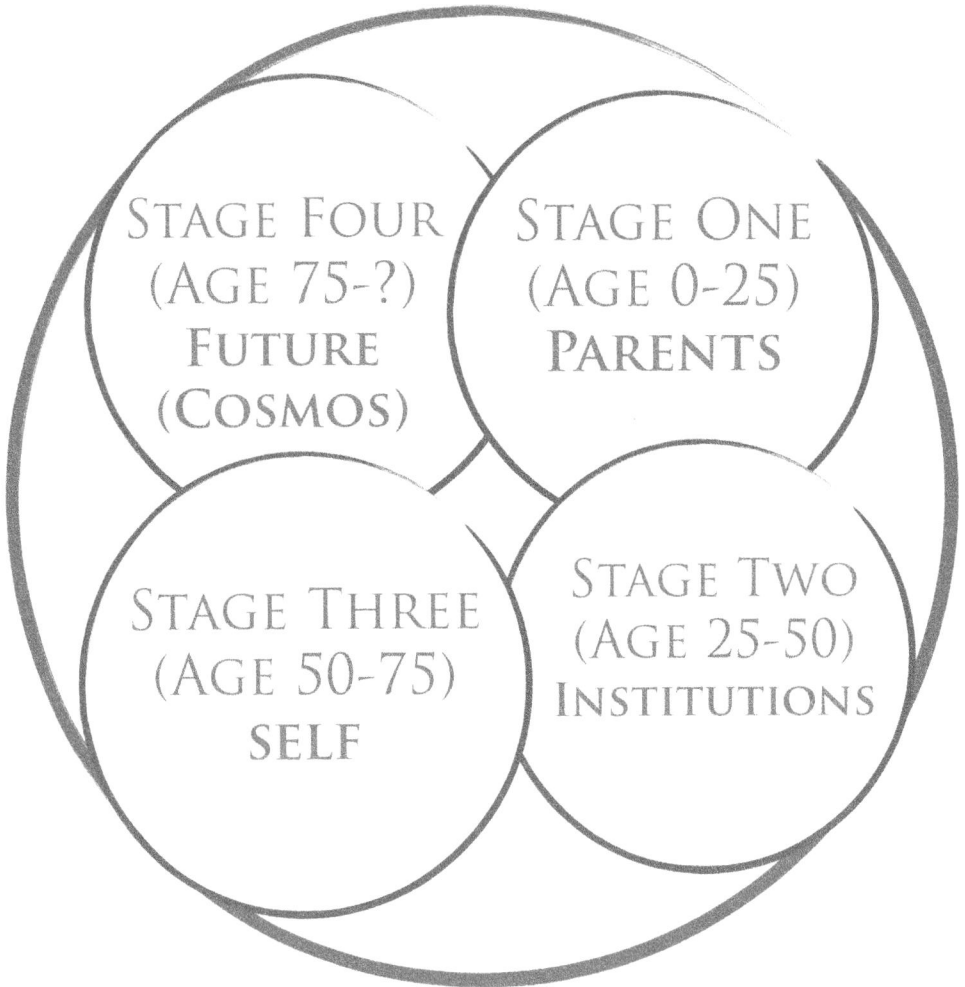

STAGE FOUR
(AGE 75-?)
FUTURE
(COSMOS)

STAGE ONE
(AGE 0-25)
PARENTS

STAGE THREE
(AGE 50-75)
SELF

STAGE TWO
(AGE 25-50)
INSTITUTIONS

PRIMARY EMPHASIS-ASPECTS OF BEING QUATERNITY

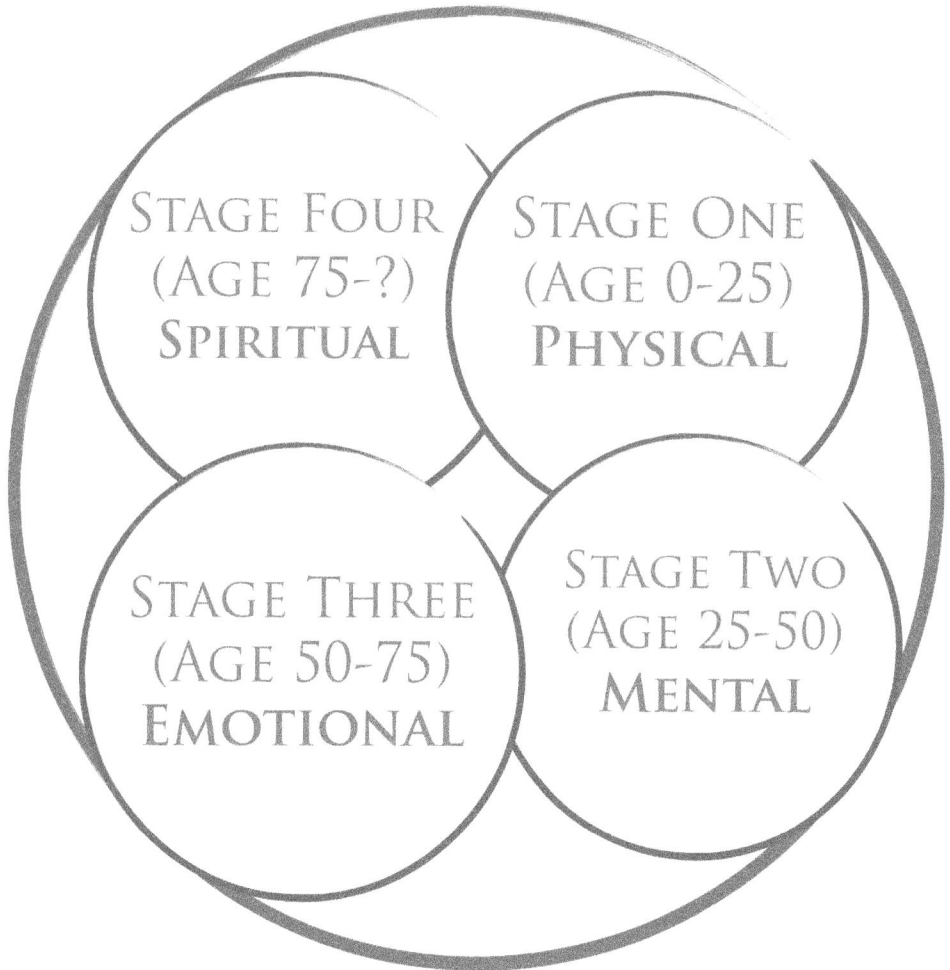

STAGE FOUR
(AGE 75-?)
SPIRITUAL

STAGE ONE
(AGE 0-25)
PHYSICAL

STAGE THREE
(AGE 50-75)
EMOTIONAL

STAGE TWO
(AGE 25-50)
MENTAL

ENLIGHTENMENT STAGE KEY TRAITS QUATERNITY

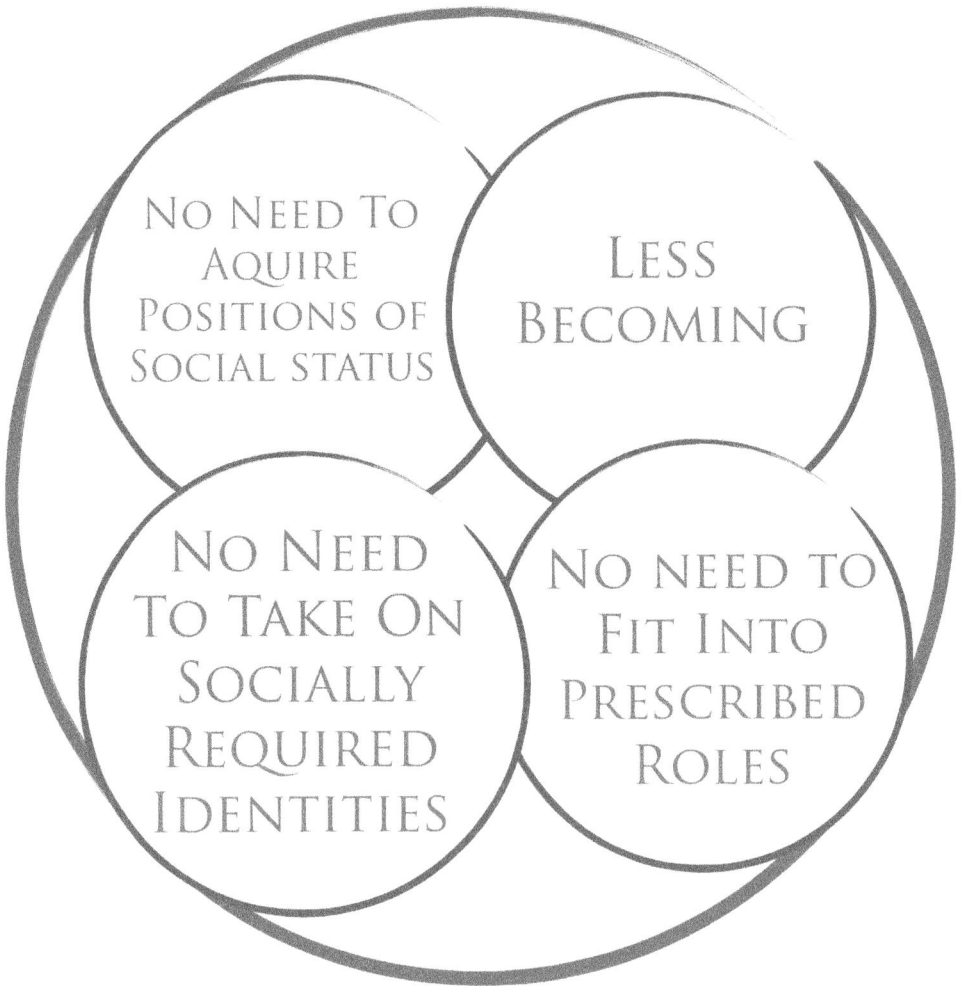

No Need To Aquire Positions of Social status

Less Becoming

No Need To Take On Socially Required Identities

No need to Fit Into Prescribed Roles

Axis of Life Quaternity

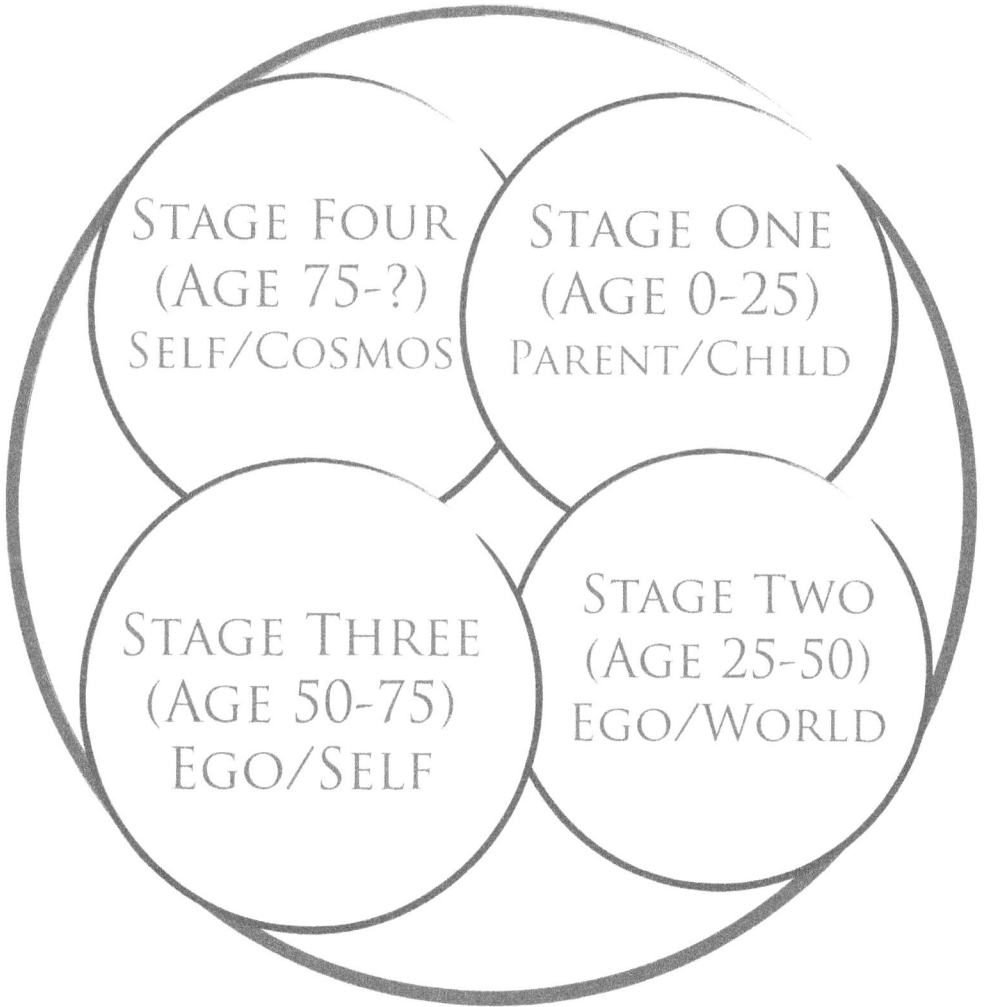

Stage Four
(Age 75-?)
Self/Cosmos

Stage One
(Age 0-25)
Parent/Child

Stage Three
(Age 50-75)
Ego/Self

Stage Two
(Age 25-50)
Ego/World

IDENTIFICATION FORMATION QUATERNITY

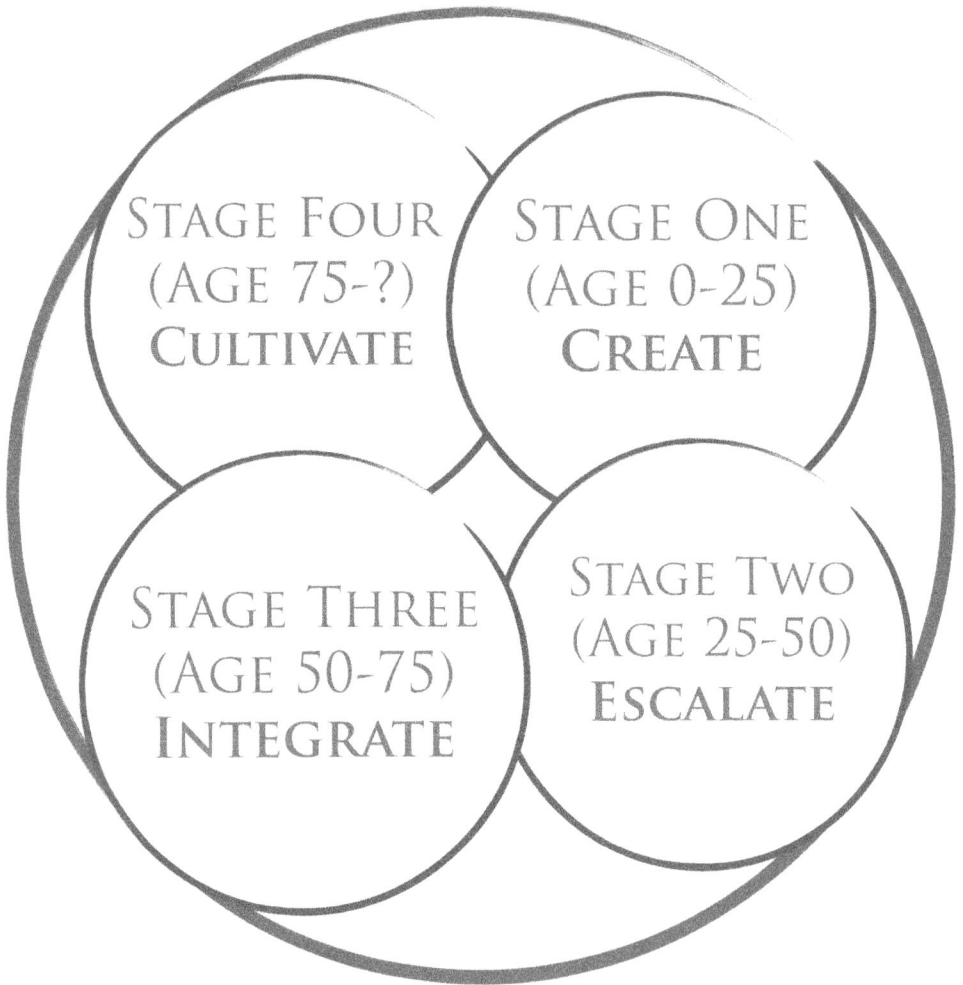

STAGE FOUR
(AGE 75-?)
CULTIVATE

STAGE ONE
(AGE 0-25)
CREATE

STAGE THREE
(AGE 50-75)
INTEGRATE

STAGE TWO
(AGE 25-50)
ESCALATE

WHOLENESS & INTEGRATION

Use a number from 1-10 to describe the current health of each aspect of your being. Which aspect are you most happy with? Surprised? Concerned? What would help them become more integrated—and bring equanimity and wholeness to your life?

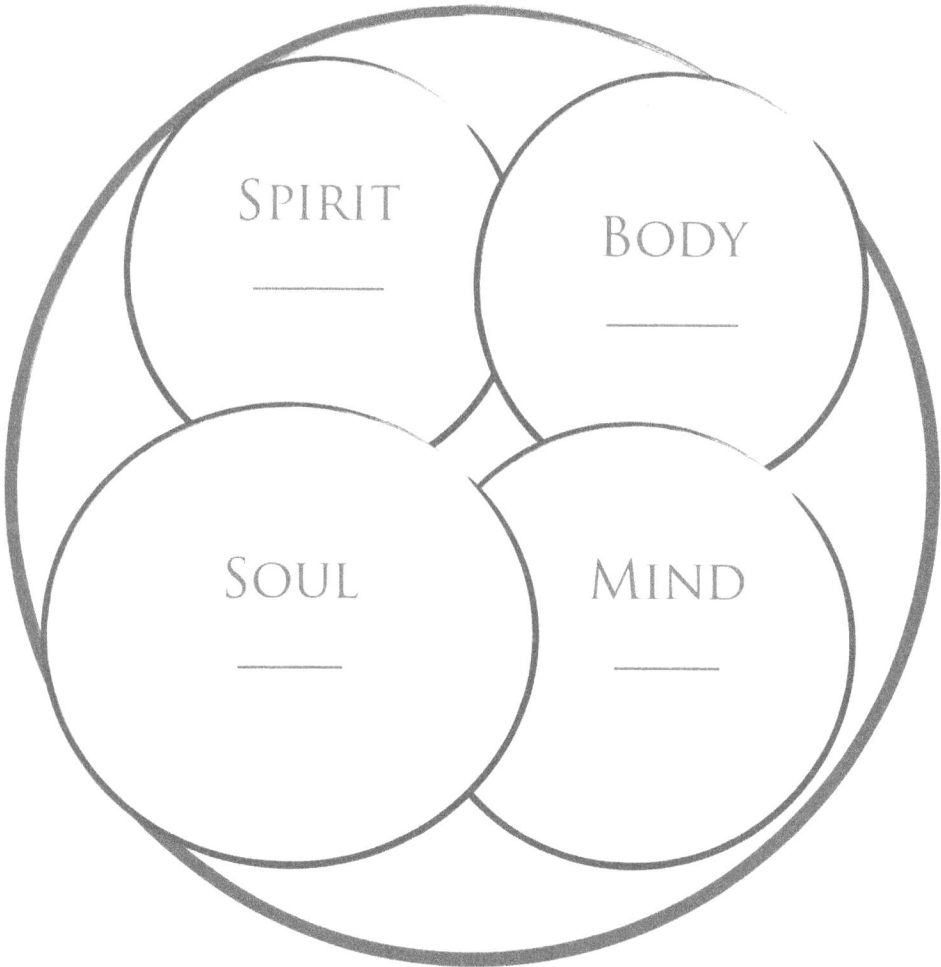

SPIRIT
_____

BODY
_____

SOUL
_____

MIND
_____

Resources

Author's Meditation Mantra

"To be whole
by integrating
body, mind, soul, and spirit;
to be playful, creative, savoring, and loving.
To be joy,
to myself, my companions, my community, and my world.
To be enlightened,
not by becoming good or perfect,
but by being whole;
and by cultivating resilience, serenity, equanimity, and transcendence.
To live my essentials daily,
sensuality, curiosity, communion, and freedom."
(repeat)

Qualities of Sages in Service

With confidence born from harvesting life experience and humility that sees service as the natural result of continued inner growth, we find ways to serve every day. This generosity of spirit elicits joy in human relations, while positively benefiting the communities and cultures we serve.

1. Respect: Affirming the worth of self and others, we strive to treat others as they want to be treated. Respect is a non-judgmental attitude and a feeling of value and care for people, places, and things. This *attitude* is linked to *behavior* in how we "treat" ourselves and others, and in how we speak and what we do.

2. **Integrity:** We practice integrity by being genuine and true to ourselves, being honest and trustworthy in relations with others, and being truthful in word and action in all circumstances.

3. **Deep Listening:** Deep listening is our ability to be present to another's story without fixing the problem or judging. Deep listening is at the core of our service, building relationships and forming community.

4. **Peacefulness:** Practicing inner calm that can come from a sense of gratitude, we speak and act in non-violent ways. Pursuing peaceful solutions to conflict, we respect and promote justice in relationships.

5. **Open Communication:** We practice effective communication by honoring mutuality in speech with language that reflects accurate, clear information and nurtures trust in relationships.

6. **Inclusiveness:** By acceptance and celebration of the rich diversity of ethnicities, lifestyles, backgrounds, ages, and spiritual/wisdom traditions in every community, we cooperate in helping others and making a difference for good in the world.

7. **Lifelong Learning:** With enduring curiosity and innovative creativity, we have a personal mission to continue to grow spiritually, cognitively, and emotionally.

8. **Joyfulness:** Through deep acceptance of our lives we remember to laugh, play, and see the humor in life. Our spirit is regularly filled with feelings of joy as we celebrate how extraordinary it is to be alive.

9. **Compassion:** With a deep awareness of the suffering of another, coupled with the wish to relieve it, we serve from a

deep passion that includes caring and understanding, reciprocity, and forgiveness.

10. **Reverence for Life:** We bring an attitude of respect and care for all living things and become stewards/trustees of our precious planet Earth. We engage in programs and projects with partnerships to nurture and sustain the well-being of the human family and planet Earth.

Written by Sage-ing® International Service Committee.
18. February. 2013.

Opportunities for Sage-Ing work

Explore the sage-ing International website *www.sage-ing.org* You can join SI with a free membership.

Attend meetings of your local SI chapter (or form one).
Go to: *https://www.sage-ing.org/about/circles-chapters*

Form or join an SI Wisdom Circle. For more information, download the free pamphlet *"Wisdom Circles: The journey from Age-ing to sage-ing"* from the SI website at:
https://www.sage-ing.org/wp-content/uploads/2020/07/WisdomCircleBooklet3rdEdition716-1.pdf

Visit SI's YouTube page: *https://www.youtube.com/channel/UCQ0CMxaqM9sWVOnBR_erjtA*

Explore conscious aging organizations: Find them:
https://www.sage-ing.org/links/conscious-aging-alliance

Suggested Reading

A Brief History of Time. Stephen Hawking. Bantam. 2011.

The Ageless Self. Sharon R. Kaufman. University of Wisconsin Press. 1986.

A Renaissance Redneck In A Mega-Church Pulpit. Randy Elrod. re:Create Publishing. 2014.

Arousal: The Secret Logic of Sexual Fantasies. Michael J. Bader. St. Martin's Griffin. 2003.

Attached: The New Science of Adult Attachment and How It Can Help You Find—and Keep—Love. Amir Levine and Rachel Heller. TarcherPerigee Publishing. 2010.

A Thing of Beauty: Travels in Mythical and Modern Greece. Peter Fiennes. Oneworld Publications. 2021.

At the Existentialist Cafe: Freedom, Being, and Apricot Cocktails. Sarah Bakewell. Other Press. 2016.

Authentic Happiness. Martin Seligman. Simon & Schuster. 2002.

Aware: The Science and Practice of Presence--The Groundbreaking Meditation Practice. Daniel J.Siegel. TarcherPerigee. 2018.

Being A Human: Adventures in Forty Thousand Years of Consciousness. Charles Foster. Metropolitan Books. 2021.

Beyond the Hero. Allan B. Chinen. Xlibris. 1993.

Catharsis in Healing, Ritual, and Drama. Thomas J. Scheff. An Author's Guild BackInPrint Edition. 1979, 2001.

Circe. Madeline Miller. Little, Brown and Company. 2018.

Creativity: Flow and the Psychology of Discovery and Invention. Mihaly Csikszentmihalyi. Harper Collins. 2009.

Deathing: An Intelligent Alternative for the Final Moments of Life. Anya Foos-Graber. Nicolas-Hays, Inc. 1989.

Ecstasy: Understanding the Psychology of Joy. Robert A. Johnson. Harper. 1989.

Elderhood: Redefining Aging, Transforming Medicine, Reimagining Life. Louise Aronson. Bloomsbury Publishing; 1st edition. 2019.

Exploring Affect. Silvan Tomkins, Ed. Virginia Demos, Cambridge University Press. 1995.

The Feminine in Fairy Tales (C. G. Jung Foundation Books Series). Marie-Louise von Franz. Shambhala; Revised ed. edition. 2017.

Finding Meaning in the Second Half of Life. James Hollis. Avery. 2005.

From Age-ing to Sageing. Schachter-Shalomi and Miller. Grand Central Publishing. 2008.

The Greek and Roman Myths: A Guide to the Classical Stories. Philip Matyszak. Thames & Hudson. 2010.

How To Be Idle: A Loafer's Manifesto. Tom Hodgkinson. Harper Perennial. 2005.

How To Change Your Mind. Michael Pollan. Penguin Books. 2019.

The Heroine's Journey. Maureen Murdock. Shambhala. 1990.

The Inner Work of Age: Shifting From Role To Soul. Connie Zweig. Park Street Press. 2021.

In The Ever After. Allan B. Chinen. Chiron Publications. 2018.

Iron John. Robert Bly. Hachette Books. 1990.

The Joy of Reading. Charles Van Doren. Sourcebooks. 2008.

The Loss of Belonging: Ten Steps To A New (and Better) Tribe. Randy Elrod. re:Create Books. 2019.

Leaving the Fold: A Guide for Former Fundamentalists and Others Leaving Their Religion. Marlene Winell. Apocryphile Press. 2006.

Long Engagements. David W. Plath. Stanford University Press. 1980.

The Longevity Project: Surprising Discoveries for Health and Long Life from the Landmark Eight-Decade Study. Howard S. Friedman Ph.D. and Leslie R. Martin Ph.D. Plume. 2011.

Man and His Symbols. Carl Jung. Doubleday & Company. 1964.

Mandala Symbolism. Carl Jung. Princeton University Press. 1959, 1969.

Man Seeks God: My Flirtations with the Divine. Eric Weiner. Twelve: Hachette Book Group. 2012.

Meanings of Life. Roy F. Baumeister. Guilford Press. 1991.

Memories, Dreams, Reflections. C.G. Jung. Vintage Books. 1961.

Modern Man In Search of a Soul. Carl Jung. Martino Fine Books. 2017.

The Mythical Quest. Retold by Rosalind Kerven. Pomegranate art Books. 1996.

The Myth of the Birth of the Hero. Otto Rank. JHUP. Updated Version. 2015.

Myths and Symbols. Kitagawa & Long. University of Chicago Press. 1969.

Norse Mythology. Neil Gaiman. W. W. Norton & Company. 2017.

Observing the Erotic Imagination. Robert J. Stoller. Yale University Press. 1985.

Pathways to Bliss: Mythology and Personal Transformation. Joseph Campbell. Stillpoint Digital Press. 2004.

Phallos. Eugene Monick. Inner City Books. 1987.

The Philosophical Baby: What Children's Minds Tell Us About Truth, Love, and the Meaning of Life. Alison Gopnik. Farrar, Straus and Giroux. 2010.

Porn: Myths for the Twentieth Century. Robert J. Stoller. Yale University Press. 1991.

The Portable Jung. Ed. Joseph Campbell. Penguin Group. 1976.

Psychology of the Unconscious. Carl Jung. Dover Publications. 1947. 2002.

The Pursuit of Pleasure. Lionel Tiger. Routledge. 2017.

The Quest of the Holy Grail. Penguin Books. 1969.

Reflections on Your Life Journal. Ken Gire. Chariot Victor Publishing. 1998.

Ritual: A Very Short Introduction (Very Short Introductions). Barry Stephenson. Oxford University Press. 2015.

Sacred Prostitute. Nancy Qualls-Corbett. Inner City Books. 1998.

Shame and Pride: Affect, Sex, and the Birth of Self. Donald L. Nathanson. W.W. Norton & Company. 1994.

The Song of Achilles: A Novel. Madeline Miller. Ecco. 2012.

The Undiscovered Self. Carl Jung. New American Library. 1957.

The Upside of Your Dark Side. Todd B. Kashdan & Robert Biswas-Diener. Plume. 2014.

Waking Up. Sam Harris. Simon & Schuster. 2014.

What Are People For?: Essays. Wendell Berry. Counterpoint; Second Edition. 2010.

Why Good People Do Bad Things. James Hollis. Penguin Publishing Group. 2008.

The Wisdom of the Shamans. Don Jose Ruiz. Heirophant Publishing. 2018.

Wired To Create. Scott Barry Kaufman & Carolyn Gregoire. Perigee Books. 2015.

Women Who Run With the Wolves: Myths and Stories of the Wild Woman Archetype. Clarissa Pinkola Estes. Ballantine Books; Reissue Edition. 1996.

The World of Shamanism. Roger Walsh. Llewellyn Publications. 2007.

References

1 Why I Hope to Die at 75. The Atlantic. https://www.law.wvu.edu/files/d/1f55427f-0bfc-4159-837f-9d9ca2971c69/why-i-hope-to-die-at-75-the-atlantic.pdf

2 Ed. Joseph Campbell. The Portable Jung. Penguin Group. 1976. p. 17.

3 *A Snapshot of the Age Distribution of Psychological Well-Being in the United States. Proceedings of the National Academy of Sciences.* 107(22) 9985-9990. Stone, A.A., Schwartz, J.E., Broderick, J.E., and Deaton, A. 2010.

4 Allan B. Chinen. *Beyond the Hero.* Xlibris. 1993. p. 218.

5 Shrek – Shrek script | Genius. https://genius.com/Shrek-shrek-script-annotated

6 What Is the Medicine Wheel – History and Meaning - Symbol Sage. https://symbolsage.com/medicine-wheel-symbol-explained/

7 David Whyte. *The Three Marriages: Reimagining Work, Self, and Relationship.* Riverhead Books; 1st edition (January 20, 2009). Kindle Edition. p.36.

8 "The Middle Passage: From Misery to Meaning in Midlife" by .... https://www.goodreads.com/book/show/47849.The_Middle_Passage

9 Hollis, James. *Why Good People Do Bad Things.* Penguin Publishing Group. 2008. Kindle Edition. p. 198.

10 Robert Bly. *Iron John.* Hachette Books. 1990. p. 221.

11 Understanding Gender. https://genderspectrum.org/articles/understanding-gender Accessed 28 February 2022.

12 Gender. Merriam-Webster.com Dictionary, Merriam-Webster, https://www.merriam-webster.com/dictionary/gender. Accessed 31 January 2022.

13 Gender. Psychology Today. https://www.psychologytoday.com/us/basics/gender

14 Understanding Gender. https://genderspectrum.org/articles/understanding-gender Accessed 28 February 2022.

15 Understanding Gender. https://genderspectrum.org/articles/understanding-gender Accessed 28 February 2022.

16 Understanding Gender. https://genderspectrum.org/articles/understanding-gender Accessed 28 February 2022.

17 Gender. https://www.psychologytoday.com/us/basics/gender. Accessed 26 January 2022.

18 Ibid.

19 Allan B. Chinen. *Beyond the Hero.* Xlibris. 1993. p. 60.

[20] Clarissa Pinkola Estes. *Women Who Run With the Wolves: Myths and Stories of the Wild Woman Archetype.* Ballantine Books; Reissue edition. 1996. pp. 312-318.

[21] Understanding Gender. https://genderspectrum.org/articles/understanding-gender Accessed 28 February 2022.

[22] Myth. *Merriam-Webster.com Dictionary.* Merriam-Webster. https://www.merriam-webster.com/dictionary/myth. Accessed 19 January 2021.

[23] Allan B. Chinen. *Beyond the Hero.* Xlibris. 1993. p. 278.

[24] Robert Bly. *Iron John* . Hachette Books. 1990. p. 113.

[25] Peter Fiennes. *A Thing of Beauty: Travels in Mythical and Modern Greece.* Oneworld Publications. 2021. Kindle Edition. Location 196-206.

[26] Robert Bly. *Iron John.* Hachette Books. 1990. p. 27.

[27] Joseph Campbell. *Encyclopædia-Britannica.com.* Encyclopedia-Brittanica. https://www.britannica.com/biography/Joseph-Campbell-American-author. Accessed 19 January 2021.

[28] "Asclepius." *Encyclopædia Britannica,* https://www.britannica.com/topic/Asclepius. Accessed 19 January 2021.

[29] Michael Brown, as cited by Roger Walsh, 2007. *The World of Shamanism.* Kindle Edition. p. 17.

[30] Don Jose Ruiz, *The Wisdom of the Shamans.* Heirophant Publishing. 2018. *pp. vii and viii.*

[31] Roger Walsh. *The World of Shamanism.* Llewellyn Publications. 2007. p. 271.

[32] *Myths and Symbols.* R.C. Zaehner. Ed. Kitagawa and Long. Chicago University Press. 1969. pp. 209-215.

[33] A Brief Cultural History Of Sex. Independent Online Newspaper. Independent. https://www.independent.co.uk/life-style/love-sex/culture-of-love/brief-cultural-history-sex-938527.html. Accessed 3 January, 2021.

[34] A Brief Cultural History of Sex. The Independent. https://www.independent.co.uk/life-style/love-sex/culture-of-love/a-brief-cultural-history-of-sex-938527.html

[35] Nancy Qualls-Corbett. *Sacred Prostitute.* Inner City Books. 1998. p. 12.

[36] http://melammu-project.eu/database. Accessed 21 January 2021.

[37] https://www.independent.co.uk/news/world/europe/medieval-fertility-ritual-leaves-czech-women-s-rights-in-the-dark-ages-659005.html Accessed 21 Jan. 2021.

[38] Robert J. Stoller. *Porn: Myths for the Twentieth Century.* Yale University Press. 1991. *p. 215.*

[39] Man and His Symbols. Carl Gustav Jung, Marie-Luise von Franz, Joseph Lewis Henderson, Aniela Jaffé, Jolande Jacobi. Doubleday. 1961. p. 291.

[40] Charles Foster. *Being A Human: Adventures in Forty Thousand Years of Consciousness.* Metropolitan Books. 2021. p. 64.

[41] https://www.arts.gov Accessed 11 September 2019.

[42] Charles Van Doren. *The Joy of Reading.* Sourcebooks. 2008. p. 335.

[43] Shrek – Shrek script | Genius. https://genius.com/Shrek-shrek-script-annotated

[44] Gore Vidal. *Palimpsest: A Memoir.* 1996.

[45] Complementary Colors - Designbar. https://www.designbaronline.com/complementary_colors Accessed 19 March. 2021.

[46] Before I Die - You Must Know This About The Future. https://www.youtube.com/watch?v=vsWnynNMCzk

[47] The 3 Steps Of Essentialism: How To Achieve More By Doing. https://www.forbes.com/sites/francesbridges/2018/11/29/the-3-steps-of-essentialism-achieving-more-by-doing-less-according-to-greg-mckeown Accessed 19 March 2021.

[48] The Four Aspects of Self. Dimensions of Light. https://balancingmindbodysoul.wordpress.com/2012/01/10/the-four-aspects-of-self/

[49] The Four Aspects of "Self" - Balancing Mind, Body & Soul. http://www.balancingmindbodysoul.co.uk/spiritual-development/the-four-aspects-of-self Accessed May 21, 2021.

[50] The Four Aspects of "Self" - Balancing Mind, Body & Soul. http://www.balancingmindbodysoul.co.uk/spiritual-development/the-four-aspects-of-self Accessed May 20, 2021.

[51] Centenarians are the Fastest Growing Demographic. http://www.annuitydigest.com/news/centenarians-are-fastest-growing-demographic. Annuity Digest. Accessed 2 Feb. 2021.

[52] Robert Bly. *Iron John.* Hachette Books. 1990. p. 172.

[53] Amir Levine and Rachel Heller. *Attached: The New Science of Adult Attachment and How It Can Help You Find—and Keep—Love.* TarcherPerigee Publishing. 2010. Kindle Edition. Loc. 293.

[54] https://www.attachmentproject.com/blog/10-attachment-style-tests-used-in-research

[55] C.G. Jung. *Memories, Dreams, Reflections.* Vintage Books. 1961. pp.173-175.

[56] Donald L. Nathanson. *Shame and Pride: Affect, Sex, and the Birth of Self.* W.W. Norton & Company. 1994. pp. 159-160.

[57] New Statistics Reveal the Shape of Plastic Surgery. https://www.plasticsurgery.org/news/press-releases/new-statistics-reveal-the-shape-of-plastic-surgery Accessed 5 August 2019.

58 Donald L. Nathanson. *Shame and Pride: Affect, Sex, and the Birth of Self*. W.W. Norton & Company. 1994. p. 179.

59 Debate: A Biblical Debate: Total Depravity (CALVINISM). https://www.debate.org/ debates/A-Biblical-Debate-Total-Depravity-CALVINISM/1/

60 27 Greatest Sir Ken Robinson Quotes - BrandonGaille.com. https://brandongaille.com/ 27-greatest-sir-ken-robinson-quotes/

61 Randy Elrod. *A Renaissance Redneck In A Mega-Church Pulpit*. cre:ate 2.0 Publishing. 2014. pp. 47-48.

62 Social Influence. https://www.psychologistworld.com/influence/social-influence#references. Psychologist World. Accessed 4 Feburary 2021.

63 Stanley Milgram. *Behavioral Study of Obedience*. The Journal of Abnormal and Social Psychology, 67(4). pp. 371-378.

64 4 Unique Working Styles: What's Yours?. https://www.inc.com/shelley-prevost/4-unique-working-styles-whats-yours.html. Inc. com. Accessed 5 Feburary 2021.

65 David Brooks: The Nuclear Family Was a Mistake - The Atlantic. https:// www.theatlantic.com/magazine/archive/2020/03/the-nuclear-family-was-a-mistake/ 605536/

66 The Nuclear Family Was A Mistake. https://www.theatlantic.com/magazine/archive/ 2020/03/the-nuclear-family-was-a-mistake/605536. The Atlantic. Accessed 5 Feburary 2021.

67 https://www.census.gov/hhes/migration/about/cal-mig-exp.html

68 Wells, William D. "Psychographics: A Critical Review". *Journal of Marketing Research*. 1975. 12: 196—213.

69 http://www.teachthesoul.com/about-the-author Accessed 2 March 2022.

70 Religious Trauma Syndrome. Marlene Winell. https://journeyfree.org/rts/ Accessed 19 April 2021.

71 Carl G Jung. Collected Works, 7, paragraph 112.

72 Deathing: An Intelligent Alternative for the Final Moments of Life. Anya Foos-Graber. Nicolas-Hays, Inc. 1989.

73 The Healing Journey. https://heroinejourneys.com/healing-journey/ Accessed 4 January 2022.

74 Tomkins Institute » Vernon Kelly: A Primer of Affect .... https://www.tomkins.org/what-tomkins-said/what-others-said-about-tomkins/vernon-kelly-a-primer-of-affect-psychology/

75 Tomkins Institute » Biography and Timeline. https://www.tomkins.org/what-tomkins-said/bio-quotes-excerpts/bio/

76 Donald L. Nathanson. *Shame and Pride: Affect, Sex, and the Birth of Self.* W.W. Norton & Company. 1994. p. 45.

77 Ibid. p.74.

78 Ibid. p. 59.

79 Ibid. p. 79.

80 Ibid. p.73.

81 Ibid. p. 94.

82 Ibid. p.124.

83 Justin Cronin. *City of Mirrors.* Ballantine Books. 2016. Kindle Ed. Loc. 2011.

84 Donald L. Nathanson. *Shame and Pride: Affect, Sex, and the Birth of Self.* W.W. Norton & Company. 1994. p. 128.

85 Ibid. p. 133.

86 Ibid. p. 251.

87 Donald L. Nathanson. *Shame and Pride: Affect, Sex, and the Birth of Self.* W.W. Norton & Company. 1994. p. 144.

88 Tomkins, Ed. Virginia Demos. *Exploring Affect.* Cambridge University Press. 199.

89 Donald L. Nathanson. *Shame and Pride: Affect, Sex, and the Birth of Self.* W.W. Norton & Company. 1994. p. 315.

90 Services – Counselling and Psychotherapy Sevices. https://cbitpeel.ca/Services

91 Donald L. Nathanson. *Shame and Pride: Affect, Sex, and the Birth of Self.* W.W. Norton & Company. 1994. p. 55.

92 Ibid. p.131.

93 Matthew 18:1-6 - MSG - At about the same time, the d.... https://www.christianity.com/bible/msg/matthew/18-1-6

94 Alison Gopnik. *The Philosophical Baby: What Children's Minds Tell Us About Truth, Love, and the Meaning of Life.* Farrar, Straus and Giroux. Kindle edition.

95 How to Change Your Mind: What the New Science of .... https://silo.pub/how-to-change-your-mind-what-the-new-science-of-psychedelics-teaches-us-about-consciousness-dying-addiction-depression-and-transcendence.html

96 Sense and Sensitivity. https://www.psychologytoday.com/us/articles/201107/sense-and-sensitivity Accessed 3 March 2018.

97 Suffered Trauma? 7 Keys to Unlocking Post-traumatic Growth. https://www.psychologytoday.com/us/blog/relationship-and-trauma-insights/202104/suffered-trauma-7-keys-unlocking-post-traumatic-growth Accessed 12 January. 2021.

98 Walden: Important Quotes Explained, page 3 | SparkNotes. https://www.sparknotes.com/lit/walden/quotes/page/3/

99 Ken Gire. *Reflections on Your Life Journal*. Chariot Victor Publishing. 1998. p. 84.

100 Mary Oliver. "Sometimes." Red Bird. Beacon Press. 2008.

101 Zweig, Connie. *The Inner Work of Age: Shifting From Role To Soul*. Kindle Edition. Loc. 1,139

102 "Mantra." Merriam-Webster.com Dictionary, Merriam-Webster, https://www.merriam-webster.com/dictionary/mantra. Accessed 8 Feburary 2022.

103 Transcendental Meditation for Anxiety. https://www.tm.org/Anxiety

104 Eric Weiner. *Man Seeks God: My Flirtations with the Divine*. Twelve: Hachette Book Group. 2012. p. 328.

105 wakingup.com Sam Harris. "How Is Waking Up Different?" Accessed. 13 October 2021.

106 How To Practice Mindfulness Meditation - Mindful. https://www.mindful.org/mindfulness-how-to-do-it/

107 Metta Meditation: 5 Benefits and Tips for Beginners. https://www.healthline.com/health/metta-meditation

108 Tom Hodgkinson. *How To Be Idle: A Loafer's Manifesto*. Harper Perennial. 2005. p. 278.

109 Charles Foster. *Being A Human: Adventures in Forty Thousand Years of Consciousness*. Metropolitan Books.2021. p. 71.

110 Jung's Imagination Technique | Ancient Templar Knowledge. https://commanderysaintmichael.wordpress.com/2020/04/14/jungs-methode/

111 The Inner Work Of Age: Shifting From Role To Soul https://idoc.pub/documents/the-inner-work-of-age-shifting-from-role-to-soul-546j12d9j8n8

112 Roger Walsh. *The World of Shamanism*. Llewellyn Publications. 2007. p. 238.

113 Sarah Bakewell. *At the Existentialist Cafe: Freedom, Being, and Apricot Cocktails*. Other Press. 2016. p. 3.

114 No Man Is an Island by John Donne - Famous ... - All Poetry. https://allpoetry.com/No-man-is-an-island

115 Martin Seligman. *Authentic Happiness*. Simon & Schuster. Kindle Edition. p. 90.

116 https://www.brainyquote.com/topics/gratitude-quotes Accessed 24 January 2022.

117 What is the Meaning of Being Gentle?. https://psichologyanswers.com/library/lecture/read/519336-what-is-the-meaning-of-being-gentle

118 The Fruit of the Spirit Is … Gentleness – A Clarion Issues …. https://candytroutman.com/2011/07/07/the-fruit-of-the-spirit-is-gentleness/

119 99 Interesting Facts That Are As Random As They Are Fun. https://allthatsinteresting.com/interesting-facts

120 Carey Elwes. *As You Wish: Inconceivable Tales from the Making of The Princess Bride.* Atria Books. 2014.

121 Leo Buscaglia - Only the Weak are Cruel. Gentleness can…. https://www.brainyquote.com/quotes/leo_buscaglia_131976

122 Proverbs 16:18-19 KJV

123 Francis J. Broucek. *Shame and the Self.* The Guilford Press; 1st edition. 1991.

124 Compassion. Merriam-Webster.com Dictionary, Merriam-Webster, https://www.merriam-webster.com/dictionary/compassion. Accessed 7 Feburary 2022.

125Louise Aronson. *Elderhood: Redefining Aging, Transforming Medicine, Reimagining Life.* Bloomsbury Publishing; 1st edition (June 11, 2019). Kindle Edition.

126 The Golden Age of Neuroscience Has Arrived. https://www.wsj.com/articles/michio-kaku-the-golden-age-of-neuroscience-has-arrived-1408577023 Accessed 26 October 2017.

127 Donald L. Nathanson. *Shame and Pride: Affect, Sex, and the Birth of Self.* W.W. Norton & Company. 1994. p.32.

128 Greg Epstein. *Good Without God.* Harper Collins Ebook. 2009. Kindle Edition. p. 20.

129 Unexplainable. Vox. https://www.vox.com/unexplainable/22348461/ocean-twilight-zone-mysteries-unexplainable-podcast. Accessed 12 December 2021.

130 Gulf of Mexico — Houston Wilderness. https://houstonwilderness.org/gulf-of-mexico

131 James Hollis. *Why Good People Do Bad Things: Understanding our Darker Selves.* Gotham Books. 2008. p.28.

132 Joseph Campbell. *Pathways to Bliss: Mythology and Personal Transformation.* Stillpoint Digital Press. 2004. p.28.

133 The World's First Images of the Brain on LSD. https://www.beckleyfoundation.org/the-brain-on-lsd-revealed-first-scans-show-how-the-drug-affects-the-brain/ Accessed 18 January 2022.

134 https://www.beckleyfoundation.org/wp-content/uploads/2021/05/Scientific-Programme__27-05-DIGITAL-1.pdf

135 Michael Pollan. *How To Change Your Mind*. Penguin Books. 2019. Kindle Edition. Location: 5,637.

136 https://brucecockburn.com/discography

137 Attachment-Based Therapy. https://www.psychologytoday.com/us/therapy-types/attachment-based-therapy Accessed 14 January 2021.

138 Attachment-Based Family Therapy (ABFT). https://www.goodtherapy.org/learn-about-therapy/types/attachment-based-family-therapy Accessed 14 January 2021.

139 https://www.goodreads.com/quotes/45102-dreams-are-illustrations-from-the-book-your-soul-is-writing Accessed 26 Jan. 2022.

140 Carl Jung Quotations 7 – Carl Jung Depth Psychology. https://carljungdepthpsychologysite.blog/2020/03/02/carl-jung-quotations-7/

141 Carl Jung. *Man and His Symbols*. Doubleday & Company. 1964. p. 49.

142 Ibid. p. 50.

143 What is the Emotional Catharsis? - Psychology Spot. https://psychology-spot.com/what-is-the-emotional-catharsis/

144 Thomas J. Scheff. *Catharsis in Healing, Ritual, and Drama*. An Author's Guild BackInPrint Edition. 1979, 2001. p.12.

145 Zweig, Connie. *The Inner Work of Age: Shifting From Role To Soul*. Park Street Press. p. 150.

146 Zweig, Connie. *The Inner Work of Age: Shifting From Role To Soul*. Park Street Press. Kindle Edition. Loc. 4624.

147 Ibid. Loc. 3993.

148 Martin Seligman. *Authentic Happiness*. Simon & Schuster. Kindle Edition. Loc: 1,806.

149 Savoring : A New Model of Positive Experience. https://searchworks.stanford.edu/view/6749204 Accessed 17 January 2017.

150 Focus on What Is Strong, Not What ... - Acknowledge Alliance. https://www.acknowledgealliance.org/news/strengths

151 https://www.viacharacter.org

152 Martin Seligman. *Authentic Happiness*. Simon & Schuster. Kindle Edition. p. 246.

153 Mihaly Csikszentmihalyi. *Creativity: Flow and the Psychology of Discovery and Invention*. Harper Collins. Author's Synopsis.

154 A Survey of the Old Testament Instructor's Manual. https://zondervanacademic-cdn.sfo2.digitaloceanspaces.com/resources/9780310280958_A_Survey_of_the_Old_Testament_Instructor_Manual_updated.docx

[155] Louise Aronson. *Elderhood: Redefining Aging, Transforming Medicine, Reimagining Life.* Bloomsbury Publishing; 1st edition (June 11, 2019). Kindle Edition. Location: 2,627.

[156] Stone, A.A., Schwartz, J.E., Broderick, J.E., and Deaton, A. *"A snapshot of the age distribution of psychological well-being in the United States."* Proceedings of the National Academy of Sciences. 2010. 107(22) 9985-9990.

[157] https://livingto100.com/calculator

[158] Sharon Kaufman. *The Ageless Self.* The University of Wisconsin Press. 1986. p. 28.

[159] Louise Aronson. *Elderhood: Redefining Aging, Transforming Medicine, Reimagining Life.* Bloomsbury Publishing; 1st edition (June 11, 2019). Kindle Edition.

[160] Zweig, Connie. *The Inner Work of Age: Shifting From Role To Soul.* Park Street Press. p. 15.

[161] Ranier Marie Rilke. *Letters To A Young Poet.* 1903.

[162] Equanimity. Merriam-Webster.com Dictionary, Merriam-Webster, https://www.merriam-webster.com/dictionary/equanimity. Accessed 30 Dec. 2021.

[163] David Whyte. *The Three Marriages: Reimagining work, self, and Relationship.* Riverhead Books; 1st edition (January 20, 2009). Kindle Edition. p. 5.

[164] Cosmology. Merriam-Webster.com Dictionary, Merriam-Webster, https://www.merriam-webster.com/dictionary/cosmology. Accessed 30 Dec. 2021.

[165] Transcendent. Merriam-Webster.com Dictionary, Merriam-Webster, https://www.merriam-webster.com/dictionary/transcendent. Accessed 30 Dec. 2021.

[166] Schachter-Shalomi and Miller. *From Age-ing to Sageing.* Grand Central Publishing. 2008. loc. 239.

[167] Ibid. p.14.

[168] Ibid. p.15.

[169] Ibid. p. 244.

[170] Ibid. p. 12.

[171] Sharon Kaufman. *The Ageless Self.* The University of Wisconsin Press. 1986. p. 14.

[172] Zweig, Connie. *The Inner Work of Age: Shifting From Role To Soul.* Park Street Press. p. 14.

[173] Schachter-Shalomi and Miller. *From Age-ing to Sageing.* Grand Central Publishing. 2008. p.2.

[174] J. Hillman. *The Essential James Hillman: A Blue Fire.* p. 286.

[175] https://www.theatlantic.com/ideas/archive/2021/12/terminal-cancer-neuroscientist-prepares-death/621114/ Accessed 1 March 2022.

176 Ram Dass. Death Quotes. https://www.ramdass.org/ram-dass-quotes Accessed 12 December 2021.

177 Stanley Keleman. *Living Your Dying.* Random House. 1974.

178 https://www.mirror.co.uk/3am/parties-dont-last-forever-ricky-25543590 Accessed 23 December 2021.

179 Anya Foos-Graber. *Deathing.* Nicolas-Hays. 1989. Kindle Edition. Loc: 9.

180 https://deathdoulas.com/whatdeathdoulasdo Accessed 3 January 2022.

181 Schachter-Shalomi and Miller. *From Age-ing to Sage-ing.* Grand Central Publishing. 2008. p.113.

182 Abraham H. Maslow. *The Farther Reaches of Human Nature.* Esalen. 1971.

183 Roger Walsh, M.D., Ph.D. *The World of Shamanism.* Llewellyn Publications. 2007. Page 109.

www.ingramcontent.com/pod-product-compliance
Lightning Source LLC
Chambersburg PA
CBHW030002290326
41934CB00005B/197